Letters to a
Young Theologian

Letters to a
Young Theologian

Edited by
Henco van der Westhuizen

Fortress Press
Minneapolis

LETTERS TO A YOUNG THEOLOGIAN

Chapter 10 is a version of an article that originally appeared as Stanley Hauerwas, "Go with God: An Open Letter to Young Christians on Their Way to College," *First Things*, November 2010, https://www.firstthings.com/article/2010/10/go-with-god. Reprinted with permission.

Chapter 16 is a version of an article that originally appeared as Kevin Vanhoozer, "Letter to an Aspiring Theologian: How to Speak of God Truly," *First Things*, August 2018, https://www.firstthings.com/article/2018/08/letter-to-an-aspiring-theologian. Reprinted with permission.

Cover design: Kristin Miller

Print ISBN: 978-1-5064-7879-1
eBook ISBN: 978-1-5064-7880-7

Contents

On Healing, Wholeness, Dignity

On Public Life, Science, Interreligious Dialogue

On Fun, Joy, Imagination

Introduction

By the way, it would be very nice if you didn't throw away my theological letters. . . . Perhaps I might want to read them again later. . . . One writes some things more freely and more vividly in a letter than in a book, and often I have better thoughts in a conversation by correspondence than by myself.

—Dietrich Bonhoeffer, "To Eberhard Bethge, Tegel, July 8 and 9, 1944"

Letter-writing is a great way to do theology.

—John de Gruchy, "On Locusts and Wild Honey— Letter Writing as Doing Theology"

Although there have been many books with the title *Letters to a Young . . .* , the title of this book by no means speaks for itself. In fact, all five of the words in the title—*theologian, young, a, to,* and *letters*—are significant.

I will begin with the end of the title, with *theologian*.

With theologian, I have in mind those interested in *why* we study theology; in what it means to *study* theology, to really study *theology*; in what makes theology *theology*; in what it means to *be* a theologian. Why do many say that studying theology is an odyssey, a pilgrimage, a sojourn? Whereto does this lead? What will we have to look out for? Who do we listen to, what do we touch or taste?

With theologian, I also have in mind those who *are* theologians, those who would *want* to be theologians, those interested in theology and the *doing* thereof, particularly those doing theology in and through *these* letters.

But I also and foremostly have in mind those who are interested in theology—interested in God, in the triune God, and therefore in ways to and in theology; in hermeneutics, reading, and writing; in flourishing, blossoming, and liberating; in healing, wholeness, and dignity; in fun, joy, and imagination; in dialogue and conversation.

Thus with *theologian* I have in mind those intrigued by questions, for whom asking good questions is more interesting than answering those that are bad.

The letters, so the title reads, are for *young* theologians.

The young in these letters refers, of course, to those who are young to or in the field of theology. For them, I want these letters to be the pictures on postcards from afar—a door, a window to where others have been, to what others have heard, seen, felt, and tasted.

But like postcards, they are just that—doors and windows through which each and every young will have to pass in their own ways. They aren't *the* picture, for the young will take their own.

With young, however, I also have in mind those who look back on being young, who, like Schleiermacher, would year after year prefix their signatures with *stud, Theo.*—that is, stating that they are not merely still theology students but students in theology. As I was reminded by Barth in *Evangelical Theology*, "Theological study and the impulse which compels it are not passing stages of life. The forms which this study assumes may and must change slightly with the times. But the theologian, if [they] were in fact a *studiosus theologiae*, remains so [i.e., a student]."[1]

I deliberately decided on *letters*.

There are a lot of letters related to theology, but theology itself is also related to letters, to words, to sentences, to paragraphs—also as they are inscribed in letters.

Letters were for years and years the way in which theology was done, without the writers thinking about the letter or the writing thereof as such as theological. Letters were the medium.

Think of letters in the biblical traditions, of the *evangelion* in and through letters, of the epistles—but later also Augustine's *Enchiridion*, his thoughts on the *evangelion*, itself a letter.

Or think of Luther or Calvin. This was oftentimes not merely the medium but the way that these theologians did their theology—that is, in and through letters. Both Luther and Calvin wrote hundreds of letters. Think, for example, of the forewords of the many editions of the *Institutes* that allow one to understand the different addressees with whom Calvin wanted to engage and that are also, of course, of importance for those who want to engage with and understand the *Institutes* today.

Think of Bonhoeffer and Barth, not only the former's letters in and from prison but the letters of both throughout their lives.

Also think of more recent letters—for example, those in and from South Africa, from where I write this introduction—letters that accompanied a *status confessionis*, that accompanied the *Confession of Belhar*.

Or think of letters in and amidst troubled times, of Denise Ackermann and her letters in *After the Locusts*:

> I wanted to write . . . to . . . anyone who might be interested in the theological reflections of a white South African woman on the life of faith. Eventually I found what I wanted, a vehicle. . . . I would write letters to people who mattered to me, about the themes that have been at the core of my search for healing. . . . [I would write] about my efforts to discover what is worth living for in the midst of troubled times. Taking complex theological doctrines and philosophical concepts and attempting to make them simple and straightforward lays me open to [many] charges [but] I am passionate about theology. I believe in its potential to change people, to deepen faith and understanding, and to heal our wounds.[2]

Thus a mere look at these theological letters, of letters with a theological tone, highlights why I entitled this book *Letters to a Young Theologian*.

But it is about more than that. Letters themselves are also a way of doing theology. There is theology in the writing of letters *itself*.

The letters in this book are written not merely by someone but by a particular someone. They are, in many ways, handwritten.

The letters, in this way, transcribe something of those who wrote them, as they are often part autobiography. And like autobiographies, they allow us, at least in part, into the biography of the other—the otherness of the other.

In the otherness, however, we are also allowed to look at our own biographies. They are pathways through the other to who we are, as we are who we are in and through them, particularly because of their being other.

They are, as with letters, accompanied by an address from somewhere such as Sydney, Stellenbosch, Cape Town, Amsterdam, Oxford, Cambridge,

Aberdeen, Tübingen, Berlin, Heidelberg, Princeton, Yale, and elsewhere. The letters are from a place, they are *emplaced* (Ricoeur).

They are written in these times, in time in our time. They are, so to say, stamped. They have a date and a time and are therefore not dated but timely.

In short, they are *from* someone, somewhere, at some time.

These letters are *for* someone, somewhere, at some time. Letters are posted; they are sent.

With letters being posted, they are in letter boxes, in envelopes. They have to be unboxed, unenveloped. With their being sent, there is boxed and enveloped within them what is unexpected. There is an unexpectedness to a letter that allows it to be an *event*:

> What a joy for me to hear from you at such length! It's really quite wonderful that we are still keeping up our dialogue, and for me it is always the most rewarding one that I have. It must be one of the laws of the way our minds work that when one's own thoughts have been understood by another, they are also transformed and stimulated through the medium of that other person. This is what makes a letter such an "event."[3]

A letter has an address; it is addressed to a particular someone. And *in* its particularity, in its being addressed to someone *particular*, it is addressed to whoever takes the time to engage it—to be engaged by it. It was written not from the abstract all to the particular, or from the particular to the abstract all, but from the particular to the particular and therein for *all* in their particularity.

The letter *itself* is a medium. In and through the letter, the writer becomes bodily present. The letter becomes an embodied presence in its physicality. It has a signature not only on it but to it. It is in the embodied presence *there* that it is heard, seen, felt, and tasted.

Of course, also what is written in the letter is a medium. In whatever is written in the letter, there *already* is calligraphic engagement, there is engaged conversation. And through these letters, these conversations are continued elsewhere, in other conversations already engaged in calligraphically.

Thus I want these letters to be received, to be read, and in the end, to be truly received. I want these letters to allow those who receive and read them to also receive what the letter writers have been writing throughout the years, to also add an address to *that*.

I end off with the *a* in the title. The *a* doesn't speak for itself. These are letters to *a* young theologian, not merely letters to theologians. This is because I want these letters to be for *a* theologian in all their particularity and diversity. Theology—also theology in and through letters—is done by *a* theologian in conversation with other theologians in their particular differences. How we do theology, how we speak about God, will only ever be someone somewhere at some time speaking about God—who within Godself has room for diversity—to someone somewhere at some time spoken to about God.

It is for this reason that Barth, in his last letter (written with the handwriting of Busch), says, "Nun ist es Eure Aufgabe, in eurer neuen, anderen, und eigenen Lage mit Kopf und Hertz, mit Mund und Händen christlichen Theologie zu treiben" (It is now your task, in your new, different and own situation, to practise Christian theology with head and heart, with mouth and hands). He continues, "Ich kann Euch dazu nur Mut machen: Ja, tut das nur—sagt das, was Ihr um Gottes willen als Christen zu sagen habt, verantwortlich und konkret wirklich mit Euren eigenen Worten und Gedanken, Vorstellungen und Handlungsweisen! Je verantwortlicher und konkreter, desto Besser, desto christlicher!" (I can only embolden you to do that: yes, just do it—say, for the sake of God, what you have to say as Christians, responsibly and concretely, really with your own words and thoughts, images and actions! The more responsible and concrete, the better, the more Christian!)[4]

It is in this manner that we who are letters written by God (2 Cor 3:2)—*are* letters for God and, therefore, to all.

I thank Adam Neder, Alister E. McGrath, Allan Boesak, Bram van de Beek, Catherine Keller, Christoph Schwoebel, Cynthia L. Rigby, Daniel Migliore, David Fergusson, Denise Ackermann, Douglas F. Ottati, Ellen T. Charry, Emmanuel Katongole, Gijsbert van den Brink, Graham Ward, Hanna Reichel, Heinrich Bedford-Strohm, Jan-Olav Henriksen, Johan Cilliers, John de Gruchy, Jürgen Moltmann, Karen Kilby, Katherine Sonderegger, Kevin Vanhoozer, Michael Mawson, Michael Welker, Miroslav Volf, Mitzi Smith, Nicholas Wolterstorff, Paul T. Nimmo, Piet Naudé, Rachel Muers, Richard Kearney, Robert Vosloo, Stanley Hauerwas, Traci C. West, Veli-Matti Kärkkäinen, Willie James Jennings, and Wolfgang Huber for not only writing but being these letters for young theologians like myself.

Henco van der Westhuizen
Bloemfontein

Notes

1 Karl Barth, *Evangelical Theology: An Introduction* (Grand Rapids, MI: William B. Eerdmans, 1963), 172.

2 Denise Ackermann, *After the Locusts: Letters from a Landscape of Faith* (Grand Rapids, MI: Eerdmans, 2003), xii–xiii.

3 Dietrich Bonhoffer, "To Eberhard Bethge, Tegel, March 24, 25, and 27, 1944," in *Letters and Papers from Prison*, English ed., ed. John de Gruchy, trans. Christian Gremmels, Eberhard Bethge, and Renate Bethge, with Ilse Tödt (Minneapolis: Fortress, 2010), 328.

4 Karl Barth, "An Christen in Südostasien," in *Offene Briefe 1945–1968. Karl Barth Gesamtausgabe V. Briefe* (Zürich: Theologischer Verlag Zürich, 1984), 551–56.

On Ways to Theology

I

Hanna Reichel

Questions

I don't know about you, but I have *so many questions*. They ring loudly within me with the questions I find in the Scriptures.

"How long shall the wicked, how long shall the wicked exult?" (Ps 94:3 ESV).

When I see that there is no justice. When I see that those who crush the dignity of others walk unperturbed while thousands and thousands are locked away in prisons, cages, asylums, and clinics. When I see that some are definitely more equal than others in their access to education, health care, jobs, housing, and opportunities to pursue their own and other people's happiness. When I see that our societies are divided by opportunities and recognition, by segregation and alienation, by hatred and resentment. When I see that in our political system, lies and self-interest, narcissism and chauvinism reign and that all over the world, "democracy" is becoming a farce. When I see how quick we are to wage wars.

"What have we done?" "Where are you, Lord?" "Where are—we?"

When I see that we have probably passed the planetary tipping point, but nothing, *nothing* can shake us out of the stupor of our mass consumption, exploitation, and complacency. Let the world go to hell, let continents burn, let apparently natural disasters and societal upheavals shake the earth—but sure, let us continue to build infrastructures around cars, let us enjoy our take-out burger and our convenient plane travel, and let's just build bigger walls to insulate ourselves from the issues we cause.

"What have we done?" "Where are you, Lord?" "Where are—we?"

When I see how random, chance events can so easily crush life and hope. When I see that your Word fails to give comfort, or is even weaponized. When I see that supposedly "Christian values" are used to exclude and discriminate. When I see that the name of the Lord is wielded for religious, national, and racial supremacy.

"What have we done?" "Where are you, Lord?" "Where are—we?"

When I see that even in such an intentional community as this one, there are walls dividing us. That many of our members are lonely and isolated and do not feel like they belong. That many of our members are poor and insecure. That many of our members suffer emotional and sometimes even physical violence in this community. That many of our members are afraid to speak, are not sure whether they are accepted, whether they will be respected, whether their voice will count as much as that of others.

"What have we done?" "Where are you, Lord?" "Where are—we?"

I have so many questions.

And among them, on top of them, the nagging superquestion: What am I even doing here? Deciphering texts. Mincing words. And maybe—maybe!—small-scale institutional reform, trickle-down education, and a thesis or a sermon that just might change someone's mind.

In all of the turmoil of the world, doing theology is a very questionable business. *How dare we* sit here in this prestigious, beautiful, neat place and read and write our books "as if nothing had happened" (like Karl Barth said in the face of the Nazi rise to power).[1]

And aren't we—who aspire to be leaders of the church and of society, light on the hill and salt for the world—the ones who are supposed to help people find answers? Solutions? Provide comfort and closure for people's burning questions?

I must admit that in the years that I have been doing theology, my questions have become more rather than less. What *are* we doing here?

Theology as Wrestling with God and the World

This morning, I opened an intro to theology class with Luke's story of the disciples on the road to Emmaus. And I claimed along the lines of this story that *theology is a conversation*, a conversation we are having among ourselves on the road.

I didn't exactly lie. But I may have made it sound much more peaceful, much more serene than I myself feel most of the time.

Let me read you a story of a different encounter on a different road, from Genesis 32:24–32:

Jacob was left alone; and a man wrestled with him until daybreak. When the man saw that he did not prevail against Jacob, he struck him on the hip socket; and Jacob's hip was put out of joint as he wrestled with him. Then he said, "Let me go, for the day is breaking." But Jacob said, "I will not let you go, unless you bless me." So he said to him, "What is your name?" And he said, "Jacob." Then the man said, "You shall no longer be called Jacob, but Israel, for you have striven with God and with humans, and have prevailed." Then Jacob asked him, "Please tell me your name." But he said, "Why is it that you ask my name?" And there he blessed him. So Jacob called the place Peniel, saying, "For I have seen God face to face, and yet my life is preserved." The sun rose upon him as he passed Penuel, limping because of his hip. Therefore to this day the Israelites do not eat the thigh muscle that is on the hip socket, because he struck Jacob on the hip socket at the thigh muscle.

In Jacob's story, it becomes clear that the road is a rather perilous place and that the encounter with the Other may be far from peaceful. So to amend or complement the conversation metaphor I used this morning, let me now suggest the following: doing theology, as we are doing here, *means wrestling with God and the world.*

And even on the road to Emmaus, the disciples were wrestling, wrestling with the hard questions and not having any answers, really. Remember, this story picks up right after the Gospel of Mark ends: the grave that marks the end of our hope, disillusionment, frustration, fear, and trembling. The disciples are moving away—even if not moving on, precisely—not knowing what to make of the strange experiences and the even stranger appearances that are haunting them. Their conversation, far from being serene, is marked by deep wrestling.

Jacob, on the road, is also wrestling. Wrestling with his guilt, with the brother he has betrayed, with his anxiety of what the future will bring and whether he will have a place in it. Jacob is wrestling with all that assails him in the darkest hour of the night. And before he knows it, he finds himself wrestling physically, trying to cross over to the other side, but he cannot: God stands in his way: "You cannot pass."

Jacob may not even understand who or what he is actually wrestling with, *or does he*? Do we ever? At the bottom of our questions, it is not God who gives us answers; it is God who stands in our way. God draws us into this fight.

Is it possible to wrestle with God and the world—and to prevail? Or, maybe more precisely, What would *prevailing* even mean in such a conflict?

From Jacob's story, we get a glimpse. At the very least, he is no longer running, no longer running from his past and his demons; he confronts them, confronts God, he is now committed not to let go, even if it means the end of him, he won't be overcome, he *will* wrestle through this.

In the darkness of this stubbornness—of this desperation, really—Jacob, who had first been assailed, now becomes the assailant. And God is not able to disentangle Godself either: "I will not let you go," says Jacob, "unless you bless me" (Gen 32:26).

Does Jacob . . . win? Well, he survives the fight. He doesn't get answers or solutions, but he is transformed, and he is allowed to continue his journey *changed*. He comes away with a new name and a blessing that will be with him on the road he continues to travel—with all the anxieties, the guilt, and the new beginnings. He also comes away with a limp: this fight marks him for life, it makes him who he is, down to his name and to his physical appearance.

In the hard questions that we raise today, with all our anxieties and all our guilt, we too may ask, Is it possible to wrestle with God and the world and to prevail—even as we cannot come out unscathed?

God's Questions

Because God is limping too. God does not come out of God's wrestling with this world unscathed, pristine, and vastly superior. God has wounds to show from God's wrestling with us, as well, wounds that will forever mark who God is. Look at Christ's hands, feet, and side.

Because it is not just *we* who are "wrestling with God and the world" and asking all the hard questions. God has questions too, even as we all too often conveniently ignore them or betray them by prematurely pretending that they have all already been answered (the ultimate temptation of every theologian, let me tell you).

That God asks us these questions is both terrifying and a ground for hope.

Terrifying and a ground for hope because it shows that God is faithful. God is not *done* with us. God stays in conversation with us and won't let us go. God is still waiting for our reply.

Terrifying and a ground for hope because it shows that God moved. God suffers from this world, its injustice, its despair, its god-forsakenness as much as we do. (Maybe more than we, finite creatures, can fathom.) And God is asking us to *stand with God* in this suffering, to not let go.

Being Christian: Staying with the Trouble, Stubbornly Faithful

Maybe God can be wrestled with? Maybe the world can be wrestled with? Maybe that is precisely the faithfulness that is demanded of us?

Bonhoeffer's poem "Who Am I?" puts our questions and suffering, our need and our longing, in deep solidarity with the questions and suffering, the need and the longing of all the world. *All* have questions, *all* are in distress, *all* need redemption.[2]

We are not smarter than anyone else. We are not holier than anyone else. And, I regret to tell you, at the end of the day, we may not have any more answers than anyone else.

The only thing that may set us apart is that (maybe!) we are just a little bit more *stubborn*. That we refuse to give up on God and the world. That we stubbornly cling to God's faithfulness, to God's faithfulness to this unredeemed world.

If we are stubbornly faithful, that means we do not walk away from God. We do not let God go. We do not let God off the hook, but we also do not leave God alone with the weight of the world. We do not give easy answers; instead, we lean into the questions, hard, and we confront God with them. Lifting the world's suffering and injustices, our fragmentation and brokenness and despair, and this whole unredeemed existence up and holding it before God—a defiant prayer that refuses to let go because things are *just not right*. We demand a response, we demand a blessing: You have promised, God! Why have you forsaken us? Where are you? What is your *name*?

If we are stubbornly faithful, that also means we do not walk away from the world. We sit with God in God's suffering from this world, and we confront the world. We hold God's suffering and despair, God's own wounds before the world, and we demand a response, demand a blessing. We have been called to be God's creatures, God's people. What have we done? What *are* we doing? Where (the fuck) are we?

That's what being a Christian, that's what doing theology is about: being stubbornly faithful, staying with the trouble, and wrestling with God and the world until they yield a blessing.

Somewhere in this faithful wrestling, there may even be a strange peace to be found.

The restless peace *Abraham found*, who refused to accept certain doom and who bargained with God for the lives of the world.

The restless peace *Hagar found*, who called God by a new name and claimed God's promises for those whom God had overlooked.

The restless peace *Jacob found*, wrestling with whatever assailed him on his dark and crooked road and finding that it may have been God.

The restless peace who found the disciples on the road to Emmaus.

With the promise of their peace, we too continue this conversation. We too wrestle with the promises, with our distress, with our lack of understanding, and with the *queer hope* that sometimes, a stranger on the road will encounter us; that sometimes, our hearts will burn inside of us and open up new beginnings; that sometimes, God will meet us on this road; and that sometimes, even as we are still unaware of God's presence, we are being blessed, we are being nourished, and we are being sent back on the road— with a limp, a new name, and the dawn of a new day on our faces.

The restless peace of God in all its stubborn faithfulness to this unredeemed world, a peace that will greet the next traveler whom we meet.

And may this *peace of God*, which surpasses all our understanding, keep our hearts and minds in Christ Jesus.

Best,
H
Princeton

Notes

1 Karl Barth, *Theological Existence Today! A Plea for Theological Freedom* (London: Hodder & Stoughton, 1933), 9.

2 Dietrich Bonhoeffer, "Who Am I? Tegel, Summer 1944," in *Letters and Papers from Prison*, English ed., ed. John de Gruchy, trans. Christian Gremmels, Eberhard Bethge, and Renate Bethge, with Ilse Tödt (Minneapolis: Fortress, 2010), 459–60.

2

Jürgen Moltmann

Every Believer Is a Theologian

Some people may think that a proper theologian must at least have studied at the famous Yale Divinity School or at one of the no-less-famous two theological faculties in Tübingen. Proper theologians have to know Hebrew, Greek, and Latin. They have to have successfully passed diverse theological exams and must have at least a PhD or a doctorate in theology. But the real top dog in theology has a chair, and preferably a chair for systemic theology, because systematic theology is the crown of all the theological disciplines. No one is higher than the professor of theology—except God himself. And God is curious to discover what the professor has to say about him and consequently puts up with him with a degree of divine irony. But so that the professors of theology don't get too much above themselves, something very unpleasant happened at their creation. The German academic legend runs as follows:

> After God had created human beings, he created from among them the most beautiful, the cleverest, and the most wonderful creature he could think of: the German professor of theology. And the angels came and marveled over him. But on the evening of the same day, the devil came along and created the ugliest, the stupidest, and the most odious creature imaginable, and that was the professor's colleague.

Of course, this is profoundly mortifying for the arrogant professor, but when all is said and done, his colleague is a professor too. So all the rivalries and conflicts remain in the family, so to speak.

But the students present a much sadder problem. The professors—I am talking about Germany—teach what they can, and put themselves forward, for what they are. What they see in front of them in the lecture rooms are potential doctoral students, helpful assistants, and future professors who are destined one day to carry on their scholarly work. In actual fact, most of the students in their lecture rooms don't want to take up an academic career at all. They want to be pastors for their congregations in the church. They want to know what good all the theological theories will do them later, in their sermons, in their pastoral work, and in the building up of their congregations. But about that, a great many professors haven't a notion because they were never congregational pastors themselves and—at least in Germany—have sometimes an extremely detached relationship to their local church. So in the theological faculties, a gulf opens up between academic theory on the one hand and pastoral practice on the other, a broad and repellent ditch.

And students, who then arrive in their congregations, proudly equipped with a Tübingen doctorate in theology or a Princeton PhD, have become strange and alien to normal Christians, and so they have to make a painful leap over that broad ditch between the educated and the uneducated and have first to learn again that in Christ, the difference between "Greeks and barbarians" counts for nothing and that all are "one." After all, the apostles, men and women both, had no PhDs, and—except perhaps for Paul—none of them would have passed our theological exams.

I have vivid memories of my first congregation. I had studied theology in Göttingen, had a doctorate in theology, and came to a little country church near Bremen. Sixty farms, five hundred souls, and three thousand cows. So there I stood in the pulpit with all my learning and felt pretty much of a fool. Fortunately, I had earlier spent more than three years in the hard "school of life" and had lived with farmers and workers in prisoner of war camps in Scotland and England. It was out of those experiences that I then preached, not out of the lecture notes I had taken in Göttingen. I wasn't perhaps a great teacher for my congregation in Wasserhorst, but I did learn something there: I learnt, and came to understand, the "theology of the people." Every Christian—man or woman, young or old—who believes and thinks at all about that belief is a theologian. In those farming families, I learnt to value "the general/common theology of all believers." I came to understand what Luther meant when he said: "Omnes sumus Theologi." We are all theologians.[1]

Ever since then, I have known that if academic theologians don't go to the people, picking up and learning the general theology of the people and working for the people, they lose their basis. Their theology becomes abstract and sterile, and they no longer have much to say to the students, who are studying in the theological faculties so that they can minister to the congregations at the grass roots. But this means that theology isn't just a task for the theological specialists at academic faculties. It is a task for the whole people of God: the faith of the whole Christian community on earth seeks understanding.

Academic theology is nothing other than the methodical, scholarly, and scientific penetration and illumination of what Christians in the congregations are thinking themselves if they believe and live with Christ. Good theology—I am thinking of Athanasius, Augustine, Luther, Schleiermacher, and Barth—is basically simple because it is clear. It is only unclear theology that is complicated and difficult. The fundamental ideas of every great theological system require no more than a single page: It is true that Karl Barth needed more than eight thousand pages for his *Church Dogmatics*, and even then, it was still unfinished. But even friendly critics have rightly objected that "truth can't be as long as that."

Barth knew that himself, and he wrote brief introductions and summaries of theology too. The many pages of *Church Dogmatics* are theological doxologies of "the infinitely bounteous God," as Barth liked to call God; and as we know, the theological praise of God knows no end.

I said that everyone who believes and thinks about that belief is a theologian. That is why there is this general/common theology of all believers as the basis for the scholarly theology of the theological faculties. But does that mean that Christian theology can only be "the doctrine of faith," to take the name Schleiermacher gave his theology? Does it mean that only people who are "believers" or "born again" can study and understand theology? Faith is of the essence for theology, and the experience of being "born again to a living hope" is a wonderful experience.

But for all that, theology isn't just there for believers, because God is not just a God of believers. He is the Creator of heaven and earth. God is not particularistic, like belief in God is. He is universal, like sunrise on the evil and the good. A theology for believers only would be the religious ideology of the Christian religious community, a sectarian in-group mentality, an esoteric, arcane teaching capable of being understood only by the group of the initiated. But that would be in contradiction to the God of public revelation; the God of Abraham, Isaac, and Jacob; the Father of Jesus Christ. German Pietism cherished the ideal of a theology of the reborn. But that theology didn't lead to the public proclamation of the gospel and to missionary universalism.

Atheists Can Be Theologians Too

In disputing the limitation of theology to Christians, let me ask, Isn't every unbeliever, who has some reason for his or her atheism, a theologian too? Atheists, who have something against God and consequently deny his existence, usually know very well what they are rejecting—sometimes even much better than believers, who more or less acknowledge God. Before I began to study theology, I was full of enthusiasm for a time for Friedrich Nietzsche, who influenced modern atheism, nihilism, and today's postmodernism. But when I read his book *The Anti-Christ*,[2] I knew that it was Christianity with its morality of compassion that was right, not Nietzsche with his immorality of the superman. The very thing he condemned was, for me, the best of all.

There is a protest atheism, which denies the existence of God because of the suffering of the innocent, that cries out to high heaven. This atheism is profoundly theological, for the theodicy question—If there is a God, why all this suffering?—is the fundamental question of every theologian too, from Job down to the Jesus, dying on the cross with the cry, "My God, why have you forsaken me?"

Dostoevsky splendidly depicts theology's two sides, the believing side and the doubting side, in the brothers Karamazov, Alyosha and Ivan.[3] Both of them wrestle with God in the face of the senseless suffering in the world. But Alyosha believes and Ivan protests. The one submits, the other rebels. The story Ivan tells is horrible enough: A Russian landowner sets his hounds on a little boy and allows them to tear him to pieces. The boy's mother is forced to look on. "What kind of harmony is that, in which there are hells like this?" Ivan cries out, and then he declares, "Is there anyone in the whole world, who could forgive, and who is permitted to forgive? I don't like the harmony. I don't like it, because of my love for the world. I would rather keep the unreconciled suffering. It isn't that I acknowledge God, but I am respectfully giving him back my ticket to a world like this. Understand me, I accept God, but I don't accept the world, God made. I cannot resolve to accept it." And his brother Alyosha answers softly, "That is rebellion. You say: 'Is there a being in the whole world, who could forgive and who is permitted to forgive?' There is someone, and he can forgive everything, all and everyone, and for everything, because he himself poured out his innocent blood for everyone and everything. You have forgotten him. It is on him alone, that the building [kingdom of God] will be built. To him we can cry: 'Just art Thou Lord, for all Thy ways have been revealed.'"

Protest atheism here, theology of the cross there. Dostoevsky portrays himself in the dissimilar brothers Karamazov. And I think the same thing goes for the theologians too. We are conscious of both sides in ourselves, rebellion against God, who permits so much meaningless suffering, and faith in the crucified Christ, who suffers with the victims and forgives the perpetrators. The person who has never "contended" with God like Job doesn't understand the crucified Christ. And conversely, the person who doesn't believe in God and his justice ends up no longer rebelling against this unjust world either.

True faith in God isn't a naive, childish trust. It is a continually surmounted unfaith: "Lord, I believe; help thou mine unbelief" (Mark 9:24 KJV). Profound faith grows up out of the pains and the doubts, the torments, and the rebellions, which we permit: "Life is not just, but God is good." True faith is the strength to say "Nevertheless . . ." and to stand fast while being assailed.

People who recognize God in the face of the crucified Christ have protest atheism within themselves—but as something they have overcome.

So I can quite well understand the atheists, who can no more free themselves from their atheism than they can free themselves from the God they deny. "I don't like these atheists," said the Catholic writer Heinrich Böll, who was so important for us all in postwar Germany. "They are always talking about God." I experienced the same thing as a student pastor in the godless city of Bremen. I liked the company of the "unchurched" atheists because they had something against God. When I was with them, I left completely free to talk about God and faith, sometimes freer, even, than in the company of the good and the pious. My experience at that time taught me that theology is not just something for "insiders"; it is for "outsiders" just as much. So theologians mustn't just get to know the devout and the religious. They must know the godless too.

Luther describes this out of his own experience in his second lecture on the Psalms of 1519: "Vivendo, immo moriendo et damnando fit theologus, non intelligendo, legendo aut speculando" (By living—no, much more still by dying and by being damned to hell—doth one become a theologian, not by knowing, reading or speculation).[4]

Jürgen Moltmann
Tübingen

Notes

1 Martin Luther, *D. Martin Luthers Werke. Kritische Gesamtausgabe. Weimarer Ausgabe* 41 (Berlin: Springer-Verlag, 1990), 11.

2 Friedrich Nietzsche, *The Anti-Christ* (London: SoHo Books, 2010).

3 Fyodor Dostoevsky, *The Brothers Karamazov* (Oxford: Oxford University Press, 2008).

4 Martin Luther, *D. Martin Luthers Werke. Kritische Gesamtausgabe. Weimarer Ausgabe* 5 (Berlin: Springer-Verlag, 1990), 163.

3

Miroslav Volf (I)

So, you've decided to study theology! That's splendid news! It's a noble vocation being a theologian, which, let's be clear from the outset, never amounts to more than committing yourself to being a *student* of theology. I am delighted you are joining the tribe.[1] It's not as if the world is flooded with good theologians; we need good theology today more than ever. I'll tell you shortly why, but first I must warn you. I don't want false hopes to seduce you; the more you love these gilded nothings, the more destructive they become.

Though good theologians are in short supply, many young theologians struggle to find anyone willing (or able!) to pay them enough to keep their body and soul together. I know some of them personally. It is a long and hard road completing basic theological training with a terminal degree. To get a PhD, it often takes as long as eight years of post-collegiate studies and almost never less than five. But then, armed with all your degrees and all that knowledge, you might end up unemployed. And even if you do get a job, you might be paid less than your high school friend who skipped college and decided to become a plumber, which isn't to begrudge anything to plumbers but to note that if money is more important to you than Jesus said it should be, you might think twice before starting your theological studies.

There's a reason why theologians, on the average, aren't paid more than good plumbers. Earlier I called theology a noble vocation. But theology's reputation has plummeted in the course of the last fifty years or so. You might have heard the medieval description of theology as the "queen of the sciences." The idea behind the phrase is simple: the discipline concerned with what matters the most and what is at the foundation of everything should be held in the highest esteem. That's theology, the intellectual endeavor of which the subject matter is God and everything in relation to God. But if you want to be treated like intellectual royalty today, go study artificial intelligence, neuroscience, or medicine, and forget about theology! In venerable old *universities* (like Oxford or Harvard), the queen has long been dethroned and now lives, metaphorically speaking, in a shack on the margins of her erstwhile realm. A "brand new" university might devote some resources to the study of religion (like Stanford does), but it is unlikely to have a department of *theology*.

Interestingly enough, and even more troublingly, *churches* often don't esteem theology any higher than do universities. I'm not entirely sure whether that's the fault of the way churches think about their identity and mission or of the way theologians practice their craft; my sense is that the blame is shared. Either way, as a theologian, you are likely to be as much on the margins of church life as of university life.

Do you still want to study theology? I hope you do, in which case, you must be after something other than a comfortable life and recognition, let alone "fame" (which, in my book, is a nonvalue, especially today when so few people care about keeping fame and infamy apart). Congratulations! You've passed a key qualifying exam for a student of theology.

The thought may cross your mind that I may not be the most credible person to downplay the importance of a secure job and of recognition in the life of a theologian. I am a tenured professor at Yale, and as theologians go, I have it made. But Yale isn't where my theological journey started. The theology bug bit me when I was sixteen, living in Novi Sad, a city in the now nonexistent Yugoslavia, son of a confectioner-turned-Pentecostal-minister. Ours was a fragile little Christian community living in a hostile environment, both culturally and politically. In the courtyard of a small house at the end of a dirt road, my father had built a small structure, and in one of its two rooms, graced with a splendid view of an electrical substation at the edge of a swamp, I started spending days and nights reading theological books and, in the process, teaching myself English and Koine Greek. My older friend and an inspiration to me, Tomislav Simić, had it worse. Together with his mother and stepfather, he lived in a two-room shack with a corrugated roof, and when he became a Christian, it was there, under the onslaught of derision from his parents, that he read his Bible cover to cover thirteen times in a single year and, later on, studied the works of many of the great theologians and philosophers.[2]

Theology became my vocation before I was legally permitted to hold a job. I'd like to think that I'd be doing theology even without a teaching post or advanced degrees in theology. (I'd like to think that . . . but I've also learned over the years that I often don't do what I'd like to think that I would do.) Had I had to go that route, I wouldn't have been alone in having done so. After all, some of the very best Christian theologians—the great Augustine of Hippo, to name just one—were never trained and never worked as "professional" theologians. And Karl Barth, the greatest twentieth-century theologian, had only a basic theological degree, and he wrote one of his most important books, *The Epistle to the Romans* (1919), while working as a parish minister.

Don't feel too sorry for theologians, including your own future self. Consider the experience of many aspiring writers—poets, novelists, and essayists. They often have a day job and practice their craft in their spare time, in the evenings or on weekends. Naguib Mahfouz, for instance, was a civil servant for much of his life, and early on, Margaret Atwood was a barista. Why do they write? Because they love writing. Because they have something to say. Deeper still, because they see themselves as writers, because they *are* writers even before they have become such in the eyes of their readers. The same applies to theologians. For "true" theologians—I hate to use the adjective, but I cannot think of a better one—doing theology is love and identity. I'll grant that love alone won't suffice to sustain a theologian or a writer. Like unrelenting dense fog bearing on a fledgling fire until even its embers die, circumstances often conspire against writers and theologians, pressing them to readjust their sense of identity and redirect their loves. But though you'll need more than love for the sustained practice of theology, love will be indispensable.

So let me ask you: Do you feel "a burning fire" (Jer 20:9), as the prophet Jeremiah did, a fire that made his prophetic work less his decision than a divinely imposed destiny and that helped him endure in face of great adversity? If not, stop and think. Perhaps take a closer look at what has led you to decide to study theology. You may discover sparks, with nothing obviously divine about them, that you could fan into fire. Though theologians need not be prophets, you'll need a fire, for which another word might be more appropriate: *eros*, theological *eros*. Here's another way to say roughly the same thing: you'll do best as a theologian not if you are first of all seeking to gain something for yourself by being a theologian but rather if you're looking for something great to lose yourself in.

Best,
Miroslav

Notes

1 This text, like most things I write these days, has benefited much from the community of scholars with whom I work at the Yale Center for Faith & Culture: Drew Collins, Matthew Croasmun, Karin Fransen, and Ryan-McAnnally-Linz. Like many things in life, theology is best enjoyed in collaborative company with those who do and enjoy it as well.

2 If you want to read my tribute to him, see "A Death of a Friend," in *Against the Tide: Love in a Time of Petty Dreams and Persisting Enmities*, by Miroslav Volf (Grand Rapids, MI: Eerdmans, 2010), 209–11.

4

Michael Welker

Ways to Theology and Ways in Theology

There are several ways to reach the decision to start studying theology. It can be influenced by, for example, experiences of vocation or religious revival. It can be conveyed by role models in the family, among friends, at school, or in church. Or an interest in God and God's work and the desire for their deeper understanding can trigger the decision to study theology.

Perhaps amazingly, a firm personal faith is not an indispensable prerequisite.[1] Probably the greatest Christian theologian of all times, the apostle Paul, writes in his letter to the Philippians, "Not that I have already obtained *it* or have already become perfect, but I press on so that I may lay hold of that for which also I was laid hold of by Christ Jesus" (Phil 3:12 NASB1995).

These words address perhaps the most important prerequisite for studying theology. Not an unshakable subjective faith but the serious readiness to better recognize Jesus Christ, God, God's Spirit, and God's work and to exchange this knowledge with other people should stand at the beginning of the study of Christian theology and continue to accompany it. All academic work in theology should also serve this search for knowledge.

Truth-Seeking Communities

A student of Christian theology belongs to two truth-seeking communities—namely, a religious community (usually with an ecclesiastical profile) and the academy (with a humanities profile). But what are truth-seeking communities?

Truth-seeking communities are not groups of people who grope around as if in a fog to discover any more or less interesting things and events as supposed truths. Neither are they associations in which people claim to have finally found the truth—with the claim that they must now offer it to all other people without compromise or even force it upon them.

Truth-seeking communities are communities in which substantiated claims to truth are raised, expressed, examined, and put up for discussion. In religious communities and in the academy, the student of theology encounters such truth-seeking and truth-representing communities—in a shared joy of discovery and a shared sense of responsibility. A wonderful experience!

The scene of Martin Luther before emperor and empire at the imperial diet in Worms in 1521 has often been conjured up as a shining example of the representation of truth claims in theology and the Church. There, in the midst of all the attacks and threats from church and politics, he is said to have spoken his famous sentence, "Here I stand; I cannot do otherwise, God help me! Amen." Is this not a wonderful expression of certainty of faith and deep awareness of truth? Unfortunately—no!

We don't even know for sure whether Luther actually said this sentence. The words certainly attested to are these: "If I am not overcome by obvious arguments of reason and testimonies of the Scriptures, then I am overcome and my conscience is caught in God's words!" Perhaps this was followed by a "God help me! Amen." It is precisely this combination of a firmly tested conviction and a readiness to learn, not a rigid, subjective certainty, that characterizes truth-seeking communities. They make firm claims to truth and indicate under what conditions they are prepared to put these claims up for discussion and then possibly change them: "If I am not overcome by obvious . . . reason and testimonies of the Scriptures . . ." The aim is to consolidate, broaden, and deepen knowledge, not encourage stubborn dogmatism (bossiness).

Truth claims can be supported in different ways. On one hand by subjective certainty, which is stated, for example, in the words, "Here I stand . . . ," but such certainty can be based on deception. This is vividly expressed in the German evening song: "Do you see the moon standing there? It is only half visible and yet is round and beautiful." Claims to truth can, on the other hand, be supported by agreement and consensus in the community. However, it should be noted that even large communities can err, that they can be seduced and—intentionally and unintentionally—are even themselves seducers. If truth claims are made, they must be examined for correctness, coherence, and rationality—even if their correctness and coherence sometimes have only limited range and validity. These limits of scope also apply to empirical and historical evidence. That is why we need not only study, education, the exchange of knowledge and experience, the joy of discovery but also constant critical examination and self-examination in the study of theology and in academic and ecclesial theological practice.

Sources of Critical Theological Examination and Self-Examination

Henco van der Westhuizen asked, What should the students of theology be looking for, what should they listen to, what should they avoid? What can prevent them from becoming good theologians?

All serious theology students should be wary of the so-called simple, ultimate, supreme thoughts about God, which are meant to complete and spare them the pursuit of a deeper knowledge of God. They should also beware of empty and clouded ideas of God, which try to convince them that not knowing is the truly pious, the humbly believing way to God. The abstract opposites of faith and knowledge, understanding and feeling are poison for theology and for a mature faith.

All students of theology should—both in their faith communities but also vis-à-vis all other religious or religion-critical communities—firmly insist on this statement: only a God who reveals himself is a true God. A so-called God who does not reveal himself at all is, at best, a thought idol, devised by obscurantists and the domineering. Dullness and thoughtlessness are not attitudes of faith.

To adhere to God's revelation, however, requires modesty. The fullness of the living God—God's preserving, saving, and uplifting creative work—can be so overwhelming that escape from it into simple, empty thoughts of God can appear like a lifeline.

The awareness of being part of truth-seeking communities in which we are all witnesses is comforting and helpful. Our knowledge of God always lags behind the fullness of the living God and the divine Spirit; it does not exhaust the richness of divine revelation. Nevertheless, the respective, quite perspectival, and fragmentary testimonies contribute to the shared knowledge of truth as long as they refuse the deceptive simplifications and empty ideas of God.

In Christian faith, it is the christological, the biblical-theological orientation, and the orientation toward the working of the Holy Spirit that keep theology and faith on the paths of true knowledge of God. These orientations are the reliable sources of testing and self-examination.

God has revealed Godself in Jesus Christ—in the pre-Easter Jesus and in the risen and exalted Christ. This source of revelation is opened up in the testimony of the Holy Scriptures. Therefore, the thorough study of the biblical traditions is a major task of the study of theology. The biblical traditions have been developed over centuries and in very different times and environments. A solid historical and philological education is very helpful in understanding the many different contexts in which they were written.

Many people are disturbed by the polyphony of biblical truth claims. In them, Jesus is depicted in continuity and discontinuity with Moses. He is represented in continuity and discontinuity with the prophetic "men of God." He is the one filled with the Spirit of God from early on. He is essentially the Crucified and the Risen One. He is the Son of God from eternity to eternity. What applies now? Does not this polyphony contradict all claims to truth?

A very decisive task of the study of theology is to convey the knowledge that it is precisely in this polyphony that the liveliness of Jesus Christ and his saving work are grasped. Not only the testimonies of the New Testament but also the other biblical traditions—prepared, collected, compared, related to one another, coordinated, and tested against one another over at least a thousand years—refer to the liveliness of God and the richness of divine activity. They open up a great variety of individual and communal experiences with God in situations of greatest need and despair but also in joyful experiences of liberation, freedom, and peace.

The study of theology also helps students and those who profit from their studies reflect not only critically and self-critically but also gratefully and enthusiastically on the immense radiant power of the biblical testimonies and the divine Spirit in history and today. In doing so, the anchoring of theology in the academy, especially in the worldwide network of research universities, is of utmost importance. It imposes on theology the responsibility to examine and prudently represent its claims to truth in the world of multidisciplinary science, in the world of international and interreligious conflicts and relations, in the web of diverse ideological, political, and ethical concerns and claims.

Pure Academic and Pure Ecclesiastical Theology?

The high praise of an academically trained and cultivated theology is unfortunately not shared by all religious communities and certainly not by many religious skeptics. Many religious skeptics fundamentally deny that theology is capable of academic work. Some religious communities shy away from the critical voices of the academy and of science and would like to replace academic self-examination with the instructions of religious leaders. They may point to the threat of one-sidedness in the academic search for truth, to educational processes that alienate the students of theology from their childhood faith, from the piety of their youth, and ultimately, from the authorities at home and in religious communities. These tensions must be endured for the sake of the search for truth, but they do not always have to be decided unilaterally in favor of the academy.

With due respect for our passion for an academically cultivated theology, we must experience time and again that some theologians distinguish themselves as historians, language experts, or specialists in religious studies, in the philosophy of religion, in sociology, or in all possible fields of psychology. A purely academic theology, however, misses the full range of tasks of theological existence and ultimately leads to a disintegration of theology. Does this mean that all theologians should be pastors at the same time?

The double qualification and double service in church and academic practice is a great asset. Those who choose this dual ministry face the vastness and liveliness, the tribulations and joys of truth-seeking communities in all their fullness. Any academic theology should pay great respect to truth-bound church practice and be able to understand and identify itself as a service also to church practice.

But just as a purely academic theology is an endangered theology, so is a purely ecclesiastical theology that does not face academic critical self-examination often endangered. It is all too easily subject to church-political and power-political interests of so-called religious leaders and interest groups. The churches, which were completely corrupted in German fascism and South African apartheid, are a deeply deterrent example of self-satisfied churchliness. However, academic self-examination alone could not prevent these ideological and demonic developments. What helps in this muddled situation?

The event of the crucifixion of Jesus Christ, which is central to Christian faith, should make all students of theology aware of the ways of prophetic vigilance. Jesus Christ is crucified in the name of the world power Rome. But he is also crucified in the name of the ruling religion, a topic that many religious communities like to suppress. He is crucified with reference to the Mosaic law and justice and with reference to the Roman law and justice. He is crucified in the name of fickle public morals and opinion, which soon cry "Hosanna!" and then again cry "Crucify him!"

Theologians, academically educated and spiritually educated, are called, according to Karl Barth, to a "watchmen's office opposite the guards."[2] In critical and self-critical, biblically trained, and christologically oriented academic and spiritual education, they can take on this great task—in the joy of liberating truth.

Ever yours,
Michael
Heidelberg

Notes

1 That is why we should not draw too sharp a line between theologians and laypeople. Unfortunately, there are superficial theologians who may have made a career after their studies. And there are so-called laypeople without an academic degree, but with a great spiritual education and a nobleness (great formation or education) of the heart, whose theological insight is clearly superior to that of many a church leader and professor.

2 Translated from Karl Barth, *Karl Barth Gesamtausgabe: Band 19: Vorträge Und Kleinere Arbeiten 1922–1925* (Zürich: Theologischer Verlag Zürich, 1990), 678.

5

David Fergusson

There are many ways of coming to faith, and it would be unwise to be too prescriptive about any one of these. Strategies that advocate a single approach quickly become too restrictive—these overlook the myriad stories that can be told of how the grace of God has worked in our lives. We can find faith through friendship, the example of other Christians, the influence of parents and teachers, uplifting worship, the power of preaching, reading a Gospel, a crisis in our lives, or more probably, some combination of these. The mirror image of this is the sad diversity of accounts that can be offered of how faith is lost and the church forsaken. Sometimes this has more to do with the lack of love or friendship in a congregation or the gradual weariness of unwelcome burdens imposed upon the faithful few. Although a crisis of belief can occur when, for example, a student enters a philosophy course at university or someone reads a book by an avowed atheist, there are many other reasons why faith is abandoned over the course of a lifetime.

So it goes with theology. There are different points of entry. For some of us, the call to ordination led us into theological study followed by a sense of vocation to teach. I include myself in that group. For others, the deep questions posed by theology have exercised a lifelong intellectual and spiritual fascination, while the liberating potential of theology can inspire social action and personal transformation. Or perhaps the spiritual force of Augustine, Aquinas, Luther, Barth, or a contemporary figure of significance sparked an enthusiasm that blossomed into a lifetime of study. Again, the likelihood is that some combination of these is obtained. The various contexts of theological study across the world also alert us to its diverse functions and the disparate reasons people have for enrolling in a course of study. For me, one of the most enriching features of teaching theology for over thirty years has been the age range of my students and how well this admixture can work. They range from school leavers, who bring a capacity to grasp new ideas together with a willingness to tackle difficult tasks, to more mature students with a greater life experience and an intuitive discernment of what makes sense.

An obvious challenge for professional theologians is that the impulse that first led them to the subject may not persist over the course of a lifetime. This is an issue for clergy too. There are many diversions along the way, not least the necessary task of contributing to the management and administration of the institutions where we work and that support the study of theology. It's likely too that those deeply held convictions that shaped us in early life will evolve or be replaced by others. On occasion, these adjustments can lead to a crisis of vocation or at least the need to turn to different projects that are more compatible with the shift in one's interests. The pressures of an institutionalised research agenda will also constrain what work one chooses to undertake. This can sometimes result in the production of outputs intended for a specialised audience, with the consequence that one's work fails to reach a wider public. I am often dismayed by the obscurity of much theological writing. To obviate this, one may need to develop a balancing strategy that enables one to write for different audiences. We should follow Thomas Aquinas in praying for subtlety of interpretation, clarity of thought, and grace of expression.

In undertaking theological research, one enters a community, both real and virtual. The stimulus of attending seminars and conferences, of drinking coffee and beer, of meeting the authors of the books and articles we've read, and of discussing one's research with one's peer group is part of what makes theological (and other forms of) study enriching. Doctoral students often worry about the dearth of professional prospects. This is not an unreasonable anxiety, especially in the current climate, though I'm always surprised by the ways in which they find their way in different forms of ministry, teaching, and professional service, even when these have not been envisaged at the outset. Today's graduate students will need much more than a Plan A as they embark upon their projects.

But for all of us, our commitment to theology will recall our teachers who set an example of intellectual seriousness, pastoral care, and personal encouragement. And as we become teachers, so we rely on the support and responsiveness of our students, probably more than they realise. I have often been inspired by students who returned to me in later years to recall something I had said or done that I had long forgotten. This reminds me of my father, who worked as a general practitioner. He would often reflect on the gratitude of patients for whom he'd done very little, or so he thought. Some of them turned up at his funeral many years later.

For me, the relationship of the theologian to the church remains paramount. It is one's rootedness in the primary community of faith that makes the discipline most rewarding and endlessly fascinating. Our work ought to have a positive relationship to the lives of fellow Christians for the sake of their upbuilding, encouraging, and consoling (1 Cor 14:3). Good theology should display a capacity to command a *consensus fidelium*, the resonant voice of the faithful who recognise its power and authenticity. Without this, theologians become more prone to cynicism or to strategies that relentlessly deconstruct or debunk the faith. This is a particular temptation at a time of ecclesiastical decline in the West, though those who travel to study here from overseas remind us of the vibrancy of church life in other parts of the world.

Vital to every Christian life, the regular activities of prayer and worship are also necessary for the pursuit of theology. Without these, it is too easy to be cast adrift and to lose one's bearings. I say this (I hope) not from an excess of pious sentiment or in a partisan spirit but in the conviction that theology is about faith seeking an understanding that will inevitably elude us as we reflect on the mystery of God. I have often returned to the haunting words of Simone Weil: "One can never wrestle enough with God, if one does so out of pure regard for the truth. Christ likes us to prefer truth to him, because being Christ, he is truth. If one turns aside from him, to go towards the truth, one will not go far before falling into his arms."[1]

All good wishes,
David

Note

1 Simone Weil, *Waiting for God* (London: Routledge, 1951), 36.

6

Nicholas Wolterstorff

We were talking, that morning over coffee, about your future career. You asked me whether I would recommend your going into systematic theology and, if so, what I thought was important to do in it. I gave you only a moderately competent answer. Your questions, after all, were big ones; and though I can't say that I had never thought about them before, still you caught me off guard. Now, after a bit of reflection, I'd like to try again.

I suppose I don't really have to remind you that I'm not a professional theologian. I'm a philosopher by trade. I feel I should mention this because my being a philosopher rather than a theologian will naturally shape my answers to your questions. Also, I'll keep in mind that, as our conversation made clear, you had decided that *if* you would pursue the career of systematic theologian, it would be in the context of the Reformed church of which you are a member. You weren't wondering whether you should pursue it in some nonconfessional, ecumenical context.

It's my firm impression that systematic theology on the American scene has fallen on bad days. I don't really keep up with it; but one thing that strikes me when I do dip into it is that American theologians have become Tractarians. They are constantly saying that we ought to have a theology of this and we ought to have a theology of that; but the called-for theologies seem never to appear. I regard such Tractarianism as marking a lack of intellectual seriousness.

Then, too, it seems that contemporary philosophy has struck terror into the minds of theologians. I would certainly be the last to argue that philosophy is irrelevant to the work of the theologian. In fact, I think it's indispensable. But I find it pitiful that shortly after Whitehead's process philosophy became well known, theologians began declaring that Christian theology must now be harmonized with process philosophy; that shortly after Heidegger's philosophy became well known, theologians began declaring that Christian theology must now be harmonized with Heideggerianism; that shortly after logical positivism became well known, theologians began declaring that Christian theology must now be harmonized with logical positivism. I admire the guts of Karl Barth, who thumbed his nose at us philosophers and said no to all such one-sided harmonizing.

So it seems to me that if you become a serious systematic theologian working with Christian integrity on the American scene, you'll be rather lonely. While I'm on the topic, though, let me urge you, nonetheless, to maintain the contacts you've already built up with American theologians. Don't become a hole-and-corner theologian. We have enough Reformed theologians who have no interaction with the American theological scene. We who are academics have responsibilities toward many different, overlapping communities. The Reformed theologian has responsibilities not only to the community of Reformed theologians but to the whole community of American theologians as well.

But *should* you become a systematic theologian? Certainly. I can't think of anything more worth your becoming. I'm taking for granted that you've already made the decision—as you told me you had—to go into some form of academic work.

I'll give you my reasons shortly. But first let me set something off to the side as *not* my reason. In the Reformed churches, it has long and often been thought that the heart of a person's appropriate response to the gospel is the acceptance of certain beliefs. On occasion, I have called that view *doctrinalism*. It was, as I look back, the view that I imbibed as a child. Furthermore, in the tradition, there was often no distinction drawn between the beliefs that someone as a follower of Christ is obliged to hold and the articulation given those beliefs by the classical Reformed theologians. These were blurred together. So what came out was the conviction that the heart of a person's appropriate response to the gospel is the acceptance of Reformed doctrine—total depravity, unconditional election, limited atonement, and so forth. No doubt if you had put it straight to any one of those doctrinalists, they would have said that *life* is also important.

But a member was always far more likely to be put out of the church for denying total depravity than for cheating on their taxes.

Now in that way of thinking, systematic theology is obviously of immense importance. Yet ironically, that way of thinking has always had the effect of thwarting all fresh and imaginative theological efforts. It's not hard to see why. All such efforts will appear either as revisions of the true gospel or as needless additions. Thus the Reformed churches have always been in the position of canonizing a few theologians, recognizing a somewhat larger group as loyal camp followers, and consigning the others to limbo. If you had put your first question to some Reformed doctrinalist, they would almost certainly have advised you to go into systematic theology, emphasizing its great importance. But they would have expected you to repeat loyally what Calvin said, what Bavinck said, what Berkhof said—with possibly some rearrangement for pedagogical purposes. They would have expected you to hand on unrevised, classical Reformed theology.

I think this view, that the acceptance of Reformed doctrine constitutes the heart of our faithful response to the gospel, is mistaken on two counts. I agree that faithful followers of Christ are required to hold certain beliefs. God cares what we think. Let's not go down the existentialist road of saying that there is no "propositional content" to the faith. But beliefs are only part of what is required. What is required is obedience *in our lives as a whole*. It is indeed required that we *believe* that Jesus Christ rose from the dead. But so too it is required that we celebrate the supper of our Lord and stand at the side of the poor and the oppressed as friends and defenders.

But then, second, I don't for a minute believe that as faithful followers of Jesus Christ, we must embrace all that stands in the books of classical Reformed theology, even if it were all true. And I hope you never believe that about any books you yourself may eventually publish. That is to confuse the belief content of the faith with the elaborate theoretical structure developed by the theologian concerning God and God's relation to humankind and the world. The theologian presumably believes that what they write is true. But they must also admit that not all of what they write is required to be believed if one is to be a faithful follower of Christ.

Incidentally, as a reaction against these two mistakes that have been so prominent in our tradition—the mistake of identifying our loyal following of Christ with our assenting to the belief content of the faith and the mistake of identifying the belief content of the faith with Reformed doctrine—there are those in our community who want nothing to do with systematic theology. They regard it as a curse. Such an attitude is just as misguided as the other. I mention it because you had better be aware that your very existence as an imaginative theologian will provoke critics on the left as well as on the right.

My principal reason for thinking that the work of the professional systematic theologian is important goes along the following lines: Systematic theology is unavoidable for Christians. The systematic theology of most of us is rudimentary, piecemeal, and inarticulate; but it's there nonetheless. The calling of the professional systematic theologian is to do more deeply, more systematically, more articulately what all of us do in our own less-than-competent ways.

We study our Bibles and try to put together what we read there about God and God's relation to human beings and the world. Then we read commentaries, go to church, talk with fellow Christians, and read Christian literature, trying to put all that together with what we had already concluded. And then we read some psychology, some philosophy, some comparative religion, some biology, trying to fit that together with the rest. What emerges is a body of beliefs, a body of theories, on God and God's relation to human beings and the world. What emerges is a systematic theology of an informal sort.

But usually it's rudimentary, not thought through. Usually it's fragmented, not tied together. Usually it's inarticulate, not expressed with any precision of thought. The professional theologian does the same thing that we all do, but better. Their work, as I see it, is not qualitatively different from the hasty efforts of the rest of us. Their work, for example, does not mark the incursion of theory where there was none before. Rather, it's an *intensification* of what we all do.

When there are professional theologians working within the community and making their work available to us, then we all benefit, each at our own level. For then we can go to someone for assistance in working out our own framework of beliefs. Naturally, the theologian to whom we go for assistance will have to be someone to whom we are willing to listen. But I think that confessional theologians usually exaggerate the degree of acceptance that must exist between them and their audience. Not finding it, they are paralyzed into timidity, inactivity, or privacy. Don't expect everybody to accept anything you say, and don't expect anybody to accept everything you say. Your contribution to your own confessional community (not to speak here of your wider contribution) will not lie in everybody's just going along with what you say. We laypeople can and will make up our own minds. What we need is assistance in that.

Another way of getting at these matters is to ask what goes wrong in a confessional community when solid and imaginative systematic theology is missing. Many things. For one thing, the community becomes susceptible to a multitude of fads, arising both within and without. A new method of evangelism is proposed, or a new method of counseling, and no one has thought things through well enough to know whether the proposal should be accepted. The rapid rise and fall of fads within the church is a pretty good sign that professional systematic theology is not doing its work.

Professional systematic theology is of particular importance in a confessional community within the Reformed tradition—and here, of course, I speak directly to your loyalty and to mine. In great measure, what holds the Anglican community together is its common liturgy. In great measure, what holds the Roman Catholic community together is its shared authority structure. In great measure, what holds the Reformed community together is a certain perception of God's relation to human beings and the world, plus an impulse that flows from that perception to see every legitimate occupation as a calling from God and to seek the reform of the surrounding society. Because a certain mode of understanding is thus at the heart of what holds a Reformed community together, the Reformed tradition has always had a very intellectual tone. For the same reason, systematic theology has always been of great importance in it. Its importance lies in the fact that if we do not have professional systematic theologians within the community who are fundamentally Reformed in their perspective, assisting us in each shaping our own informal systematic theology, that particular contour of beliefs that one might call "Reformed" is bound to fall apart and disappear in most of us. As a matter of fact, I think that is happening in most Reformed churches. Seeing it happen makes me sad, for I believe that the Reformed tradition represents a profound perception of the shape of the gospel and has the promise of continuing to be of great benefit to Christendom and Western civilization. I think the disappearance of good systematic theology is, in great measure, responsible for the decline. I see in you, and in some other young theologians, the promise of a renascence.

Perhaps here is the place to tuck in my advice that because you see it as part of your calling to enliven the Reformed tradition in the twentieth century, you must become acquainted with that tradition deeply enough so that you can distinguish between what lies at its heart and what constitutes irrelevant accretions picked up over the centuries. Include that in your program of studies.

I want to highlight two implications of what I've been saying. One is that in your professional work, you must keep an ear open for the perplexities of those of us who are not professional theologians and address yourself to those perplexities. That follows from my having said that the rationale for the work of the *professional* systematic theologian is that they give assistance and guidance to the rest of us. One thing that distresses me about many of our theologians is that they seem strangely unconcerned to give guidance to us nonprofessionals on the issues that vex us. For example, all of us today are concerned—and confused, I might say—about the nature and task of the church. Yet we who are not professional theologians are forced to work out our ideas by ourselves. That is defection from responsibility on the part of our professional theologians. So at the beginning of your career, let me say to you as emphatically as I can: part of your calling as a professional theologian will be to listen to us and to address yourself to answering *our* perplexities.

A second implication is that the systematic theology that you produce must be *systematic* systematic theology. That sounds odd. What I mean is this: one of the chief flaws in the systematic theology of us laypeople is that it isn't very systematic. There are theologians around who are interesting to read and sometimes helpful, but many of them are also unsystematic. They are *dabblers*. They do not, with passion and intensity, follow out the consequences of their ideas, probe their foundations, and fit it all together. Such theologians are of little permanent benefit. For really to know whether an idea is acceptable, you have to know where it goes, what underlies it, and how it fits together with other ideas. The great contribution of Karl Barth to twentieth-century theology is that he was a passionately *systematic* systematic theologian. After his work, we know, very much better than we ever did before, where certain ideas go. To be a *systematic* systematic theologian takes a great deal of intellectual determination and single-mindedness (Latin, *monomania*). It's so much easier to be a genial dabbler. I hope you've got what it takes. I know you do; so instead I say, *cultivate* what it takes.

Already I've written you a sizeable letter, and I still haven't gotten around to what I think is important for you and others to do in systematic theology. So let me hurry on to that.

(1) Over the years, I've come to the conviction that one of the most fateful decisions ever made in the classical tradition of Western theology was to explicate God's relation to time in terms of eternity rather than in terms of everlastingness. God, it's said, is outside of time. The alternative would have been to say that though God is without beginning and without end, and though God is Lord of what takes place in history, yet God's own life incorporates succession. Once the decision is made that God is eternal, vast consequences follow. Then God is immutable, then God does not really respond to the actions of human beings, then God does not do one thing before another—create, say, before sending his son into the world—and so on. The Bible, of course, pervasively speaks of God as acting in sequence. The theologian committed to God as eternal must somehow explain that all away.

I myself have concluded that the classical theologians made the wrong choice, and I have argued the case in some detail in my essay "God Everlasting."[1] When I first delved into the matter, I expected to find a great number of biblical texts that would give trouble for the "God everlasting" position. To my surprise, I discovered that there are only two or three texts that are ever cited in favor of the "God eternal" position and that these, when read in context, clearly say not that God is outside of time and unchanging but that God is faithful to God's covenant promises.

(2) More recently, I have come to think that an even more crucial stone in the edifice of classical Western theology is the doctrine that God is simple—that within God, there are no distinctions of any sort. God's exemplification of any one attribute is identical with God's exemplification of any other attribute, God as such is identical with God's exemplification of any attribute, there is no earlier part of God's history distinct from any later part, and so on. What this means, of course, is that the whole categorical structure with which we think and speak of God does not, in fact, apply to God. For we, of course, make and presuppose a multitude of distinctions, unavoidably so. Thus as I now see it, the doctrine of

divine simplicity functions not so much as a distinct doctrine in theology but as a preface to theology. What it says is that none of what follows in the theological discussion is really true. What *is* really true of God is, of course, never said. It is inexpressible. I think you can easily see why it was that their doctrine of divine simplicity led the classical theologians to formulate a doctrine of analogy when they were discussing our predications concerning God.

Now, some have seen it as a mark of piety to say that none of what we say about God can be really true of God. They say that we must humbly confine ourselves to thinking and speaking of God as God has revealed to us that God wants us to think and speak of God and that we must never suppose that that is how God is. To me, that seems a matter not of piety but of extreme skepticism. And if those who espouse this position *really* hold it, they will also have to say that God does not *really* reveal Godself and is not *really* an object of our worship.

But more relevant is to ask why theologians have held this view. Here one finds the biblical evidence even more meager than it was for God as eternal. The historical truth of the matter, so it seems to me, is that later theologians have followed in the path of the early theologians, and the early theologians took over from the Greek philosophers the two doctrines of God as eternal and God as simple. It was Parmenides who first thought of the divine along these lines. I think both doctrines must be rejected as incoherent and as unfaithful to the Scriptures. Christian theology must be dehellenized.

But for the theologian to reject these doctrines is to commit themselves to a massive project of reconstruction, the scope of which I have only hinted at. I myself see the prospect of that reconstruction as both enormously exciting and—I admit—rather frightening. But the outcome, I am persuaded, will be a theology both more biblically faithful and more coherent.

(3) I have also slowly over the years come to see that fundamental to the whole biblical witness is a certain understanding of how God acts—namely, that God acts in great part by human beings acting. By Jesus doing what he did, says Paul, God was reconciling the world to himself. By the prophet saying what he did, says the writer of Deuteronomy, God was speaking. In short, by persons acting, God acts. Yet in spite of the centrality of this understanding in the biblical witness, theologians have given it little attention. The early Christian theologians began to worry over questions

of identity: Was Jesus identical with God or not? Did he have a nature identical with God's or not? The whole notion of God acting by men acting fell from view. And once again, what they began, others have continued. Here, I think, is a whole rich and important area of theological—and philosophical—investigation.

The implications, again, are many. I don't see, for example, how we can ever formulate a coherent evangelical doctrine of Scripture without achieving clarity on this matter. For surely, the evangelical confession is that by way of Paul saying what he did in his letters, *God* spoke to the Corinthians and speaks yet to us. So too the Calvinist understanding of the sermon requires clarity on this matter. For Calvin was of the view that by the minister saying what they say, God speaks.

Thus far, I have spoken of various matters that need exploration in the foundations of theology. I have suggested that what is called for is considerable reconstruction. Let me now move to important, but less foundational, matters.

(4) I think the doctrine of election needs to be explored anew. (When didn't it?) As I see it, Reformed theologians have thought of election as God's making persons be and do something—God's producing conversion in a person, say. That conception of election gets expressed in vast stretches of Reformed thought. But in the Scriptures, there is another—and I would guess far more prominent—way of thinking of election. Election consists of God's *choosing* a person (or a people) to do or become something. And to such a choice, such a call, there are many biblical examples of the called person saying no. I don't know where a doctrine of election thus conceived would go. But it seems to me to bear the promise both of being more faithful to the Scriptures than the concept of election as God's making someone do or be something and of delivering us from a morass of traditional impasses.

(5) I think the relation of creation and redemption must be explored anew. That's pretty vague; unfortunately, I can't do better. In great measure, this seems to me to be an issue raised for the theologian not so much by the perplexities of us laypeople as by occurrences in twentieth-century theology. In Barth, for example, there is a systematic reluctance to see redemption as occurring within the context of, and for the fulfilment of, creation. Rather, creation is seen as for the sake of redemption. Barth's greatness, as I earlier suggested, lies in carrying out this idea with astounding single-mindedness and imagination. For example, the basic task of the

state in his view is to make the preaching of the gospel possible. Christianity, in his view, is not a religion but opposed to all religions; it is a word of God, whereas they are all words of humans. In his view, when the gospel is preached, there are no beliefs, and perhaps not even any concerns, in the auditor to which the preacher can attach their proclamation. And so forth. I don't think that theologians have even begun to work through the issues that Barth raised.

(6) An issue raised for the theologian by the perplexities of us laypeople is the nature and task of the church—whether now you understand the church as the people of God or as the ecclesiastical institution. We are confused about both and about their relation. Consequently, we don't know what form evangelism should take. We don't know what role the church should have with respect to social justice. And we don't know very well whether the church is the company of the committed ones, the covenant community of the baptized ones (believers and their children), or some combination of these.

(7) Last, the church's confrontation with Marxism—and with many other "isms"—requires that we begin to develop a theology of history, or as it was traditionally called, of eschatology. Do we as human beings have a role to play in the coming of the Kingdom? If so, what is it? Do only Christians have a role to play, or does everyone? How do their roles differ? Do nations have a role? Are there some favored nations in God's scheme? Do we now have only the promise of a new life, and will the age of the resurrection for the first time introduce that new life? Or do we already have new life, and does the age of the resurrection mark its fulfilment? If the latter, what does that mean as to how Christians should be living today? Should they be living in model communities committed to communism of goods and to pacifism?

In reading over this letter, I find that I myself can get excited about the prospect of being a systematic theologian today. Actually, I once considered becoming one, as I told you. Now I almost regret having made the decision I did. Almost.

One last point. I suppose some concerned but rather cautious and conservative person will ask why the old Reformed theologians aren't enough for our purposes today. Why something new? Why have I been emphasizing imagination? Well, it's really fairly obvious, isn't it? Over the course of history, we come to a better understanding of the difference between biblical Christianity and classical Greek philosophy. Over the course of history, new theologies enter the public arena. Over the course of history, new concerns and perplexities grip the minds of God's people. That's why theology must always be done anew. That's why imagination is needed.

As *ever,*
Nick

Note

1 Nicholas Wolterstorff, "God Everlasting," in *Contemporary Philosophy of Religion*, ed. Steven M. Cahn and David Shatz (Oxford: Oxford University Press, 1982), 181–203.

On Hermeneutics,
Reading, Writing

7

Richard Kearney

If you are thinking of studying Christian theology, I would recommend you start by ignoring what every theologian has written and addressing Christ's question directly—"Who do you say that I am?" The hermeneutic question par excellence.

Then, I humbly suggest, you might ask why Christ never offers an abstract metaphysical solution to the riddle, but *acts*. He acts in the flesh, as word made flesh (not concept). And almost every act is one of healing. Just look at the Gospel narratives where Christ touches the wounded and welcomes embodied strangers as friends. Note how Christ heals himself by healing others.

In short, before you take up any of the great *summae theologiae* (and the best, I submit, are still those of Aquinas and the subtle Celts, Duns Scotus, and Scotus Eriugena), consider closely the stories of how God came on earth to cure the sick in body and soul.

The revolutionary meaning of incarnation was too often muted in mainstream Christianity. But it was there from the beginning. Saint Paul famously wrote in his letter to the Philippians that Christ willingly emptied himself of divinity—his "equality with God"—in order to assume human wounds in his body, offering himself as a healer for mortals. After his emptying descent (*kenosis*) into flesh, Christ spent much of his life curing sick people by touching them—laying hands on the blind, deaf, and dumb, the crippled and the dying. Think of the healing of the twelve-year-old girl: "Taking her by the hand, Jesus said, '*Talitha koum*' (Rise up, little girl)" (Mark 5:41; my translation). Or the cure of the leper: "Jesus stretched out his hand, touched him, and said, 'I do choose. Be made clean'" (Luke 5:13). Or, more graphically still, the cure of the deaf-mute in Decapolis: "He put his finger into the man's ear and, spitting, touched his tongue . . . and said, '*Ephphatha!*—Be opened!'" (Mark 7:32; my translation). It is significant, I think, that Jesus heals by touch before word and even forbids the cured leaper and deaf-mute to speak of it afterward. He enjoins both of them "not to tell anyone." And we could also cite here the other famous cures of the centurion's servant, the Syro-Phoenician's daughter, Peter's mother, or the blind man on whose eyes Jesus rubs mud before bidding him bathe in the pool of Siloam. Christ came on earth to touch the wounded. And significantly, it is a matter not only of him touching others but of *being touched* by them in turn. Jesus is eminently tangible, and Christianity is a story of "double sensation" throughout—a phenomenon vividly portrayed in the story of the hemorrhaging woman who grasps the hem of Jesus's cloak while he is not looking, a scene regularly portrayed in religious paintings throughout the centuries, in which the verb *touch* (*hapto*) is repeated four times:

> She had heard about Jesus and came up behind him in the crowd and touched his cloak. She said: "if I but touch [*hapsomai*] his clothes, I shall be cured." Immediately her flow of blood dried up. She felt in her body that she was healed of her affliction. Jesus, aware at once that power had gone out from him, turned around in the crowd and asked: "Who has touched me?" (Mark 5:27–30; my translation)

Jesus *feels* the power draining from him even though he does not actually *see* it. He turns in surprise. The contact is carnal before it is cognitive. It is a quintessential reciprocal sensation, as the Gospel keeps reminding us: "Everyone in the crowd sought to touch him because power came forth from him and healed them all" (Luke 6:19 NABRE).[1] Or again, "[They] begged him that they might touch only the tassel on his cloak; and as many as touched it were healed" (Mark 6:56 NABRE).

One might even say that Jesus is gradually apprenticed to his humanity—it takes time for Word to become flesh—by receiving the humanizing touch of *others*. From the moment he is conceived, Jesus is carried in a womb, fed at the breast, and surrounded by animals in a manger before going on to spend three decades working with his hands as a carpenter. One often forgets that Jesus was a handyman for thirty years, and maybe they were as formative as his last three. For without this basic material labor of hands on wood, Jesus might have been tempted to forget his earthly body and slip back into pure spirit. The lure of Gnosticism has haunted theology since—the great temptation of ex-carnation, denying the corporality of Christ. But it is remarkable how carnal Christ really was. How deeply

The Healing of the Blind Man, Rembrandt (photo by Sarah Kearney)

touched he was, for example, by Lazarus's death—John tells us "Jesus wept" (John 11:35 ESV)—to the point of bringing Lazarus's physical body back to life (several paintings depict Jesus carrying his friend in his arms from the tomb). And how often his gestures of healing, as noted, involve explicit moments of touching and eating. Indeed, his postpaschal appearances almost invariably involve Jesus touching and feeding his disciples: "come and have breakfast" are his words to them on Lake Galilee (John 21:12 ESV). Christ did not say "Believe this"; he said "Eat this!" "Touch this!"[2] Christ is tactile before and after death.

Healing of Bleeding Woman, anonymous fresco (photo by Sarah Kearney)

The Touch of Thomas

But if you really want to explore a radical theology of incarnation, look to the primal scene where Thomas places his hand in Jesus's side. Thomas was not just an incredulous sceptic, as received tradition has it, but a healer educator. He was the disciple who helped his master resist the erasure of scars in a Glorious Body that would be no body at all.[3] He refused the lure of ex-carnation. The risen Jesus heeds Thomas's challenge in the Upper Room to remain true to his wounds, keep his promise of ongoing incarnation as a recurring Christ who returns again and again every time a stranger (*hospes*) gives or receives food and water (Matt 25). This repetition of Christ as an infinitely returning stranger—in the reversible guise of host/guest—is what we might call *ana-carnation* (from the Greek prefix *ana-*, meaning "again," "anew" in time and space).[4] It is a story of endless carnal reanimation captured in the verse of Gerard Manley Hopkins:

Thomas touching wounds, detail from *The Incredulity of Thomas*, Caravaggio (photo by Sarah Kearney)

Christ plays in ten thousand places,
Lovely in eyes, lovely in limbs not his
To the Father through the features of men's faces.[5]

Ana-carnation is the multiple repeat act of incarnation in history—resurrecting not only in the future *after* Christ but also in the past *before* Christ, through countless identifications with wounded strangers, forgotten or remembered. It signals the tangible reiteration of Christ (BCE and CE) bringing Jesus back to earth in a continuous community of solidarity and compassion.[6] This is the kingdom come on earth invoked in the Lord's Prayer. And by this reading, Thomas ceases to be a "servant" and becomes a "friend," nay even a "mentor," of Jesus—a doctor teacher who holds Jesus to his word made *flesh*, ensuring Jesus remains faithful to his carnality. Thomas, hailed as the patron saint of medicine in India, has no time for supersensible erasure or one-way ascension into heaven. On the contrary, he reminds us that what goes up must come down and that "the last temptation of Christ" was not to marry and remain human—as Kazantzakis has it in his great novel—but to rise too quickly to heaven and lose touch with his body altogether. To disappear into pure air! In short, we might say that Thomas acts in keeping with the Samaritan woman at the well and the Syro-Phoenician woman at the table—all outsiders from the margins, teachers from the basement, reminding Jesus that his divinity is in his tangible humanity, that the right place for the infinite is in-the-finite. Otherwise, Christian in-carnation becomes ex-carnation, a fundamental betrayal of Word made flesh. Thomas will have none of it: he climbs to the Upper Room to bring Jesus back to earth.

In all these Gospel scenes, Jesus is recalled to his original healing vocation: his mission to bring full humanity to the earth. *Incarnation* means assuming a body that can touch and be touched and doing so with the wisdom of two-way tact. In Christ, as the first letter of John tells us, God became a person we can touch with our hands. To forget this is to forget the basic message: "I came that they may have life, and have it abundantly" (John 10:10).

The history of Christianity, I am suggesting to you, is a story of being in and out of touch with flesh. It is out of touch when it betrays the truth of Word made flesh, veering toward notions of anticarnal Gnosticism and puritanism. Witch-hunting and the inquisitorial persecution of "pagan" earth religions and carnal sexuality were symptoms of such puritanical zeal. And it was this history of suppressing the body that prompted Nietzsche's ire: "Christianity is the hatred of the *senses*, of joy in the senses, of joy itself. . . . It leaves others the *body*, wanting only the *soul*."[7] The resultant pathologies of sexual repression and abuse, misogyny and repudiation of bodily joy, tell their own story. But it is only half the story, as my admonition to you on the ana-carnational character of Christianity hopes to show—especially concerning the power of healing touch.

So dear aspiring student of theology, once you have taken the flesh of Christ to heart, you should then—and only then—feel ready to take up the great metaphysical summae and inquire how each of them is an attempt, directly or indirectly, to respond to the call of incarnation. And doing so, consider carefully Aquinas's praise of eucharistic taste and touch, Duns Scotus's celebration of the unique "thisness" (*haecceitas*) of things, Eriugena's panentheist embrace of the "running God" (*deus currens*), and Bonaventure's fascination with the divine fingerprint (*vestigia dei*) in all creatures. When you witness the mystery of Christian ana-carnation, you can take seriously the Augustinian summons—*tolle lege*, take up the book and read.

      All good things,
      Richard

Notes

1 See also Mark 3:10: "He had cured many and, as a result, those who had diseases were pressing upon him to touch him" (NABRE).

2 See the radically incarnational claim of John 6:51: "I am the living bread that came down from heaven; whoever eats this bread will live forever; and the bread that I will give is my flesh for the life of the world" (NABRE). On the claim that God becomes flesh (John 1:14), the Franciscan Richard Rohr writes, "Incarnation is scandalous, shocking, intimate, sexual. Christ did not say 'think about this, fight about this, stare at this'; he said 'eat this!' A dynamic, interactive event that makes one out of two. . . . As Gandhi said, 'There are so many hungry people in the world that God could only come into the world in the form of food. It is marvelous that God would enter our lives not just in the form of sermons or Bibles, but as food.' God comes to feed us more than just teach us. Lovers understand that" (qtd. in Richard Kearney, *Touch: Recovering Our Most Vital Sense* [New York: Columbia University Press, 2021], 166).

3 See Giorgio Agamben, "The Glorious Body," in *Nudities*, trans. David Kishik and Stefan Pedatella (Palo Alto, CA: Stanford University Press, 2010), 91–103.

4 Richard Kearney, *Anatheism: Returning to God after God* (New York: Columbia University Press, 2010).

5 Gerard Manley Hopkins, *Poems and Prose* (London: Penguin, 1953), 51.

6 See Shelly Rambo, *Resurrecting Wounds: Living in the Afterlife of Trauma* (Waco, TX: Baylor University Press, 2018); and Tomas Halik, *Touch the Wounds* (Notre Dame, IN: Notre Dame University Press, 2021). See also the interdisciplinary work of Jacob Meiring, "Theology in the Flesh—Embodied Sensing, Consciousness and the Mapping of the Body," *Theological Studies* 72, no. 4 (2016): 1–11, where he explicitly engages our project of carnal hermeneutics.

7 Nietzsche's *The Anti-Christ* quoted in Alice Miller, *The Untouched Key* (New York: Anchor Books, 1990), 112.

8

Piet Naudé

And you show that you are a letter from Christ delivered by us, written not with ink but with the Spirit of the living God, not on tablets of stone but on tablets of human hearts.

—2 Corinthians 3:3 RSV

Once in a circle of professional people, everyone had to explain briefly what they did. The lawyer applies the law, the doctor diagnoses illness and promotes health, the architect designs new buildings, the accountant signs off on financial statements, the psychologist offers therapy, and the civil engineer builds roads and bridges.

When my turn came, I simply signaled: "Theologians read."

The invitation to study and practice theology is an invitation to start on a hermeneutic journey. Hermes, from which *hermeneutics* is derived, was the Greek god of translators and interpreters. He acted as a messenger for all other gods. Hermes was involved in reading, messaging, translating, interpreting, conveying meaning, clarifying from Mount Olympus—site of all the gods—and crossing the boundaries between the realms of gods and humanity.

Christian theologians carry the huge responsibility and have the enormous honor to attain *theos logos* (knowledge of God). We then act as readers, translators, and interpreters to convey to other humans—in the most truthful way possible—the will and words (Word) of God.

What do theologians read?

The first and obvious answer is that we read written texts, the most important of which is the canon, a gathering of books collectively called and confessed as the Bible, the Word of God. Canon history, the story of how these books became authoritative, is in itself an interesting read. But the most basic task of a theologian is reading the Scriptures—and for good reason in the original languages of Hebrew, Aramaic, and Greek (grammatical criticism). This is no simple task. And not only because one has to learn ancient languages but because reading itself is a complex process.

Reading is both a science and an art.

In traditional exegetical theory, we read the world "behind" the biblical texts (historical criticism). We need to understand the ancient Near Eastern world in which most of the Old Testament was constructed and the Roman-Hellenistic world of the New Testament. We read the world "of" the texts by careful distinction of the great variation of literary genres found in the Bible—each requiring a distinct and appropriate reading mode (form criticism). Reading the Bible as a literary collection richly rewards the theologian and interpreter (literary criticism).

As far as historical research assists us, we need to understand who the author(s) are—whether individuals or oral communities—as well as the intended or actual first recipients/audiences. In this way, the reconstructed "original" communication events (as contained in the written text) assist us in discerning the meaning of the texts, taking into account their own formation into the final canonical form (tradition and redaction criticism).

Reading theology does not only mean a reading of distinct texts and books and testaments contained in the canon and assisted by different exegetical methods. No, reading is also aimed at making sense of the canon as a whole. For this to happen, exegetes construct specific theological themes as interpreted from the original text. One then speaks about the theology (constructed meaning) of the Yahwist, the Deuteronomist, Luke, Paul, or John. Or one selects a specific hermeneutical angle (feminist, ecological, materialist) or theme (covenant, people of God) to aid in making sense of Scriptures, abiding by the ancient rule that the Scriptures interpret themselves best!

But it is a humble realization that we in the twenty-first century—with all our scientific (historical-philological) knowledge—are not the first readers.

This realization requires us to also read the interpretation history, or the world "in front of" the text. Instead of viewing the historical and cultural distance between us and the biblical texts as a difficult chasm we need to overcome, that distance constitutes the creative *Wirkungsgeschichte* (reception history; Gadamer) of the text, transforming interpretative distance into creative modes of understanding.

We see this already happening intracanonically where earlier events and texts are adopted and reinterpreted in later biblical texts. See, for example, the mighty reinterpretation of the law by Jesus in the Sermon on the Mount (as reported by the three first Gospels) or the gallery of the faithful accounted for in Hebrews 11.

Then follows the postcanonical times, which we can divide into the periods of the Church Fathers; the Middle Ages; the Protestant Reformation; the modern, secular period; right up to the Pentecostal and Independent Churches' readings of the Scriptures today. Early schools like Antioch and Alexandria and names like Origen, Augustine, Aquinas, Luther, Calvin, Barth, Bultmann, Gutiérrez, Radford Ruether, and many others are all good reading companions providing us with a layered reading tradition.

Reading theology always happens within a certain theological tradition— even more so for those who claim to be "just reading the Bible without any creeds." There are at least six of these traditions, each providing helpful lenses to highlight aspects of the biblical text (even where the canon itself is disputed). We know these traditions in historical order as Catholic, Orthodox, Lutheran, Reformed, Pentecostal/Independent, and Ecumenical. The best way to approach these traditions is to first survey and understand one's own tradition (with its strengths and blind spots) and then enter into fruitful dialogue to gain additional perspectives from other traditions.

These traditions yielded us the ecumenical creeds like Nicea and the Apostolicum and confessions like the Heidelberg Catechism, the Barmen Declaration, the Belhar Confession, and the Accra Declaration. One then discerns the shoulders of the church as a "reading community" on which we stand and from which we derive enormous wisdom and benefit.

Reading theology is not only interested in the past—namely, the world from which the text arose and how it was read through the ages. The interest in the past is exactly aimed at reading the present so that a creative fusion of horizons (Gadamer) can occur where the text speaks afresh in new and different contexts.

Theology has always read the Zeitgeist (spirit of the present time) with philosophy as its primary partner. By reading Aristotle or Erasmus and the humanists, or Enlightenment philosophers like Descartes and Kant, or postmodern thinkers in the twentieth century, theology could understand both the ancient text and the text of contemporary society. Philosophy remains key, but there are additional disciplinary languages required to read dominant social systems (Luhmann) in our current situation.

One immediately thinks of the powerful hold of economics (the Market is god, says Cox; capitalism is a religion, says Harari) and the embeddedness of our total existence in technologies (in the beginning, there was the Word; now there is the Update, says Jarzombek). These two social realities merge to form the enormous power of "data economics" and point in dramatic fashion to the exciting, ever-shifting task of reading for the sake of *kairos*—expressing the right word at the right time at the right audience.

Yes, reading theology is not an action in and for itself. With the rise of "public theology" (Tracy, Moltmann, Bedford-Strohm), theologians overtly distinguish their reading audiences or publics. Academic reading is meant for the public of professional theologians, pastoral and confessional readings are meant for the public of the church, and social-political reading is meant for the public domain in its broadest sense. Reading theology always includes speaking theology—as is required by the public and the context.

This guarantees theology's continued relevance and makes reading theology an adventure with ever-new interpretative challenges. Never a dull moment for reading theologians!

Reading theology is also a future-oriented, or eschatological, task. This is not in the first instance a reference to the "future-telling" prophets who are so popular in some Pentecostal and Independent traditions. (They know our fascination with the future and also know that "how God is going to act" at such and such a time is a drawing card for followers and the media.)

Reading theology as a future-ing task implies a continuous pointing toward the transcendence of God in relation to both living space and time. God and God's kingdom are both immanently present (via creation and incarnation) and are always transcending our current social realities (via the resurrection of Jesus, the Christ). For God, a thousand years is like a day (Ps 90:4), whilst Jesus Christ is the same yesterday, today, and forevermore (Heb 13:8).

This future-ing task prevents human existence from both a collapsed, impoverished immanence and from false transcendent promises arising from different ideologies that purport to bring hope for tomorrow by the mere realization of restricted current possibilities. Theology reads and tells of the radically Other who makes all things new.

Reading theology, finally, requires as precondition self-reading or self-understanding. We are reflexively reading the reader as well. Calvin, in the opening paragraphs of the *Institutes of the Christian Religion*, refers to the inexorable tie between knowledge of self and knowledge of God. He holds that "it is evident that man never attains a true self-knowledge until he has previously contemplated the face of God, and come down after such contemplation to look into himself."[1]

Self-understanding is important, because we always already have some idea of the text we read and cannot jump over the shadow of our own presuppositions (Bultmann). Every exegesis is always also eis-egesis. By acknowledging the character of our *Vorverständnis*, we become aware of both its inhibiting and its enabling power to read responsibly. Such a pre-understanding includes our theological tradition, social location, assumptions about gender, and pious ideas about the Bible.

This reading of the self leads to a transformation toward *becoming a text*.

Theology is an academic discipline aimed at knowledge of God. The spiritual purpose of theologians' reading different texts in the search of this knowledge of God is for ourselves to become a text to be read by others. By reading the text of Scripture and all associated "texts," we ourselves become *text*ured. We—our attitudes, writings, teachings, lifestyles—are letters from Christ, revealing knowledge of God as we are transformed by the Spirit of the living God. We could also resist or grieve the Spirit (Acts 7:51; Eph 4:30), reducing theology purely to technical hermeneutical capabilities and sophisticated philosophical reasoning, devoid of the character of whom we write and think about.

Reading theology is, in the end, being read as theologian. As Paul says in 2 Corinthians 3:2–3,

> Your very lives are a letter that anyone can read by just looking at you. Christ himself wrote it—not with ink, but with God's living Spirit; not chiseled into stone, but carved into human lives—and we publish it. (MSG)

I pray for a blessed reading journey!

Piet Naudé
Stellenbosch

Note

1 John Calvin, *Institutes of the Christian Religion*, trans. Henry Beveridge (Peabody, MA: Hendrickson, 2008), 5.

9

Karen Kilby

I feel quite pompous writing to you out of the blue—am I really so sure I have useful counsel to offer? Perhaps I will begin with advice for later in life: when you get to be an older theologian, make sure to notice when the time comes to listen and learn from the young rather than always assuming you have a lot to say that everyone else needs to hear. Otherwise, dangers of pomposity and repetition—making a fool of oneself in one direction or another—loom large.

I'm worried not only about making a fool of myself, actually, but also about whether there is advice that can usefully be given that is not specific to the person addressed. So, for instance, it's hard to think of anything more significant to being a theologian than the dispositions one brings to the task. Some desire for truth, some concern for other people, a capacity to hold the ego in check, a degree of humility—these are the first things that come to my mind. But they are absolutely pointless to commend, or worse than pointless. A reader who lacks these qualities will think, *Of course, of course, all very basic, everyone already knows about such simple things—I wouldn't have expected her to be quite so trite and obvious*, and then read on, looking for something more stimulating or novel. Someone who does possess these dispositions, on the other hand, might well be cast into doubt by my mention of them: *Do I really care for the truth? How would I know whether I do? Maybe I am just pursuing it all from a secret desire to be, or to seem, clever. Maybe I am only telling myself that I am concerned for others, but really it is all about me.*

You may notice that the list of dispositions that first came to my mind is quite generic. Aren't they, you might wonder, virtues that would be significant for any intellectual pursuit whatsoever? If I am going to be casting around for advice to give a young theologian, wouldn't it make sense to give advice more specific to theology? Shouldn't I be urging the young theologian to prayer, contemplation, a fervent faith, a deeper love, a resolute focus on God? Didn't Evagrius say that the theologian is the one who prays, and the one who prays is a theologian?

This style of advice, when I see it offered, worries me. These things are indeed important: we do all stand in need of prayer, of a deepening of our faith and hope and love. But we stand in need of this, it seems to me, just as all Christians do. This need and these practices are what unite us with others, not what mark us as distinct. I'd rather not suppose that to be a theologian is to belong to an elite club of extraholy people. In one sense, of course, to be a theologian *is* to be a member of an elite group: you have a level of education, time for thinking and study, and probably a level of intellectual ability that are not available to everyone. And precisely for this reason, it is important not *also* to imagine yourself as part of a spiritual elite. I've sometimes toyed with a slightly different motto, making a bit of a play on Evagrius: maybe the theologian is the one who prays, and who stumbles in their prayer, and who thinks about their stumbling. Maybe we have a particular gift to offer the church—not as leaders, advance guard, all-round models but as slightly odd people, average believers in other ways, involved in the practice of the faith just as others are but more inclined than others to question, probe, and puzzle over what we don't understand. And sometimes, as a result, we are able to bring back something useful to others.

It is an unheroic vision of what it is to be a theologian, I know, but it does have the advantage of underlining one thing: if you want to contribute to others, to be of some use to someone, as many of us do, this doesn't mean that you should force yourself to work on the most obviously practical or most morally urgent topic possible. Often, I think, we have most to contribute if we pursue the problems and themes that genuinely concern and interest us, even if it is only later that we learn in what way they matter to anyone else. This is particularly important early in a theological career. Later there will likely be calls on you, requests from others, and it may be natural and right to let your thinking be shaped by what others ask. But in the early years, it is worth allowing your attention to go, insofar as circumstances allow, to whatever draws you the most, to whatever bothers you the most, to wherever it is that your deepest interests lie.

I say all this because of an anxiety I felt myself as a young theologian and that I sense in quite a number of others I meet, especially other lay theologians: Is theology really a legitimate occupation for a Christian? we ask ourselves. Should we not be doing something more obviously in service to others, something that addresses the wounds and shocking injustices of our societies? In a world where so many terrible things are done and suffered, is it legitimate to try to gain a clearer grasp of the concept of divine simplicity, or an insight into the balance between Aristotelian and Neoplatonic influences on Thomas Aquinas, or the relation of philosophy to theology in the thought of Karl Rahner? The process of doing a doctorate is typically the process of becoming more and more focused on narrower and narrower matters, ever further away from the everyday concerns of others. Can that really be the shape of a Christian vocation?

I will not respond, "Yes, of course, just focus your research, no matter how obscure, and do your best to ignore any little awareness you have of the cries of those who suffer so as not to be distracted." Just as prayer is part of the Christian life, so is the effort to turn our ear towards, rather than away from, the suffering of others and the demands of justice. Like anyone else, like any other Christian, the theologian is in need of a kind of continual conversion, a conversion enabling us to attend to the pain of others and the call of justice. For some, theological work grows directly out of this; for none, I would hope, is the theological life untouched by it. But that does not mean that every theologian is obliged to cast around for what seems the most practically or morally urgent task—the most oppressed group, the greatest moral outrage or ecclesial need, the most critical crisis—and then, as a matter of principle, devote themselves to it. That would be a formula for producing stale and mechanical work, of limited use to anyone or any cause, including the cause in whose name one sets out.

The worry over whether one ought to be doing something more practical is one of a number of anxieties with which young theologians often live—we might call it the anxiety of relevance. Another anxiety is, of course, the career. Is there a job to be found at the end of a doctorate? Not everyone worries about this. Clergy, in my experience, don't—perhaps clergy are less worldly, but there is also the fact that they already have a version of employment security. In countries where PhD students are paid a good salary, I detect less anxiety—the students don't risk so much in pursuing their studies and can consider with equanimity the possibility of moving to another kind of work after the doctorate. But for many, the worry about eventually getting a job is a powerful one and can spawn a whole host of subworries: When do I need to publish, and how much? Whom do I need to impress? Are some of my colleagues cleverer than I, or better at playing the game? What else am I supposed to do to become marketable—translations, conference organising, book editing . . . ? In my experience, students get most of their advice on such questions from other students, and in the process, both misinformation and group anxiety escalate.

There is also an anxiety that arises from theology itself, from what I can only call its intellectual impossibility. To be a theologian, you ought to know classical and contemporary languages. You surely need to be up to speed with biblical scholarship if you claim to take Scripture seriously. To do theology without a serious immersion in the history of the subject is to operate in the dark, and in particular, there is a range of key figures from the past that must be encountered firsthand, at some depth, and in context. And naturally, one can't be a good theologian without serious philosophical training, both conceptually and in the history of philosophy. The list goes on. To ignore either science or social science is to be irresponsibly out of touch with the world around you. All theology is, in some way, political, and so you need to work out how you see the world politically and how you see your theology in relation to this. Without a deep and sympathetic knowledge of Christian traditions other than your own, you risk being antiecumenical and culturally blind, while it would be hopelessly narrow to be a Christian theologian without paying serious attention to non-Christian religious traditions. And surely, if one is to do theology well, and not in an anti-intellectual style, it needs to be in engagement with literature and the arts?

Each of these demands is reasonable, even undeniable. Collectively, they are impossible. As a result, nothing is easier than to be convinced one is not a proper theologian and to live in dread of the moment when one's ignorance of something every serious scholar obviously ought to know will be revealed. As a young theologian, one watches one's peers display their own particular strength, their linguistic capacity or historical knowledge or intellectual quickness or conceptual power or whatever it may be, and of course one thinks, *Yes, that is how you're supposed to do it*, and feels inadequate. None but the arrogant, I'm inclined to think, ever feel fully competent in theology.

I'm sorry to say that I don't have a cure to offer for all these anxieties. I can't tell you how to be certain that your work will prove of service in the end, or how not to worry about getting a job, or how to get around the fact that you cannot know everything you ought to know. I can only suggest that these fears need not be a sign you are doing the wrong thing, or doing it in the wrong way. Obviously, it is a great privilege, and endlessly fascinating, to be a theologian, to be able to approach from such a variety of angles such a rich and deep tradition, to enter conversations across disciplines, across continents, across centuries. Obviously, there is great fulfilment in being able to focus, intellectually, on questions that matter most, even if the answers are always beyond us. But not knowing whether this pursuit of one's deepest interests will turn out to matter to anyone else, or whether this path in which you invest so much will in the end be open to you—such uncertainty is just not easy. I am inclined to say that for many, and especially for many lay theologians, this is a form of suffering that simply needs to be endured as part of the vocation. The goal, perhaps, should be to bear this suffering lightly enough that it does not damage the integrity of your work.

I wish you, then, insight in the midst of the stumbling, peace in the midst of the anxieties, and a long and fruitful path to tread before you too end in repetition and pomposity.

All the best,
Karen

IO

Stanley Hauerwas

"The Christian religion," writes Robert Louis Wilken, "is inescapably ritualistic (one is received into the Church by a solemn washing with water), uncompromisingly moral ('be ye perfect as your Father in heaven is perfect,' said Jesus), and unapologetically intellectual (be ready to give a 'reason for the hope that is in you,' in the words of 1 Peter). Like all the major religions of the world, Christianity is more than a set of devotional practices and a moral code: it is also a way of thinking about God, about human beings, about the world and history."[1]

Ritualistic, moral, and *intellectual*. May these words, ones that Wilken uses to begin his beautiful book, *The Spirit of Early Christian Thought*, be written on your soul as you begin college and mark your life—characterize and distinguish your life—for the next four years. Be faithful in worship. In America, going to college is one of those heavily mythologized events that everybody tells you will "change your life," which is probably at least half true. So don't be foolish and imagine that you can take a vacation from church.

Be uncompromisingly moral. Undergraduate life on college campuses tends in the direction of neopagan excess. What a waste! Not only because such behavior is self-destructive but also because living this way will prevent you from doing the intellectual work the Christian faith demands. Be deeply intellectual. We—that is, the Church—need you to do well in school. That may sound strange, because many who represent Christian values seem concerned primarily with how you conduct yourself while you are in college; they relegate the Christian part of being in college to what is done outside the classroom.

The Christian fact is very straightforward: to be a student is a calling. Your parents are setting up accounts to pay the bills, or you are scraping together your own resources and taking out loans, or a scholarship is making college possible. Whatever the practical source, the end result is the same. You are privileged to enter a time—four years!—during which your main job is to listen to lectures, attend seminars, go to labs, and read books.

It is an extraordinary gift. In a world of deep injustice and violence, a people exists that thinks some can be given time to study. We need you to take seriously the calling that is yours by virtue of going to college. You may well be thinking, "What is *he* thinking? I'm just beginning my freshman year. I'm not being called to be a student. None of my peers thinks he or she is called to be a student. They're going to college because it prepares you for life. I'm going to college so I can get a better job and have a better life than I'd have if I didn't go to college. It's not a *calling.*"

But you are a Christian. This means you cannot go to college just to get a better job. These days, people talk about college as an investment because they think of education as a bank account: you deposit the knowledge and expertise you've earned, and when it comes time to get a job, you make a withdrawal, putting all that stuff on a résumé and making money off the investment of your four years. Christians need jobs just like anybody else, but the years you spend as an undergraduate are like everything else in your life. They're not yours to do with as you please. They're Christ's.

Christ's call on you as a student is a calling to meet the needs of the Church, both for its own life and the life of the world. The resurrection of Jesus, Wilken suggests, is not only the central fact of Christian worship but also the ground of all Christian thinking "about God, about human beings, about the world and history." Somebody needs to do that thinking—and that means *you.*

Don't underestimate how much the Church needs your mind. Remember your Bible study class? Christians read Isaiah's prophecy of a suffering servant as pointing to Christ. That seems obvious, but it's not; or at least, it wasn't obvious to the Ethiopian eunuch to whom the Lord sent Philip to explain things. Christ is written everywhere, not only in the prophecies of the Old Testament, but also in the pages of history and in the book of nature. The Church has been explaining, interpreting, and illuminating ever since it began. It takes an educated mind to do the Church's work of thinking about and interpreting the world in light of Christ. Physics, sociology, French literary theory—all these and more (in fact, everything you study in college) are bathed in the light of Christ. It takes the eyes of faith to see that light, and it takes an educated mind to understand and articulate it.

There's another dimension to the call of intellectual work. In the First Letter of Peter, we read, "Always be prepared to make a defense to any one who calls you to account for the hope that is in you" (3:15 RSV). Not everybody believes. In fact, the contemporary American secular university is largely a place of unbelief. Thus the Church has a job to do: it must explain why belief in the risen Lord actually makes sense. There's no one formula, no one argument, so don't imagine you will find the magic defense against all objections. You can, however, offer the reasonable defense Peter asks for. You may at least make someone think twice before they reject the risen Lord.

Anyway, defense isn't the point. Lots of people feel lost because they imagine being a sophisticated, contemporary intellectual makes faith impossible. The Church wants to reach these people, but to do so requires an ambassador at home in the intellectual world. That's you—or at least, that's what you can become if you do your work with enthusiasm. Share in a love of learning. It's a worthy love in its own right, and it will allow you to be the leaven in the lump of academia.

So, yes, to be a student is to be called to serve the Church and the world. But always remember who serves what. Colleges focus on learning; as they do so, they can create the illusion that being smart and well educated is the be-all and end-all of life. You do not need to be educated to be a Christian. That's obvious. After all, Christ is most visible to the world in the person who responds to his call of "Come, follow me." I daresay Saint Francis of Assisi was more important to the medieval Church than any intellectual. One of the most brilliant men in the history of the Church, Saint Bonaventure, a Franciscan, said as much. But the Church needs some Christians to be educated, as Saint Bonaventure also knew; this is why he taught at the University of Paris and ensured that, in their enthusiasm for the example of Saint Francis, his brother Franciscans didn't give up on education.

The best way to think about the relation between your calling as a student and the many other callings of Christians can be found in 1 Corinthians 12. In this letter, Paul is dealing with a community in turmoil as various factions claim priority. It's the same situation today. Pastors consider preaching and evangelizing the most important things. Teachers consider education the most important thing. Social activists argue for the priority of making the world more just. Still others insist that internal spiritual renewal is the key to everything. Saint Paul, however, reminds the Church at Corinth that it comprises a variety of gifts that serve to build up the Church's common good. To one person is given wisdom, to others knowledge, to still others the work of healing, prophecy, and the discernment of the spirits. By all means, honor those who are serving the Church in the ordained ministry, or through social action, or through spiritual direction. But remember: you are about to become a student—not a pastor, a social worker, or a spiritual director. Whatever you end up doing with your life, now is the time when you develop the intellectual skills the Church needs for the sake of building up the body of Christ.

Your Christian calling as a student does not require you to become a theologian, at least not in the official sense of the word. Speaking as one whose job title is "Professor of Theology," I certainly hope you will be attracted to the work of theology. These days—at least in the West, where the dominant intellectual trends have detached themselves from Christianity—the discipline of theology is in a world of hurt, often tempted by silly efforts to dress up the gospel in the latest academic fashions. So God knows we need all the help we can get.

But there is a wider sense of being a theologian, one that simply means thinking about what you are learning in light of Christ. This does not happen by making everything fit into Church doctrine or biblical preaching—that's theology in the strict, official sense. Instead, to become a Christian scholar is more a matter of intention and desire, of bearing witness to Christ in the contemporary world of science, literature, and so forth.

You can't do this on your own. You'll need friends who major in physics and biology as well as in economics, psychology, philosophy, literature, and every other discipline. These friends can be teachers and fellow students, of course, but for the most part, our intellectual friendships are channeled through books. C. S. Lewis has remained popular with Christian students for many good reasons, not the least of which is that he makes himself available to his readers as a trusted friend in Christ. That's true for many other authors too. Get to know them.

Books, moreover, are often the way in which our friendships with our fellow students and teachers begin and how these friendships become cemented. I'm not a big fan of Francis Schaeffer, but he can be a point of contact—something to agree with or argue about. The same is true for all writers who tackle big questions. Read Plato, Aristotle, Hume, and John Stuart Mill, and not just because you might learn something. Read them because doing so will provide a sharpness and depth to your conversations. To a great extent, becoming an educated person means adding lots of layers to your relationships. Sure, going to the big football game or having a beer (legally) with your buddies should be fun on its own terms, but it's also a reality ripe for analysis, discussion, and conversation. If you read Mary Douglas or Claude Levi-Strauss, you'll have something to say about the rituals of American sports. And if you read Jane Austen or T. S. Eliot, you'll find you see conversations with friends, particularly while sharing a meal, in new ways. And of course, you cannot read enough Trollope. Think of books as the fine threads of a spider's web. They link and connect.

This is especially true for your relationships with your teachers. You are not likely to become buddies with your teachers. They tend to be intimidating. But you can become intellectual friends, and this will most likely happen if you've read some of the same books. This is even true for science professors. You're unlikely to engage a physics professor in an interesting conversation about subatomic particles. As a freshman, you don't know enough. But read C. P. Snow's book *The Two Cultures*, and I'll bet your physics teacher will want to know what you're thinking.[2] Books are touchstones, common points of reference. They are the water in which our minds swim.

You cannot and should not try to avoid being identified as an intellectual. I confess I am not altogether happy with the word *intellectual* as a descriptor for those who are committed to the work of the university. The word is often associated with people who betray a kind of self-indulgence, an air that they do not need to justify why they do what they do. Knowledge for knowledge's sake is the dogma used to justify such an understanding of what it means to be an intellectual. But if you're clear about your calling as a student, you can avoid this temptation. You are called to the life of the mind to be of service to the gospel and the Church. Don't resist this call just because others are misusing it.

Fulfilling your calling as a Christian student won't be easy. It's not easy for anyone who is serious about the intellectual life, Christian or not. The curricula of many colleges and universities may seem, and in fact may be, chaotic. Many schools have no particular expectations. You check a few general education boxes—a writing course, perhaps, and some general distributional requirements—and then do as you please. Moreover, there is no guarantee that you will be encouraged to read. Some classes, even in the humanities, are based on textbooks that chop up classic texts into little snippets. You cannot become friends with an author by reading half a dozen pages. Finally, and perhaps worse because insidious, there is a strange anti-intellectualism abroad in academia. Some professors have convinced themselves that all knowledge is just political power dressed up in fancy language, or that books and ideas are simply ideological weapons in the quest for domination. Christians, of all people, should recognize that what is known and how it is known produce and reproduce power relations that are unjust, but this does not mean all questions of truth must be abandoned. As I said, it won't be easy.

You owe it to yourself and to the Church not to let the incoherence, laziness, and self-critical excesses of the contemporary university demoralize you. Be sure not to let these failures become an excuse for you to avoid an education—a Christian education. Although some universities make it quite easy to avoid being well educated, I think you will find that every university or college has teachers who deserve the titles they've been given. Your task is to find them.

But how can you find the best teachers? There are no set principles, but I can suggest some guidelines. First, ask around. Are there professors who have reputations as intellectual mentors of Christian students? You're eighteen. You don't need "substitute parents"—or, at least, you don't need parents who think you are still twelve. But you do need reliable guides. So rearrange your schedule to take the professor who teaches Dante with sensitivity to the profound theological vision of that great poet. You may end up disagreeing, both with the professor and with Dante, but you'll learn how to think as a Christian.

Also, go to the bookstore at the beginning of the term to see which professors assign books—and I mean real books, not textbooks. Textbooks can play a legitimate role in some disciplines, but not in all, and never at all levels. You want to find the teachers who have intellectual friends, as it were, and who want to share those friends with their students. If a professor has a course outline that gives two or three weeks to reading Saint Augustine's *Confessions*, you can reasonably hope that they think of Saint Augustine as someone they know (or want to know) and as someone they want to share with students.[3]

The best teachers for a Christian student aren't always Christians. In fact, a certain kind of Christian teacher can lead you astray. It's not easy to see the truth of Christ in modern science or contemporary critical theory, for example. The temptation is to compartmentalize, to assign your faith to the heart, perhaps, and then carry on with your academic work. Some professors have become very comfortable with this compartmentalization, so be careful. By all means, take spiritual encouragement wherever you can get it; these sorts of professors can be helpful in that regard. But don't compartmentalize, because that's basically putting your Christian faith outside of your work as a student.

Your calling is to be a Christian student. The *Christian* part and the *student* part are inseparable. It will be hard and frustrating because you won't see how the two go together. Nobody does, at least not in the sense of having worked it all out. But you need to remember what Christ says: "I am the Alpha and the Omega" (Rev 22:13 NIV). However uncertain we are about *how*, we know *that* being a Christian goes with being a student (and a teacher).

Although many professors are not Christians (at some schools, most aren't), many professors have a piety especially relevant to the academic life. One, for example, might be committed to the intrinsic importance of knowing Wordsworth's poetry, while another works at getting the chemistry experiment right. These professors convey a spirit of devotion. Their intellectual lives serve the subject matter rather than treating it as information to be mastered or, worse, a dead body of knowledge to be conveyed to students. English literature and modern science do not exist for their own sakes, and the university doesn't raise money for the sake of professors' careers. For these professors, the educational system exists for the sake of their disciplines, which they willingly serve. This spirit of devotion is not the same as Christian faith, but it can help shape your young intellectual desires and impulses in the right way by reminding you that your job as a student is to serve and not to be served. College isn't for you; it's for your Christian calling as an intellectual.

Eventually, you will no longer be a freshman, and American undergraduate education will force you to begin to specialize. This will present dangers as well as opportunities. You will be tempted to choose a major that will give you a sense of coherence. But be careful that your major does not narrow you in the wrong way. It's true, for example, that modern psychology provides powerful insights into the human condition, but don't allow your increasing expertise to lure you into illusions of mastery. Continue reading broadly. It may seem that the more you know about less and less, the smarter you've become; after all, you now know so much more about psychology! But in truth, the more you know about less and less should teach you humility. After a couple of years spent taking advanced courses in modern European history, you'll know more about the French Revolution, but if you're self-reflective, you'll also know how much work it takes to know anything well. And there's so much more to know about reality than modern European history.

To combat a tendency toward the complacency that comes from mastering a discipline, it is particularly important that you gain historical insight into the practice of your discipline. For example, I have nothing but high regard for those disciplines we group under the somewhat misleading category "the sciences." Too often, though, students have no idea how and why the scientific fields' research agendas developed into their current form of practice. To go back and read Isaac Newton can be a bit of a shock, because he interwove his scientific analysis with theological arguments. You shouldn't take this as a mandate for doing the same thing in the twenty-first century. It should, however, make you realize that modern science has profound metaphysical and theological dimensions that have to be cordoned off, perhaps for good reasons. Or perhaps not. The point is that knowing the history of your discipline will, inevitably, broaden the kinds of questions you ask and force you to read to be an intellectual rather than just a specialist.

It is also important that you not accept as a given the categorizations that dominate the contemporary university. For example, if you read Dante, you probably will do so in the English department. The English department has claimed Dante because it considers the *Inferno* "literature."[4] Dante obviously was a poet, and one of the most influential, but he also was a theologian, and we fail to do him justice if we ignore that quite specific theological convictions, some controversial in his own day and in ours as well, were at the center of his life and work. The same can be said for the theology department, which often imagines that a particular form of scholastic and philosophically shaped reflection defines the discipline even as the departmental theologians ignore the mystical traditions as well as the traditions of biblical commentary.

I emphasize broadening your major with historical questions and challenges to set categories because your calling is to be a *Christian* student, not a physics student or an English student. Again, I do not want to make every Christian in the university into a theologian, but it is important for you to interrogate theologically what you are learning. For example, you may major in economics, a discipline currently dominated by mathematical models and rational-choice theories. Those theories may have some utility (to use an economic expression), but they also may entail anthropological assumptions that a Christian cannot accept. You will not be in a position even to see the problem, much less address it, if you let your intellectual life be defined by your discipline.

There's more to say, and I wish I could give more practical, concrete advice. But most of academic life is "local," as Tip O'Neill once said of politics. Theology programs at some nominally Christian colleges are positively harmful to the calling of the Christian student; programs at others are wonderfully helpful. For some students, studying with a professor who avows atheism may be their first encounter with a teacher who thinks faith is relevant to the intellectual life, albeit in a purely negative way. The encounter need not harm the Christian student. It might galvanize the student's convictions and set them on the course of figuring out how faith supports and motivates the intellectual life. Still, as I have tried to emphasize, you need good mentors—men and women who are dedicated to their work and for whom a fitting humility about the limits of their expertise leads them to read broadly and thus become intellectuals rather than specialists.

Let me return to Robert Wilken's observation about the ritual, moral, and intellectual life of the Christian. Don't fool yourself. Only a man or woman who has undergone a long period of spiritual discipline can reliably pray in the solitude of a hermitage. You're young. You need the regular discipline of worship, Bible reading, and Christian fellowship. Don't neglect them in college. Also, don't underestimate the moral temptations of the contemporary college scene. We cannot help but be influenced by the behavior of our friends, so choose wisely.

To worship God and live faithfully are necessary conditions if you are to survive in college. But as a Christian, you are called to do more than survive. You are called to use the opportunity you have been given to learn to construe the world as a creature of a God who would have us enjoy—and bask in—the love that has brought us into existence. God has given your mind good work to do. As members of the Church, we're counting on you. It won't be easy. It never has been. But I can testify that it can also be a source of joy.

What a wonderful adventure you have before you. I wish you well.

Stan

Notes

1 Robert Louis Wilkin, *The Spirit of Early Christian Thought: Seeking the Face of God* (New Haven, CT: Yale University Press, 2003), xiii.

2 C. P. Snow, *The Two Cultures* (Cambridge: Cambridge University Press, 2012).

3 Augustine, *The Confessions* (Oxford: Oxford University Press, 2008).

4 Dante Alighieri, *The Divine Comedy* (Oxford: Oxford University Press, 2008).

II

Miroslav Volf (II)

I set out to write these letters to celebrate your decision to study theology and to encourage you. I hope that I have made it clear why theology really matters, even why it has never mattered more than it does today. The extrinsic rewards of theology—money and fame—may be scant, but if you come to love theology, you'll find yourself doing much-needed and highly rewarding work. But doing theology is also hard work, placing high demands not only on your intellect but on the entire orientation of your life. I stress this, and will say more about it shortly, because I want you to fall in love with the fierce beauty of the magnificent royal thing itself rather than some diminished version of it. My experience is that while the service theology demands is arduous, it is immensely rewarding—and joyful too.

You won't love theology—the real thing—for long unless you love *hard*, *intellectual* work. You've got to learn your languages, some ancient and some modern, and you've got to study history. Then there are many formidable theologians, some of whom are difficult on the surface and easier the deeper you go, while others are the other way around. There's also the cultural sea in which you swim, the many and related things on which you might want to shine the light of the gospel; its waters are turbulent and full of crosscurrents that thinkers from various disciplines try to make sense of.

For my doctoral dissertation, I wanted to explore ordinary human work, the kinds of things we do from nine to five, or whenever it is that your day job starts and ends. So I decided to write on Karl Marx, the most influential thinker to write extensively about work. But to understand Marx on work, I had to wrestle with Hegel and his *Phenomenology of the Spirit* (1807), which turned out to be a nearly impossible task. Ernst Bloch is reported to have observed that Immanuel Kant's very difficult *Critique of Pure Reason* (1781) was "train-ride reading" compared to Hegel's

Phenomenology. You may not need to read Hegel's impenetrable book to do your theological work well, but there's no avoiding texts that require an intellectual equivalent of "mule work."

Speaking of the hard intellectual work and endurance needed . . . While I was a doctoral student in Tübingen, Germany, Karl Rahner, a great Catholic theologian from the last century and a formidable thinker himself, delivered the Leopold Lukas lecture (1983). The posters—I read the one on the entrance door of the historic Gastl bookstore right across from the Stiftskirche—announced the topic: "On Intellectual Patience in Itself." The title puzzled us all; we wondered what the great theologian would say about the essence of intellectual patience. It turned out that the title was garbled in transmission. The lecture he came to deliver was "On Intellectual Patience *with Oneself*"—*in sich selbst* had replaced *mit sich selbst* on the posters.[1] Without intellectual patience with yourself, you'll likely lose heart; I certainly would have. And you'll need patience with yourself not just at the beginning of the theological journey but all the way to its end; Rahner delivered that lecture less than two years before he died, after all his major work was done.

The intellectual challenges in doing theology are out in the open, strewn like big boulders on your path; they puzzle and perplex you, they slow you down, and some you end up unable to remove and must circumvent. Less obvious and often unrecognized is another challenge. Call it *spiritual.* Like ancient Greek philosophies, theology wants to claim your whole life, not merely your mind. It isn't just done *for* a way of life, flourishing life, but is itself part of that way of life. Not all share this view. Here is why I embrace it. In my previous letter, I explained that theology's subject matter is God (and everything in relation to God), and its purpose is furthering God's mission in the world. But God isn't just out there, an object like a distant galaxy, though immensely more complex. A good argument can be made that God isn't an object among other objects at all. For God, who is uncreated, brought into being "all things," which is to say, all objects of which God cannot be one (John 1:3). But that's not the point I wish to dwell on here. I want to draw your attention to another aspect of the claim that God is not an object—namely, that if you believe in God, God is not something about which you can decide whether the concept concerns you in a deep way. Whenever we talk about God, we aren't just talking about God; we are speaking *also* and *inescapably* about ourselves. God is the source of our lives, and importantly, God sets the goal of our lives. The entire orientation of the world's history and of each of our lives is always involved, directly or indirectly, when we talk about God. We often forget that fact, and God makes it easy for us to forget because God has made it a habit to remain anonymous. God concerns in an ultimate sort of way everything we are and do.

Friedrich Nietzsche, my favorite anti-Christian and antitheologian, has somewhere written, "One ought to hold on to one's heart; for if one lets it go, one soon loses control of the head too." If he is right, and I think he is, a simple and revolutionary consequence follows: for theologians *not* to lose control of their heads—for theologians to be able to discern, articulate, and commend well a Christian vision of a flourishing life—they must keep their hearts set on God and on God's purposes with the world. Set it on something else—and set it you will—and the shape of your theology will shift, though likely not right away and not in all respects. You will find it unsustainable to discern, articulate, and commend a vision of flourishing life that runs counter to what is de facto your god. That's why an important tradition in Christian theology insists that saints, those imperfect people whose lives are stably oriented toward God, are our most reliable theologians.

Which brings me to Jesus Christ, the divine Word who became a human being and lived among us. Do you like him? I ask because the Christian faith just *is* relationship to Jesus Christ. Christian theology, therefore, either has Jesus Christ at the center or has lost its identity. In response to the question I asked you, a lot of Christians say they do like Jesus, but it often feels they are saying it because that's what's expected from them. Most of us cherry-pick from his teaching and example. For others, he has morphed into a vague source of unadulterated comfort, as if they and he were figures in a sentimental painting of "Jesus and the Little Children." In either case, lost is the heavy "cost of discipleship" of which Dietrich Bonhoeffer wrote powerfully at the time of collective nationalist and racist madness in Germany (1937). "Whoever comes to me," says Jesus, "and does not hate father and mother, wife and children, brothers and sisters, yes, and even life itself, cannot be my disciple" (Luke 14:26; see also Deut 33:9). "Hate" can mean here many things. But whatever "hate" means, all possible meanings of it are ways to carry the cross and follow him. This Jesus scares me. If I am honest, I am ambivalent about letting my three-year-old daughter be among the little children in his arms; his blessing seems more like a burden than a boon. I know about the promise he makes that "there is no one who has left house or wife or brothers or parents or children, for the sake of the kingdom of God, who will not get back very much more in this age, and in the age to come eternal life" (Luke 18:29–30). But the price still seems unreasonably high and impossible to pay. Do you like *that* Jesus?

Jesus Christ liberates captives from sin, oppression, and futility, and his Spirit renews the face of the earth. But like God in the story of Abraham's near sacrifice of Isaac, Jesus Christ also demands nothing less than what he promises to return transformed and dressed in splendor—our very lives with everything we have. The question about "liking" Jesus is, of course, wrongly phrased to heighten the provocation. It assumes that Jesus has no intrinsic value, makes him comparable to a flavor of ice cream or a make of car. In the offending verse about "hatred" of our own lives, Jesus is talking not about likes and dislikes but about ultimate allegiance, about the aspiration to orient one's whole life toward him and toward becoming like him. This shifts attention away from taste and sentiment to commitment and practice. And increases the stakes.

In case you were wondering, I haven't forgotten that I am writing you a letter about being a theologian. The work of theology presupposes spirituality, and the shape of spirituality it presupposes is that of "forgetting what lies behind and straining forward" (Phil 3:13 ESVUK) into obedience and conformity to Jesus Christ. That "spiritual" labor of the body and soul is as hard as any intellectual labor theology may require of you—and also at least as joyful too.

Yours,
Miroslav

Note

1 Karl Rahner, "Über die intellektuelle Geduld mit sich selbst," in *Über die Geduld*, by Eberhard Jüngel and Karl Rahner (Freiburg, Germany: Herder, 1986), 39–63.

On Ways in Theology

12

Jan-Olav Henriksen

I was happy to learn that you have decided to study theology! Theology is not only among the oldest disciplines in the university, but it is also a study that allows you to enter into many different realms of human existence: history, thinking, believing, worshipping, reading, and so on. Therefore, this study will not only engage you as a whole person, but it will open up further to a life in faith with understanding. It also offers you the opportunity to think through why people believe what they believe and to assess their beliefs from a critical point of view—not to make things difficult for them but to help them develop a transparent and more profound understanding of how faith can shape their lives.

Actually, theology is not one discipline. Theology consists of many different approaches and a variety of different topics that one needs to deal with in different ways. For example, it requires the skill to read Greek and understand the New Testament in its historical context but also the knowledge about present positions in philosophy and the role of religion in the contemporary society. And much more. Hence you can study theology in different ways, with different interests and concerns, and develop your skills in various directions. This diversity is part of what makes theological studies so enriching!

Your decision to study theology takes me back to my own study days and challenges me to reflect on the difference between then and now. As I embarked on my studies more than forty years ago, theology was still mostly about understanding what the Bible says and how it shapes the content of peoples' doctrinal beliefs. Accordingly, theological studies were very much oriented toward your own denomination and what your church was teaching and believing. Some would therefore say that theology was, fundamentally, a normative discipline. And it was mostly about reading, interpreting, and understanding texts. Of course, this is still the case to some extent. However, some factors have changed the shape, scope, and context of theological studies: First of all, theology has become oriented toward practice and the study of how belief and religious life actually manifest and shape people's lives. This change is reflected not only in so-called contextual theology but also in the growing interest of theological students to do empirical work in their papers. In scholarly terms, we call this the empirical turn in theology. I am very grateful for this change, because it means that in the present, theology students are enabled to work on topics related to peoples' lives and how they practice their faith. The empirical turn makes visible the experiential dimension always present in theology. This dimension is sometimes understated or forgotten—especially if one mainly focuses on theology as doctrine.

A consequence of this turn is that what was previously the main focus in theology—that is, the study of texts—has been expanded now to include how these texts are understood, used, and included in different practices. This refocusing helps us understand that a text never exists on its own, but its use is linked to conditions in the social context where it is read. This has liberated theology from being confined to a Western, white, and male-dominated expression and entailed a shift in focus, concerns, and aims for many who *do* theology. (I write "do theology" here because theology is a practice best expressed in the odd word *theologizing*.)

This first shift implies that what were previously clear boundaries between theology and religious studies have become more blurred. The introduction of the disciplines psychology of religion and sociology of religion to theological studies has also contributed to this blurring. This means that the skilled theologian needs to know not only the texts but also the context in which the texts work and *how* they work. To use a metaphor: a good theologian needs to know not only the instruction manual but also how to maneuver the tools she has acquired through her studies in different contexts and under different conditions.

A second shift, which perhaps is more visible in parts of Europe than elsewhere, is that denominational demarcations play a lesser role than they used to. That is a good thing because it allows theological studies to cross borders and learn from a broader range of perspectives. That theology has become more ecumenical is a necessary development if Christianity is to be able to avoid being hijacked for political or ethnic purposes—which is an ever-present and alluring danger.

It is not a wise thing to study theology from one perspective alone. One of the main advantages of this study is that you get the opportunity to learn from others—not only from books but from other people. Others are an opportunity to expand your world. I know of students who said that they entered their studies only to confirm what they already believed in and to get a diploma. This approach to theological studies is very narrow. I believe that such students will risk exiting their studies just as narrow-minded as they entered them if they retain this attitude. Thankfully, however, they often realize through their studies that there are other merits to be gained from their degree apart from a diploma. They learn to listen to others with convictions that differ from their own, and as a result, their own world expands. Many male students have learned from being challenged by their female peers, and both students and faculty have learned from listening to people of color or another sexual orientation than their own.

When you study theology, you study something in which you also place your own faith. However, every learning experience involves two different elements for which you need to be prepared: You need to be prepared to meet new perspectives and understandings of the Christian faith than those you are familiar with. To do so, you have to face yourself, where you come from, and who you are in new ways. Studying theology is also to enter a process of self-development, a faith process, and an ongoing process with you and your community. Hence you learn about God, faith, your community, and yourself, and this makes studying theology different from studying physics and mathematics. This said, though, I find that most students in most subjects at the university go through phases in which they have to confront and assess their own skills, aspirations, and limitations. Studying offers you opportunities to learn about the world as well as yourself, and this is important not only to realize but to grasp as a once-in-a-lifetime opportunity.

This point also has a very practical side: when I did some of my theological studies in Germany, I learned that German students were expected to study at different universities. It meant a mandatory shift in perspective. Later, I learned how important it is to go to other places to study and do research. The experience of changing one's study environment cannot be underestimated in terms of gain in insights. So whenever you get the chance, make sure that you spend a term or two abroad, preferably in a well-known university or in a cultural context that differs significantly from your own—you will not regret it!

A short story can illustrate some of the dimensions of what I am trying to convey here: In my first year as a professor, I had a student who was a piano prodigy when she was a child. She did well on her own but soon had to get a teacher to improve her skills. This teacher taught her how the different compositions were built up and structured, and thus, she had to learn how to play in a way that was no longer merely an immediate expression of the score. She confessed, "In the beginning, I felt that this teacher was ruining the compositions for me. But then, after a while, I realized that I was able to enter more deeply into what I was playing because I understood it better. And the exact same thing happened to me when I started studying theology." The point here is that the immediacy of faith is often lost when you begin to study theology. But then, after a while, you can regain it. The philosopher Paul Ricoeur talks about this regaining as entering "the second naiveté."

So to study theology is to get opportunities—many opportunities—to see things in a new light. It is hard work because studying is a practice: it is a practice you do with others, and it involves being challenged, engaging in controversy, and running the risk of being contested and changed. You yourself must also learn to contest and confront the positions of others. That means finding your own theological voice and learning to argue on the basis of what you find most convincing. You cannot do theology by merely saying, "I believe the opposite is true"—you have to offer reasons for your claims and positions.

In other words, no proper studies without learning about how to receive criticism and to criticize others yourself. Criticism means probing, analyzing, making distinctions and differentiations, and taking nothing for granted. It is by engaging in critical work that you can see things in a new light.

Against the backdrop of what I have written so far, I want to suggest what I see as the main tasks of a theologian today. Indirectly, this is an answer to the question "Why should anyone study theology?"

Theology expresses itself as the church's conscience and self-criticism. To understand what this means, we need to see the church as an institution that expresses itself through different practices: worship, *diaconia*, teaching and preaching, care and counseling, and more. These practices need to be understood, legitimized, reasoned about, justified, and critically approached.

Theology is the means for doing that. It aims at making the church's practices responsible and based on sound knowledge. Thus theology tries to make sure that the church does what it does with good conscience and insight. It also means that theology is the mode in which the church exists as self-critical.

To make sure that theology can fulfill this task, it has to be *relatively* independent of what goes on in the church it serves. This relative independence is one of the reasons you will study theology in a university context. Your studies will be determined not only by what church authorities say but also by how you learn to relate theological knowledge to other fields of knowledge that exist in the university. It is difficult to understand how one can study theology without any relationship to any church, and perhaps it is not possible. But one can also say that the reason theology is still a subject in the university is due to the historical fact that the universities emerged from an ecclesial context and that the church sees fit to relate its knowledge to a broader field of subjects in order to remain both conscientious and self-critical.

Hence to study theology is to care for the church because you care for how the church practices its faith in God when it struggles to serve others. To care for the church is to care for how faith in God is practiced and expressed in the world. Underlying this understanding is, of course, the conviction that what matters more than anything else is the God of love, who created the world in love and struggles for this love to be realized in faith, hope, justice, and peace. Jesus revealed and practiced belief in this God, and it is because we are convinced about the continued relevance of Jesus's teachings and practices that we want the church to continue and thrive.

So when you have decided to study theology, you have decided to take up the responsibility for the continued life of the church. You study to acquire tools that can help others experience the liberating force of Christian faith and witness. These tools allow you to get a comprehensive grasp on life's experiences from the point of view of Christian faith, life, and practice. By using them, you help people see why belief in God matters and can become life changing.

Finally, when you start your studies, you should know that they do not end once you leave the university. Theological studies are always unfinished business. We will never know all about God, about what it means to be human, and what God wants with our lives. You will bring along the tools, skills, and knowledge your studies offer you and find ways to practice for the rest of your life. I am sure you will realize that they serve you—and others—well.

The understanding of theology that I have written about in this letter will, I hope, not only make you understand more about why and how to study theology. It may also help you become a good pastor who can serve your congregation well—a good shepherd who offers sound advice in the difficult times we sometimes find ourselves in. A pastor who is well trained in theology knows the path to the well that God has provided and can lead others to it. Then she serves the community of those who seek to make God's love present in the world.

The news about your decision to study theology made me happy, indeed. As you can see from this letter, it also made me reflect on how much theology has changed as a discipline since I began my studies more than forty years ago. It made me think about how theology is an always-changing task that needs continuous development. The church should, therefore, be grateful that there are young people still willing to take up the responsibility and the privilege of theologizing in the future.

Best of luck!
Jan-Olav

13

Katherine Sonderegger

I think I say nothing new to you when I say that theology is absorbing, demanding, and beautiful because God is its Object, Judge, and Desire. I would hazard that very few people are drawn to this field without at some time tasting that hunger for God—the hunger to *think* God, to encounter with our intellect and our heart this Abiding Mystery who is God. In truth, our minds were made for just this task, to think of its Maker, and to think of this Creator beyond all and every act of creation. Nothing is as dazzling, as exacting, and as holy as this intellectual quest to know God.

Yet few choose theology as their life's work. Why is this? I don't think there is one simple answer to this question. There *are* cheap and easy answers; but no one who aspires to be a theologian is satisfied with them. We want a theological answer—an answer that has to do with God—in response to this query. So we might begin with the very nature of the task of theology, its surpassing difficulty. God is profoundly hidden in His own cosmos. I do not mean that there is no revelation, no Holy Scripture, no Sacraments, no saints or Church; certainly not! But God's Reality, His Surpassing Holiness, is such that He is present to our intellects and in our minds as that which can be ignored, mistaken, or forgotten. This in itself is an extraordinary Attribute of the One God! Theology has traditionally spoken of God as the Most Beautiful Being, the One Most True, Most Benevolent—the Refuge, Augustine says, of every restless heart. Such a Reality, we might well think, would on Its manifestation be an irresistible draw to every soul that encounters It. Indeed, if we conceive of God as Omnipotent, as did our ancestors in the faith, we might be even more puzzled by our widespread ability to turn away from this Almighty Source, to prefer other intellectual or spiritual tasks, or to deny altogether such a Power exists. At times, popular religious teaching explains this remarkable state of affairs—explains it away, really—with an appeal to human free will. But when this answer is examined more closely, we see it manages to restate, not answer, our dilemma. For just why can the human will turn away from the Object of its greatest desire, its greatest joy? However we reckon with the mystery of the human will, we find that in the end, all these partial answers point toward God Himself, His Mystery that stands at the end of all our questioning. It must be that the very Nature of God is such that in His presence to the cosmos, God can be looked past, looked through, passed by on the other side, rejected. Just this is His profound Humility exhibited in a world that loves Him not. We must be able to learn something about our central task, theology itself, by reflecting deeply on the paucity of theologians in intellectual circles.

We begin with the truth that God is Invisible. This is perhaps the oldest attribute of God, one we trace back to Moses, his face turned aside and sheltered in the cleft of a rock from the Invisible One who passes by. Visually, this is expressed by the Presence of God *in the night*: Abraham, fallen into deep sleep while Smokey Fire passes between meat offered in sacrifice; Jacob wrestling with the Stranger deep into the night at the Jabbok; the terrible Arm of the Lord passing through Egypt at night; Nicodemus searching for God under cover of night; and the Lord Christ denied and betrayed in the night when no one can work—all expressions of God's profound Invisibility. The early Church follows the Scriptural pattern, distinguishing God from His creation not first by notions of transcendence or increatedness but rather by Invisibility. Just this we see in Irenaeus and in Origen, the great break between creature and Creator marked by the permanent Invisibility of its Maker. This does not mean that God is not known or revealed to His cosmos; far from it! The apostle Paul notes famously in the opening to his letter to the Romans that the Invisible things of God—His Deity and Power—are known in the things He has made. Indeed, all the Scriptural exempla of Invisibility are *encounters* with God, a disclosure of Covenant or Judgement or Redemption.

As theologians, then, we are to consider Invisibility a property of God that is at once His Impenetrability, His obdurate Objectivity to the Cosmos, and His Self-Disclosure, such that He is not seen in His Presence. We should expect, then, that human creatures will not consider God one of the realities in their universe. He will not be enumerable as a substance or individual within the created order. Yet He is there! He is there as the Invisible One, unseen among the fruitful oceans of created life. The broad secularism of much of elite life—in the professions, in the academy, in the journals that house today's public intellectuals—pays tribute to the Invisibility of our God. Our aim as theologians is not to *deny* secularism or confront its adherents as if they have simply made a mistake in the calculation of reality. Rather, it is to express *doctrinally* the significance of worldly indifference, to find its root in the gracious Presence of the Invisible One. To put this in more spiritual terms, God wills to be Unseen as Mystery.

Our encounter with the larger culture that surrounds us, then, should be one of confidence and of openness. It has been the habit of some theologians over the centuries to teach a kind of combative brio in relation to the tendencies of the age. And certainly, there are worldly matters that must be opposed! But I believe that as theologians, we have principally a different habitus to exhibit: a generous and faithful curiosity. We will learn about God, as the apostle Paul has told us, by examining the world He has made. Our fellow creatures are busily unfolding lives of purpose, of invention and discovery, of the daily round that will teach us much about the discipline we are taking up. We are not to be subservient or alarmed by what we learn there! The Christian faith has no need for the kind of defense that a frightened or precarious inhabitant must wage to keep a vulnerable house in order. The depth, strength, and intellectual rigor of the Christian faith are unmatched in the cognitive domains of human thought; we speak always from the strength of our ancestors. Just this underwrites our openness and our curiosity. God is Present there in His majestic Invisibility.

Of course, this entails that we study this ancestral faith. Always there are temptations to read only the present-day literature, only to focus on the crises of the present age, only to listen to the complaints, the hopes, the puzzlements of our contemporaries. C. S. Lewis once spoke of the great value in reading "old books"—he was quite firm about this—and I think theologians will be especially well served by following Lewis's maxim. There is a clamor in a globe unified by finance and by market that demands attention always to the available, to the new, to the satisfying. Here is one of the elements of present-day culture I believe we should resist! This is *not* because theology is antiquarian, or backward facing. Christian theology is not a reactionary discipline! It is rather that theology finds its confidence, its profound resources, in the great tradition of the Church, and it is from that strength that theologians are ready to take up the fresh tasks of the contemporary world. Womanist, queer, and liberation theologians exemplify this *ressourcement* in powerful ways. These schools of theological work find their confidence and revolutionary strength in their reading of Augustine, Saint Thomas, Gregory of Nyssa, Catherine of Siena, Dame Julian. Because the Spirit of the Holy God is at work in the Church, in the midst of all its brokenness, the past can be studied with an eagerness born of trust in the Provident God. In a shallow global culture, we will invite others to put down deep roots when we take our nourishment from the past.

Above all, however, we must turn again and again to Holy Scripture. There is, in truth, no substitute for steady study of the Bible, hearing its word, and being judged by its truth. Some theologians will exhibit their exegeses in their doctrinal work: Karl Barth is one such, and I would count the magisterial Reformers, Luther and Calvin chief among them, as others. But many theologians prepare their interpretation of Scripture before they turn to dogmatic work. For those theologians, doctrinal theology *rests* upon exegesis but does not contain it. Think of the summa tradition among medieval schoolmen, the *Summa Theologica* of Saint Thomas Aquinas as the greatest. Or of the work of Friedrich Schleiermacher, who managed to write an entire systematic theology—a very great work—in a single volume. Only by assuming his exegesis rather than demonstrating it could such a feat be accomplished. Others take particular texts as central and do not exegete across the domain of Holy Scripture. Think of the Passion narratives for Jürgen Moltmann, or the exodus for Gustavo Gutiérrez and James Cone. It is easy, in the study of systematic theology, to find oneself absorbed by the technical material of this rigorous field, its precise methodologies, its careful distinctions, its heresies and dogmatic definitions, such that we lose track of the biblical texts that must always underwrite and guide such work. Holy Scripture is the well of theology: do not neglect it! For God is Present there, to teach and guide, to judge and correct, to summon. We will not be able to write about Almighty God, about His Triunity, or about the Missions of the Son and Spirit without a deep immersion in Holy Writ. And we will also not be able to write properly about poverty and wealth, about sin and sickness, about sacrifice and holiness, about slavery and oppression, or about the Kingdom of God for which we hunger without deep encounter and study of the Old and New Testaments. Women and men are seen under the Eternal Eye of God there, and it is this vision that animates all theological work on creation and creatures.

Finally, I wish for you as you begin your journey in theology a deep and steady prayer life. As we can allow our roots in Holy Scripture to atrophy, so we can avoid or desiccate our spiritual lives of prayer in the intense concentration technical theology demands. It may be possible to write *about* theology without prayer; but it is certainly not possible to write theology itself without it. To call upon the Unseen and Present Mystery, to beseech and confess, to praise and adore, to intercede: these are the gifts of prayer that nourish theology and bring up from the dead the sinful lives of theologians. The Good God has a word for you: listen for it!

Virginia Theological Seminary
Alexandria

14

Christoph Schwoebel

First of all, let me congratulate you on your chosen subject of inquiry. Looking back on a number of decades in which I have tried to become a theologian, I can only say that it is, in my experience, the most exhilarating, demanding, and truly rewarding subject of study. If the subject matter of theology is "God and everything in relation to God," then theology is an inquiry that strives to understand God as "something than which nothing greater can be thought," as Anselm of Canterbury puts it, the highest principle of rational inquiry, and the reality that makes all other things possible. On such an understanding of God, which is shared throughout the Christian traditions, it is difficult to transcend and surpass theological reflection. If God created everything out of nothing, there is nothing before God, surpassing the reality of God. And if God is the ultimate goal of everything, there is nothing after God, no goal beyond the ultimate goal of everything. If God is in this way the power of the origin of everything and the goal in which everything finds its fulfilment, theology is not only the discipline that reflects on the highest apex of thought but also the discipline that is the most wide ranging and comprehensive, since it considers everything in relation to its ultimate ground and final goal.

Such a description of theology as an intellectual pursuit can, however, literally put the fear of God in anyone who is trying to engage in the task of offering *logos* about *theos*, rational discourse about God. Was the great Swiss theologian Karl Barth not right when he confronted theologians with this dilemma: "As theologians we ought to speak of God. But we are humans and as such we cannot speak of God"?[1] Would we not have to agree that we can only speak of God if, when, and after God speaks to us, that we can only dare to know something about God when God has given himself to be known by humans? This is, of course, the core of the Christian gospel, that God has, indeed, spoken to us in the words and deeds, the life, and the death and resurrection of Jesus of Nazareth, who by encouraging us to address the God of Israel, the creator and consummator of all that is not God, as "Father" includes us through the one we address as the "Son of God" in the narrative of how God has spoken to Israel. Therefore, that we are—in the diversity of our situations in different nations, cultures, and social settings—enabled by God in his Spirit to recognise the truth of the gospel of Jesus Christ as the true account of God's relationship to the world.

What is it that God enables us to "know" through his address in Jesus, which becomes personal certainty for us through the Spirit, a personal certainty of the truth of the promise that God created this world, our world, out of love and will bring creation to fulfilment and to ultimate flourishing in communion with its creator, overcoming all the resistances, the suffering, the pain, the evil that stand in the way of its flourishing? As theologians, we will only discover the riches of this "knowledge" step-by-step, in small discoveries and great disclosures. The road of discovery that is theology is not always easy. It is, at least in my experience, not one where continuous and steady progress can be made. There will be periods of setbacks and disappointments where we as theologians become acutely aware that the "object" of our study is not in our control and not at our disposal. God and everything in relation to God are not dead objects we could dissect in the laboratory of advanced theological technology. God is a living reality, at work in everything that constitutes our world, and so we are always dependent on God's self-giving, which elicits our receptiveness, our open hands, minds, and hearts for what God has to give us. However, this reality is not a silent object but a living and free address. Our communicating about God is dependent on listening to God's communication with us and trying to respond to God's communication with our whole embodied personal responsibility, of which our theology is only a part. It is, however, the part that has relevance for the whole of our embodied existence.

Doing theology, listening to God's communication with us as the precondition of our discourse about God, has an existential depth, where the meaning of our lives as persons-in-relation is at stake. The "knowledge" that theology deals with is never "neutral" but always elicits a response from us, provokes affirmative and critical answers. Martin Luther puts this well when he notes that when theology deals with "God and everything in relation to God," it deals with "humans as they are guilty and lost and God who justifies and saves." If God is not only the source and goal of all being but also the ground of all meaning and the creative power of justice, God's relationship to us will also lay open where we have failed to respond to God's promise and have closed us off from what God has to give. Cut off from the source of life and meaning, we experience that we are lost if we, as creatures who owe everything to God, rely exclusively on our own resources. The traditional language of being in bondage to sin acquires in such situations astonishing diagnostic precision. Moments when we realise that the wonder of the gratuitous gift of God's grace becomes amazing for us and the surprise that God addresses even those of his human creatures who shut themselves off from his address fill us with joy. One is a theologian with everything one is and has, with heart, mind, soul, and body and all relationships in which we exist.

Because the Christian message has this liberating effect, it also liberates us for communion with others. Theology needs to be practised as a communal activity, in conversation with others who are also prepared to engage with God and everything in relation to God. That we tend to become solitary when we are entangled in the contradictions and hardships of our lives is an experience most of us can share. Such situations are often accompanied by a loss of language so that words seem to fail us when we try to express what we are oppressed by. I find the reassurance that God's Spirit will make intercession for us "with groanings which cannot be uttered" (Rom 8:26 NKJV) when we are at a loss for words and do not even know how to pray, one of the most hopeful promises in the New Testament. Could there be anything more comforting than the promise that God, when our words fail us, even supports and restores our ability to speak, and be it in lamenting to God? Restoring our speech to God restores our speech to one another. What would be more fitting than to celebrate the fact that the God who is conversation in the exchange between the Father, the Son, and the Spirit—the eternal speaker, the eternal word, and the eternal listener—stands in for us when we have fallen silent in theological conversations among one another. Such conversations happen at all levels and in all situations of life, with children who show themselves to be astute theologians if we can engage them with their theologies in conversation, with old people, sometimes even with those who suffer from dementia whose conversation often retains snatches of prayers and hymns, echoes of the gospel and the address to God. Would these not be the words we would want to continue to speak and to listen to, as words of comfort and encouragement, when we are no longer fully in control of our usual communicative skills?

The fact that theology is a communal activity that is pursued in communication and in listening to the voices of others and in talking to God, from God, and about God reminds us that listening to and giving a voice to those who are not attentively heard in the busy exchanges of our societies is a primary concern for theology. A theology that remains faithful to the biblical witnesses can never forget that listening to the concerns of widows and orphans, strangers and the poor and giving their concerns a voice in our societal—and theological!—discourse is a central concern of the Hebrew Bible and of the New Testament. It is one of the most crucial implications of the justice of God. When the Word becomes flesh and lives among us, the New Testament underlines, those who have no voice begin to be listened to and begin to speak, addressing God and their fellow humans. Oppression and social injustice often have their roots and pervasive symptoms in rendering those who are marginalised speechless and without a sympathetic audience. For a theology that places the fact that God speaks and listens—indeed, that God is conversation in the eternal Trinity and with all God's creatures—at the heart of its enterprise, listening to those whose voices are suppressed and ignored is a central concern that goes to the heart of its identity.

In recent years, we have experienced that social communication in its various forms can be a means of making people speechless. In the debates about fake news and the disturbing diagnosis that we might be living in a "post-truth" era, it struck me often how central the commitment to truth is for Christian theology. We are confronted not only with the prophets who defend the truth of God's promises against false prophets claiming divine authority but also with Jesus's encounters with those who claim a monopoly on religious truth. In the theological tradition, this commitment to truth has been expressed in the sharp statement "God is Truth," insisting that only God whose speech creates a world can ultimately establish and safeguard the correspondence between "things" and "signs." For theology, this should be a reminder that the commitment to truth is not negotiable and should release critical and self-critical potential for speaking the truth. It is also a liberating insight that none of our theologies, not even the dogmas of the church, can lay claim to absolute truth but are relative to the God who is truth. One of the most disturbing experiences in recent years was, for me, that the erosion of the commitment to truth in our social life reduces social interaction to the naked use of power, no longer controlled by truth, so that it becomes indistinguishable from violence. Speaking truth to power thus becomes an urgent task of theology that it can only fulfil if it remains self-critical with regard to the problematical coalitions with half-truths or strategic interests in which it finds itself entangled. The more I have engaged with that situation, the more the last judgement appears to me as a constitutive part of the gospel: the ultimate disclosure of truth, the definite end of all fake news—even we ourselves, individually and as a guild of theologians, probably find ourselves in the image of the great revelation scene in Matthew 25 as belonging, each one of us, both to the sheep and to the goats, which are hopefully goats that have been forgiven.

A Christian theological community that is committed to seeking the truth and waiting on the God who is truth cannot refrain from being in conversation with the theological communities of other faiths. This is something that has changed since the time I started studying theology, and it should be an essential element of your way of doing theology. There is first the conversation with Judaism. Christian theologians who confess the first-century Jew Jesus as the Christ, the Son of God, cannot refrain from taking Jesus's situatedness in Judaism with utmost seriousness. It is a permanent blemish on the history of Christian teaching about Jesus Christ that good news for the gentiles had as its ugly accompaniment the "teaching of contempt" (Jules Isaac) with regard to Jews and Judaism. In view of the abhorrent history of Christian anti-Judaism, which all too often forged coalitions with racist anti-Semitism, it is one of the most hopeful developments that in recent decades, Jewish scholars have "reclaimed" Jesus for the traditions of his people and that this has happened in conversation with Christian scholars. There are difficult theological problems to be tackled here with honesty and trust, in respect for the other and in tactful conversation, supported by the willingness to endure the differences that provide occasions for further exchanges.

If I consider what has changed since the time I began to do theology, one aspect is immediately obvious. Today, we live in a religiously pluralist world in which the processes of globalisation have opened up possibilities of encounter with the world religions as probably never before. At the same time, the significance of the religions for all dimensions of life has become more apparent, not least in religiously fuelled confrontations and even in religiously motivated violence. My wish would be that as many young theologians as possible engage in interfaith conversations, not as an exotic field for specialists, but as a "normal" way of doing theology. Many of the significant theological conversations I have had in recent decades have been with theologians from other religious traditions—in my case, conversations with Jewish and Islamic theologians. Often we have engaged in these conversations with central theological traditions, studying the Tanakh, the Bible, and the Qur'an together and engaging with central texts from our theological traditions. I have always found it an enrichment when we could do *theology* together, exchange our views on what it means to be human before God and how we should see the world if we view it from the perspective of faith as God's creation. Often interreligious conversations focus on our respective religions and soon get entangled in debates of what we find attractive or problematical in our own or the others' religious traditions. We should remember that religions, even in their own understanding, are very relative organisms; they live from the God they attempt to relate to in religious practices and teachings. If that's the case, why not talk about God and turn the interreligious dialogue into an intertheological conversation? One of the most important discoveries for me, a systematic theologian mostly concerned with the questions of modern theology, was that there are rich materials of such intertheological discussions from earlier periods of theology, perhaps in the most developed form in medieval theology. Classic theologians like Thomas Aquinas were acutely aware of the reflections on God and creation in Jewish and Muslim traditions, often learning from them in constructive objections and critical appropriations. Should we not use the rich resources of these traditions of intellectual engagement with the theologies of the "others" to inform our own attempts at conducting intertheological conversations?

I have already written to you quite extensively about what I see as the foundations of Christian theology, about its commitments, and about my enthusiasms and concerns in doing theology. All these things come to life when one practices theology as an activity, a practice that requires skills. Doing theology is also a lifelong apprenticeship in learning basic skills and developing them through practice. Many of these skills have to do with reading. Since God communicates with the people of Israel in Jesus of Nazareth, in the early church of witnesses to the resurrection of Jesus, in time and space through the languages and cultures of their times, in the very particularity of the special circumstances, they could only witness to the truth of what had been communicated to them and what they had experienced by handing it on, in most cases, first in oral forms and then in writing. The texts that have reached us bear all the traces of complex processes of transmission. They witness, on the one hand, to the embeddedness of the original witnesses in particular historical and cultural contexts and, on the other hand, to the fact that the content of God's engagement with the concerns of God's particular human creatures, which we have in the form of their responses to the divine address, was considered to have a promise of truth that also applies to future generations. This point has a wide-ranging significance for me. God realises his universal truth by working through the particulars—the particularities of the biblical writers, readers, redactors, and traditors—and through our own particularities of listening, receiving, understanding, and responding in the particular situations in which we live.

If the particularities are theologically so important, it seems advisable to take them seriously: by learning the biblical languages, by acquiring the skills for biblical interpretation that takes the contextual character of the texts seriously, and by becoming familiar with the trajectories of the interpretation and application of the biblical witnesses in the history of the Church. It is on such a basis that we learn to pay attention to the particularities of the processes of tradition, embedded as they are in written testimonies, hymns, prayers, and theological treatises, in institutions and forms of communal and personal piety. We also wake up to the particularities of our situation with its local, regional, and global connections, as the situation to which the truth of the Gospel is meant to speak and as the situation through which God provokes and elicits our response. It is this attentiveness that makes us aware of so much theology outside the academic study of theology—not only in the visual arts, in music, in the austere works of medieval plainchant to pop songs, and in film but also in politics, in the economy, and in all forms of cultural expression. Theologians are challenged not to switch off their theological sense in engaging with the world around them but to engage with the theology outside theology attentively, openly, critically, and constructively. Of course, this will often be a critical engagement in which we are made aware that idolatry, worshipping finite entities as if they were the ground of all being and meaning, is by no means an object of study in distant times and faraway places but very much a reality at the heart of our cultures, our communities, and perhaps even our churches and our theologies, where traditions, ecclesial authorities, and theological systems take the place of the God they claim to serve. This is where our theological instincts must spring to life—above all, self-critically.

However, engaging with the theology outside academic theology is not only a critical and self-critical enterprise. When I look at sacred architecture, sometimes in their form dysfunctional, a living rejection of the "form follows function" orthodoxy because it is built for the glory of God, I am astonished by the theology embedded in stone and wood. I discover something more about the richness and splendour of the "object" of theology and the inspirational "push" it can give to human creativity. When I sing in a Bach cantata or the Brahms requiem or join in an African American spiritual, I am sometimes overwhelmed by the truth my theology can only express in the most modest conceptual forms. However, that can also be a comforting experience. Where my theology, the theology I have developed in conversation with others, falls short, there is so much more theology that will fill in the gaps, correct the mistakes, and compensate for the failures of my attempts at contributing to theology. These forms of theology outside theology are a powerful witness of the truth of the incarnation, the sanctification of creaturely means of communication as an expression of the glory of God.

Martin Luther had the audacious thought that every human being is a theologian. Just because of our creatureliness, our very existence is already engaged with God in every moment of our lives. As creatures, the *logos*—the meaning pattern—of everything we are, suffer, and do points to God as the source of our being, meaning, and fulfilment. Since this is a relationship in which we find ourselves but is not at our disposal and is beyond our control, we are also aware where we fail to be theologians, where we put ourselves at the centre of our *logos*, the meaning patterns informing our actions and passions. We also find that although we may realise that we have somehow become dislocated in the network of relationships in which we live because we do not acknowledge God as the source, meaning, and goal of everything, we are unable to put ourselves back in the right relationship to God. Our strategies of self-salvation sometimes only turn out to be pitiful manifestations of what is really wrong with us. It is in this situation that the gospel speaks to us with its promise that in Jesus, God has taken our place, the place of estrangement with God, to invite us to take his place in the power of the Spirit of God, the place that we are destined to have in a filial relationship to God. I find Luther's bold thesis fascinating because it allows us to do our theology in solidarity with all the other theologians, God's human creatures on earth.

In recent years, I have been wondering, again following Luther, whether his view of every human person as a theologian must not be extended to every creature. Every creature—a theologian? In his *Lectures on Genesis*, which Luther delivered for ten years at the University of Wittenberg (a lecturer's dream and student's nightmare), he says that every creature—sun, moon, heaven, earth, Peter, Paul, you, and I—are all words of God, part of God's vocabulary and subject to the rule of divine grammar. If we follow Luther, we would have to say yes, every creature is theology, a word of God's speech. Could we also say that for a creature as a word, the very act of existence is not only divine address but also creaturely *logos*, responding to God, so that the whole universe is a world of conversation, and we, God's human creatures, are called to respond to God in solidarity and communion with the whole of creation? Against such a backdrop, the biblical expressions "The heavens declare the glory of God" and "Day unto day utters speech" (Ps 19:1, 2 NKJV) suddenly make sense, and the phrase "Mountains and hills will burst out into song, and all the trees in the countryside will clap their hands" (Isa 55:12 CJB) conjures up an audio-image of a singing, swinging, hand-clapping creation of theologians—animal, vegetable, mineral—celebrating the advent of the creator who spoke it into being in the first place. What would it mean for us to do theology in consonance with this polyphonic, creaturely chorus?

So far, it seems that I have been inviting you to theology as a rich and comprehensive field, embracing God and the world in all its diversity and pluriformity. This raises, as a matter of course, the question of whether there is some form of shape, a centre or focus of this bewildering richness. Is there a way in which one can avoid getting lost in the abundance of creation mirroring the superabundance of the triune creator? Can we point to one ordering system that provides the ideal map for this vast continent of theologising—a systematic theology, perhaps, or a theological formula that neatly encapsulates what theology is all about? For years, I thought that the "doctrine of justification" might provide such a centre or that the doctrine of the Trinity could function as the "frame" for structuring the riches of Christian theology. I do not think that these ideas were wrong. However, I have come to feel that they do not show how the focus of theology works, how it operates not only on the level of theological concepts but on the level of embodied actions and passions, attitudes and acts of giving and receiving. In recent years, I have come to realise that Christian worship in the ordinary form of Sunday-morning service enacts such a focus liturgically. I have not always seen this so clearly as it appears to me now, and my involvement in various forms of worshipping God has been a continuous learning process about different ways of celebrating the self-giving of the triune God. It is also a process of personal formation in communion with others. From being gathered in the name of the triune God to being sent out with the blessing of the Trinitarian name, we are taken into a rich fabric of communicative exchange—of speaking to God and listening to speech from God, from being addressed by God to speaking about God. Being invited into this conversation brings our whole existence before God in thanksgiving, praise, petition, and lament, and it enfolds us in the whole of God's communicative presence. Processing, standing, sitting and kneeling, listening, singing and speaking, addressing and responding, receiving and giving, eating and drinking—we are taken into communion with others and with the God who, in his grace and truth, shares his presence with us. Since this has become clear to me, I have been keen to connect the ideas I think about theologically to the basic acts of worship in which I participate, and I have tried to find out where the right connections can be found, not only in propositions and concepts, but also in the embodied concepts of the liturgy. I have come to these connections as a relatively late discovery. Will you come to them earlier, starting at a different point in time?

Letters normally end with good wishes, or even with best wishes. Having taken up your patience with a rather long letter, I wonder what might be my good wishes for you as a young theologian. I have sometimes tried to summarise what I had understood so far about theology in my lectures in a series of rules based on the Ten Commandments. This might appear as a rather legalistic enterprise, laying down the law for doing good theology. However, I have been persuaded by Old Testament scholars who have pointed out that in its setting in the Exodus narrative, the Decalogue is concerned with preserving and maintaining the freedom the people of Israel had just been granted by being liberated from slavery in Egypt. Are the Ten Commandments advice for remaining free and never again being slaves? As an invitation to remain free, could the Ten Commandments, with all theological licence, serve as a matrix for good wishes? I shall give it a try, and so I wish you that you can hold fast to the promise "I am the Lord your God, who brought you out of Egypt, out of the land of slavery"

(Exod 20:2 NIV). Christians have radicalised this description so that the God of the exodus, the God of liberation is confessed as the "God who makes the dead live and calls into being things that are not" (Rom 4:17; my translation) or as the "God who raised our Lord Jesus from the dead" (Rom 8:11; my translation). This is pure gospel.

By trusting in this God, as is my wish for you, you will not feel any attraction to worshipping "craven images" and will be quick to detect and combat idolatry, even when it comes in theological guise. Keeping the Sabbath holy provides the background for wishing you to allow yourself rest, to remain attentive to limits of human activity, to rest from activity in order to realise anew that all our activity is rooted in the activity of the creator. This rest creates a space Christians have filled with the worship of the triune God. Can we rephrase the command to honour one's father and mother as the invitation to acknowledge the traditions in which we stand when we do theology—traditions we can use as resources to face the challenges that confront us in our situation? The traditions we come from, our fathers and mothers, are always richer and more complex than we imagined, and every serious attempt at engaging with these traditions will expand our theological possibilities in the present. Honouring our mothers and fathers does not mean that we have to become like them, but it does mean that we are invited to accept their wisdom as opening up new possibilities for our theologising. I wish you fruitful discoveries in the rich tradition of theology that will lead you to explore courageous innovations so that the process of tradition can go on. Since I have become a "Doktorvater" to quite a number of academic daughters and sons, I have to admit that I am very pleased when they take what they have learnt from me in new directions—and nevertheless continue the conversation with the "older generation." Can the commandment not to commit murder be transformed into a good wish? Already Philip Melanchthon complained in the sixteenth century about the rabies of theologians, their exaggerated eagerness to engage in polemics. I wish you the gift of being able to negotiate differences of opinion with friendliness and courtesy, and above all, I wish that you are treated in theological conversations with generous politeness. The difficulty of extending the commandment "Do not commit adultery" to doing theology is obvious. However, one can imagine that there are ways of doing theology where theology is resolutely hitched to the wagon of the latest critical theory without preserving what theology would have to say that could not be said by any other discipline. Therefore,

I wish you the courage to do theology, to delight in what theology has to bring to the table of conversations in academia. Perhaps the admonition "Do not steal" says the same thing from another perspective: I wish that you find the theological perspective so satisfying that you do not have to appropriate nontheological resources. I have already mentioned the temptation to form coalitions with untruths and half-truths in our society. Not to bear false witness simply appears as a variation on that theme. Nevertheless, I wish that you can form a covenant with truth so that telling the truth, even when it hurts and reveals our capacity to fall victim to self-deception, is experienced as a big liberation. For the practice of theology, the injunction "Do not covet" warns of the temptations of mimetic desire, of desiring what the others are and have. This can be expressed in the wish that the route you embark on as a theologian proves to be so rewarding and exciting and continues to be so interesting that you are happy with what you are: a theologian.

Blessings
Christoph Schwoebel

Note

1 Karl Barth, *The Word of God and Theology* (New York: T&T Clark, 2011), 177.

15

Paul T. Nimmo

It's great news that you have decided to study theology! Theology is one of the most interesting and engaging subjects to explore, and if you feel called to study it, then you're right to pursue that calling and to see where it leads. While the path that you've chosen is unlikely to be an easy one, and indeed may bear more than a few challenges, it's also a path that holds out the prospect of real insight and deep blessing. And along the way, it's a journey on which you will encounter some truly remarkable people.

Before I write anything else about the joys that theology will bring, it's as well to be open from the start about some of the challenges of becoming a theologian. Of course, in one sense, every Christian is a theologian, for one definition of *theology* is, simply, "speech about God," and every Christian speaks of God. It may be actions rather than words, or in hidden and small ways rather than in large and public gestures, but in the very broadest sense, all Christians speak of God. At the same time, another definition of *theology* is a narrower affair, referring to a particular field of scholarly work. Under this definition, it covers topics such as the study of the founding texts of Christianity in the Old and New Testaments, the exploration of the practical and missional consequences of what Christians believe, and the content, relevance, and coherence of Christian truth claims. It is this last-named field—theology in its most narrow definition—that you have chosen to study, and this discipline brings very particular challenges. It may help prepare you for what lies ahead by setting down a few notes about some of them. Not to discourage! But perhaps just to forewarn . . .

To begin, it's important to realise that theology, like every discipline, has its own specialist vocabulary, its own particular history, and its own various approaches. You might be loosely acquainted with some of this material already, whether from your own reading or from your church life. In time, however, it will be your job to become at least broadly familiar with all of these in order to gain a proper understanding of what the field of theology looks like and of how you position yourself and your own theological ideas within it.

First, then, there will be some vocabulary building ahead of you—in English, let alone perhaps in Hebrew, Greek, Latin, or other languages!—and it will take time until you're comfortable with all these new terms. As you will find, theology, like every other academic discipline, loves its jargon. Second, you will have to increase your knowledge of world and church history greatly as you attend to the history of theology, and in particular its various periods and characters. You will gain a real sense of the ways in which theology always takes place in conversation with the world. And third, you will realise that different scholars have at different times approached the tasks of theology in very different ways, using the various sources of theology to produce at times strikingly contrasting results. Across all these areas of study, there will be much for you to take on board and understand.

But that's all only part of the battle. From the very start, studying theology will challenge your own personal and highly cherished points of view. There will be ideas and positions you encounter that may initially strike you as eminently sensible and important; often because these same ideas and positions will conform to your prior sense of things. By contrast, other views may seem to be entirely unreasonable or deeply problematic—especially when they don't agree with your previous intuitions and beliefs. Yet if we want truly to grow as theologians, then we have to be a little more humble and a little more open rather than simply allow our existing views to be confirmed by what we want to hear.

Instead, beliefs must be tested, new voices must be heard, fresh ideas must be generated. This can be a pretty uncomfortable process, especially as other students learning alongside us begin from different starting points. We can be challenged not only by our texts but also by our colleagues and friends, and these challenges should be seen not as hostile threats but as refining fire. In response, we have to be ready both to change our views in light of greater wisdom than ours and to hold firm our opinions when they are assailed by others unjustly—and crucially, we have to seek the wisdom to know when to do what.

Theology also challenges us because, for all that we study theology as individual scholars, in truth theology is the task and responsibility of an entire community—the church. The job of studying or teaching theology may be a specialist task, requiring particular training and expertise. And the place where we learn theology may be a seminary, college, or university. But in truth, the real home of theology is the church. And that means that whenever we become theologians, we locate ourselves—explicitly or implicitly—in relation to the church.

First, the work of theology is called to be in constant conversation with the whole communion of saints: not only the saints of the current generation but also the saints of previous generations, particularly the saints who are the prophets and apostles responsible for Scripture. Theology is one of those disciplines where the past may hold more wisdom than the present. And second, the work of theology is called to guide the contemporary church and its proclamation faithfully, to call and to lead the saints in today's church into the future. Theologians bear responsibility in the church, for their voice can impact upon its clerics, its administrators, its members, and its adherents. By becoming a theologian in the church, then, you take on a fairly daunting role in respect of its past, present, and future.

And that leads me to perhaps the biggest challenge. Theology is ultimately a discipline undertaken not before your fellow students and your professors, or even before your fellow Christians and your minister, but before God. It calls you not only to be attentive to the standards of academic work and the wisdom of church tradition; it calls you also to fresh responsibility before God. Theologians seek in their work to be obedient to the living God and to be faithful to the Word of God incarnate in Jesus Christ and attested in Holy Scripture. This is a remarkable venture, and its success depends entirely on the guidance and illumination of the Holy Spirit. And therefore, the basic posture of faith that is demanded of you in theology is that of prayer for God's presence, guidance, and aid, for the practice of theology in a very real sense stands under the judgement of God.

You may be thinking that this letter has been fairly cautious—even negative!—so far, and certainly I've been trying to explain some of the challenges involved in studying theology. I do think it's important to be clear about these and prepared for them. But to be honest, the possibilities, opportunities, and joys of theology more than make up for the difficulty of these challenges. Theology was once called "queen of the sciences" because it provides the framework that contains all other fields of study and because of the divine nature of its own subject matter . . . For some, that particular title may belong to a bygone age, but it does at least hint that there are a number of very special things about this discipline.

One of those special things is the scope of the discipline, as I just mentioned. The range of topics in which theology is interested is God and all things in relation to God—in other words, everything! Theology is engaged with such a vast range of subjects because God is. And so it considers everything, from the divine life to human culture, from the salvation in Jesus Christ to the witness of the church, from the heavens to the environment. Just as nothing falls beyond God's vision, so too nothing is outwith theology's range of attention. More than this, when theology treats of all things that are related to God, it treats them *as* relating to God. Nothing is purely mundane: everything is part of the creation and under the providence of God. That insight brings a special light to bear on any topic that you can imagine, and it is the task of theologians to investigate what is illuminated by it.

Another great joy of theology is the variety of voices that it brings into discussion. One of the wonderful privileges of studying the discipline in the present is that more and more voices and perspectives are joining the discourse of theology, and these voices are genuinely being heard, challenging existing wisdom and addressing existing injustice. It shows that there is no room for complacency: as a theologian, you have to listen and hear how other people and traditions and cultures have conceived and do conceive God and how God has impacted upon their faith journeys and life experiences. And your voice too is crucial: you should speak with care and integrity but also with confidence. To share stories and beliefs in this way is a chance to embrace the full and multifaceted diversity of the communion of saints and to recognise the work of God in ways we could never anticipate.

Most of all, however, it's the material that belongs to the discipline of theology that is perhaps its most compelling feature. One of the traditional ways of conceiving of eternal life involves the beatific vision, the final encounter with the glory of God in heaven. Theology doesn't always manage to rise to such heights . . . But the chance to think and speak about God—to reflect upon the God who became one with us in Jesus Christ, to meditate upon God's Word in Holy Scripture, to think of the history of God's people through history, to discern the Spirit of God at work in the world today—is nothing if not a provisional foretaste of the joy that is to come. And because of that, to study theology is a rare privilege.

It's also a privilege with consequences: you may become engaged with your faith journey in a new and dynamic way so that your approach to life, to the church, and to the world takes on new contours. In fact, you may never be able to see things the same way again, as theology has opened your eyes in vivid and exciting ways. And just as a relationship with a friend can grow and change as you learn more about them, so too your relationship with God may evolve and develop. This doesn't mean that you will become any more or less spiritual, any more or less holy, even any more right or wrong about matters of faith! But it does mean that your journey may open up new insights and new possibilities.

Finally, theology is a special discipline because over the course of your studies, you will meet—both on the page and in the classroom—some of the most wonderful and most discerning people whom you will ever encounter. That doesn't mean, of course, that you will get on with everyone in theology, whether at the outset or down the line. And actually, theologians can be pretty horrible to each other sometimes, just as anyone can. But as you throw yourself into the conversation of theology that has been going on for millennia, as you listen out for the wisdom of others and contribute to the dialogue with your own voice, I suspect that some of the connections you forge will remain with you for the rest of your life.

One of the reasons for this is that other theologians will know exactly the kinds of joy and challenge that you will be experiencing, so you will share common terrain between you. Another of the reasons is that among your fellow theologians will be other good and faithful people, serving their churches and seeking to be humble and open yet confident witnesses of God as you do. But another reason is that theologians in conversation are forced into being honest about the very deepest-held convictions in their lives, and such a vulnerability can produce respect and bond people in surprising and wonderful ways. To study alongside other theologians may prove to be one of the greatest blessings of your calling.

And so theology stands not only under the judgement of God but also under God's grace. So as you take this next bold step, I trust that you will do so as someone deeply aware of its challenges but keenly excited by its possibilities. In all your doings in theology, act justly, love kindness, and walk humbly. And may every blessing be yours on all the paths ahead.

With warm regards—
Paul T. Nimmo
University of Aberdeen

16

Kevin Vanhoozer

I was delighted to receive your letter asking about the best route to becoming a theologian. Let me confess up front: I'm still *in via* myself. My business card should identify me not as a research professor but as a perpetual pupil of theology—though if it did, you probably wouldn't be writing to me. I need to underline the point: theology is neither a nine-to-five job nor a career. To know and speak truly of God is a vocation that requires more than academic or professional qualifications. The image you should have in mind is not the professor with a tweed jacket but rather the disciples who dropped everything to follow Jesus. Becoming a theologian means following God's Word where it leads with all one's mind, heart, soul, and strength.

Let me say a few more things about what theology is and why it matters, just to make sure we're on the same page. Theology is the study of how to speak truly of God and of all things in relation to God. But theologians can't approach the object of their study the way biologists study living creatures or geologists the earth. God cannot be empirically examined. God is the creator of all things, not to be identified with any part of the universe or even with the universe as a whole. Speaking of God thus poses unique challenges. If God had not condescended to communicate to creatures something of his light, we would be in the dark.

Are you familiar with Thomas Aquinas's definition? "Theology is taught by God, teaches of God, and leads to God." It's worth pondering these three prepositions.

By God. Only God can make himself known. There is a prior divine self-communication to which all theologians are accountable. You can't deploy God's name simply to add support to your pet ideas or favorite agenda. Theologians aren't fiction writers either: we're not making this up, Marx, Freud, and Nietzsche notwithstanding. We're simply children who love their father and want to know him better, who trust their father's wisdom (Matt 18:3–4), and for that very reason, we keep asking "Why?" (This is my gloss on Anselm's famous definition of theology as "faith seeking understanding.")

Of God. There are theologies of marriage, the body, leisure, the imagination, and so forth, but they are theological only to the extent that they relate their objects to God, their author and finisher. Theology is thinking hard about what God has taught about himself and all things in relation to himself.

To God. William Ames, a Puritan, uses language much like Aquinas's: "Theology is the doctrine of living to God." Theology is more than an academic exercise, more even than knowing God; it's ultimately about cultivating godliness in oneself and one's community. Theology's proper ends are both contemplative (I dare not say "theoretical") and practical.

It's true, there is a guild of "professional" theologians—mostly academics who populate colleges, seminaries, and university divinity schools—and there are scholarly journals and awards to be had, not to mention salaries and sabbaticals. I know it's tempting, especially when you're still a student, to revere or perhaps romanticize your teachers and the lives they lead. The reality—grading papers, committee meetings, critical reviews, and so on—is different. It gets worse: theology ranks very low on the totem pole of academic status. Banish, therefore, all thought of "success," and don't confuse making a living as a theologian with living out the knowledge of God. If you aspire to speak of God, do so to please God, not people (Gal 1:10; 1 Thess 2:4)—neither the professionals nor their popularly cultured despisers.

In short, if you see God as a means to worldly fame, power, or popularity, please don't. There are already plenty of people, too many, who speak of God for the wrong reasons, which means they are not speaking truly of the one true God. You aspire to theology, you believe in God, you do well. Yet "even the demons believe—and shudder" (Jas 2:19). Becoming a theologian involves not only coming to know God (theology is simultaneously art, science, and craft) but also becoming a certain kind of person, one whose created intelligence has been illumined by the Holy Spirit.

Knowing God, the gospel of God (what God has done in Christ), and all things in relation to God and the gospel is to know reality. Are you surprised? You shouldn't be. When theology proclaims the deep mystery—God's plan of redemption conceived "before the foundation of the world" (John 17:24; Eph 1:4; 1 Pet 1:20) and executed in history—it doesn't promote cleverly devised myths. It awakens disciples to reality. Philosophers study *what is*, but the Christian theologian sets forth in speech *what is in Christ*: reconciliation, a new creation (2 Cor 5:17–18). The world is passing away (even scientists agree, acknowledging that our sun will eventually burn out), but God's Word endures forever (Matt 24:35).

All this to say, I affirm your general aspiration, but have you prayerfully considered whether academic theology is your vocation rather than, say, doing theology in the church, perhaps as a pastor or priest? Assuming I haven't dissuaded you, I'll now try to address your specific questions by commending four adjectives that characterize the practice of theology and then three pairs of virtues that characterize its best practitioners. I haven't forgotten that you also asked about *where* you might best flourish as a theologian, and I'll conclude with some thoughts on that.

As to learning how to think theologically, let me begin with four adjectives (*Trinitarian*, *biblical*, *catholic*, and *systematic*) that qualify Christian theological thinking. Each describes a theological habit of mind that has proved useful in getting the understanding faith seeks.

Becoming a Christian theologian means developing a Trinitarian habit of mind. On the one hand, everything begins with divine initiatives, the speak-acting of God. God's creative and redemptive words—"Let there be light" (Gen 1:3), "Your sins are forgiven" (Luke 7:48)—precede all theologizing. Yet we have to approach God's Word in three ways: God speaks, God speaks himself, God speaks himself through himself. You must always and everywhere give priority to theology's principal subject matter, the being and activity of the triune God: the Father speaking the Word through the Spirit.

Theology means thinking about all things in relation to God, and it helps to remember that all three persons are engaged in everything God does. (I'm speaking as one who, on occasion, has been accused of "forgetting" the Holy Spirit!) Commit this patristic adage to memory, in Latin and English: *opera trinitatis ad extra indivisa sunt* (the outward works of the Trinity are indivisible). Why is there something rather than nothing? Because God the Father created all things in and through the Son in the

Spirit. Why is there good news rather than no news (silence)? Because God the Father has reconciled the world to himself in Christ through the Spirit (what Irenaeus calls the "two hands" of God).

Second, the best way to stay focused on the subject matter of theology is to stay focused on Scripture. John Calvin viewed his *Institutes* as help for aspiring disciples "to find the sum of what God meant to teach us in his Word." It's no coincidence that the most important figures in the history of theology—Augustine, Aquinas, Luther, Calvin, Barth—also wrote biblical commentaries. Roman Catholics enthusiastically agree. When Benedict XVI called Scripture the "soul of theology," he echoed Vatican II's claim that "the study of the sacred page" is the very soul of theology (in *Dei Verbum*).

Given the fragmentation of theological studies in the modern university, I fear that you may find it challenging to establish your biblical bona fides. Some biblical scholars insist on reading the Bible like any other text, and some theologians think that doing theology is a matter of compiling "proof texts" that establish doctrines. There are better ways of reading the Bible theologically.

C. S. Lewis's distinction between looking *at* a beam of light and looking *along* it clarifies what's at stake. Those who look *at* the biblical text analyze it from a critical distance. They see the text, but not necessarily what it's talking about. In contrast, those who look *along* the text enter into its strange new world. Looking along the text is the best way to resist what Hans Frei calls the "great reversal" in hermeneutics that took place in the eighteenth century—namely, the exchange of the biblical narrative as our framework for understanding the world for some other story (e.g., neo-Darwinism, existentialism, process philosophy—their name is Legion).

The Bible is not an object to examine under this or that hermeneutical microscope. God addresses us in Scripture and requires our response, and that means we do theology in the first and second person (cf. Martin Buber's *I-Thou*). Scripture is not a textbook but the Church's holy script, and understanding it involves reading all the books in the Old and New Testaments as parts of an overarching story. It's more than narrative, it's drama: story made flesh, in which readers today have speaking parts. Karl Barth spoke of exploring the "strange new world of the Bible," and that's an apt image. The theologian is a kind of cartographer of this new world, this new life, this "theodrama": the story made flesh of God's two-handed outreach to the world.

The third thing you must do to acquire a theological habit of mind is to read the Word of God with and for the people of God. You may be tempted to say something original about God. Let me urge you to make sure your brilliant insights are in line with the consensus of the catholic tradition. Those who swim against the stream of Christian tradition risk subverting the logic of the gospel. We're apprentices to Scripture and to those who have read it well before us. To become a theologian is to enter into a centuries-long conversation, started by (who knows?) those two disciples on the way to Emmaus who wondered about the significance of what happened to Jesus in Jerusalem (Luke 24:13–24).

The best theologians are apprentices to Scripture and to the consensual tradition of its interpretation. By the way, that tradition, viewed theologically, is the result of the Spirit leading the whole Church into all truth (John 16:13). Thanks to the Council of Nicaea, you don't have to reinvent the Trinitarian wheel. And speaking of Nicaea, every aspiring theologian should study the way Athanasius read Scripture to see how the logic of the gospel gave rise to Trinitarian theology. Catholicity is a well-known mark of the Church; it ought also to characterize theologians. Let the gospel be the center of your thinking, but let catholic tradition fill out its content and fix its circumference. *Evangelical* and *catholic* are bedfellows, not rivals.

The fourth theological habit of mind involves thinking *systematically* as we read the Word of God with the people of God. The Bible is much more than a collection of truths to be organized into a comprehensive system. That way leads to what we might call *hard* systematic theology. I recommend a "soft" systematics that acknowledges a unity to truth, though not like the truth of geometric axioms, which are not suitable for expressing redemptive history. There are things that theologians must make known, but they primarily concern what God has said and done in history. What unifies Scripture is the story of God's determination to see through his purpose for creation to the end, a story in which Israel and the Church loom large, with Jesus Christ as its hinge and center. If you aspire to "systematic" theology in the sense of articulating the general coherence of what the Church proclaims on the basis of Scripture, you do well. Doctrines such as the Trinity or the atonement are typically either identifications of key persons or elaborations of the meaning of key events in the story.

One more thing: you might learn these four habits of mind by apprenticing yourself to an established theologian, dead or alive, and reading all their works. You don't have to agree with every detail; the point is to gain a sense of how to think theologically.

Now that we've sketched the kinds of things theologians do, let's turn to your question about the kind of person you need to become. The short answer is "wise": a person with understanding, who knows how to live out what they know and does so in ways appropriate to their circumstances. Wisdom is the virtue that regulates and balances all the other virtues, so let me provide a sketch of the wise theologian by describing three pairs of contrasting qualities.

First, faith and reason. Theologians need to believe firmly and think clearly. Wisdom begins with the fear of the Lord and theology with trust in God's Word. Anselm says we must believe *in order* to understand. Every science has to start somewhere, with some given; theology starts by believing that God has spoken in Scripture (the written Word) and Christ (the revealed Word). Only those who read the Bible in faith can read it as Scripture (authoritative divine address). In general, theologians do well to reason *from*, not *to*, Scripture.

Logic is but ethics (honesty) applied to the life of the mind. In this sense, reason is neutral. It does not legislate what Christians can believe but rather tells us what follows from the articles of faith revealed in Scripture. Reason exercises a ministerial function in theology. Reason is best viewed in terms of created, fallen, and redeemed human intelligence. Notice what I just did: I practiced what I've been preaching about thinking theologically. I thought about human reason *in relation to God*. Relating things to the triune God by thinking biblically is the reflex of a mature theologian.

Don't let knowledge go to your head. (How's that for an oxymoron?) As the apostle Paul warned, knowledge "puffs up" (1 Cor 8:1) and inflates our pride. The best remedy for this is constant prayer. Helmut Thielicke's *A Little Exercise for Young Theologians* reveals well the dangerous gap between what we know intellectually about God and our actual spiritual growth. He points out that a "conceptual experience" is no substitute for genuine faith. Theologians must never be content with living at second hand. That's why prayer is so powerful: unless we are praying to God, we are talking, as it were, behind his back. In Thielicke's words, "A theological thought can breathe only in the atmosphere of dialogue with God."[1]

Anselm embodied the tension between faith and reason by writing his *Proslogion* in the form of a prayer.

Second, joyful truth speaking and hopeful truth suffering. To become a theologian, you must be willing to bear true witness and call out false witnesses, casting down idols and ideologies. That's the shadow side of theology, but the best part is speaking light and truth in astonished indications of God's goodness. I love John Webster's definition of *theology*: "that delightful activity in which the Church praises God by ordering its thinking towards the gospel of Christ."[2] Being a theologian means getting to have not necessarily the last word but the word about last things, "the end for which God created the world" (to cite the title of a dissertation by Jonathan Edwards). It's not only a good word but the best of all possible words—namely, that God glorifies humans and all creation, magnifying his own glory and subjecting all things to the Lordship of Christ so that "God may be all in all" (1 Cor 15:28 NIV). It's the privilege of the theologian to bear witness to the length, depth, breadth, and width of the cross and resurrection. Karl Barth is right: "The theologian who has no joy in his work is not a theologian at all."

Theologians need to be thick-skinned witnesses (martyrs) to the truth. Paul was accused by the Corinthians of "misrepresenting God" (1 Cor 15:15) in testifying to Jesus's resurrection. Fortunately, present-day Western theologians need fear nothing more than metaphorical crucifixion in the courts of academic or popular opinion. You may know of Richard Dawkins's letter to a London newspaper complaining, "If all the achievements of theologians were wiped out tomorrow, would anyone notice the smallest difference?" Yes, I know all about "sticks and stones," but still . . . Well, you'll discover that what hurts even more than the slings and arrows of secular critics is the indifference to doctrine in the Church itself.

An Evangelical theologian who shall remain nameless once advised a student, "Be prepared to be misunderstood and undervalued." I would add, prepare to be unpopular: many people resent being told they are not lords of their own lives. Theologians ought not be nags, but they must be "the conscience of the congregation,"[3] reminding people that faith is not the same as anti-intellectualism and that God is not a supporting actor in their stories, but we have bit parts in his.

Third, whether you're an introvert or an extrovert, becoming a theologian requires a measure of boldness and humility—yet another tension you'll need to preserve. Paul speaks about both in connection to his ministry. To adapt a saying of Luther's, "A theologian is a perfectly free lord of all disciplines, subject to none." Theologians are free from the methodological constraints of other disciplines. The theologian must not let any other discipline into the driver's seat. God is the origin and destiny of all things, and theology knows all things *in their relatedness to God*. By the way, if and when you need a booster shot in your rhetorical right arm, you may find inspiration in the display of bold theology often in the *International Journal of Systematic Theology*. In the present political climate and blogosphere, however, it's harder to find good examples of humility. That, incidentally, is why Augustine is one of my favorite theologians: he published a whole book rehearsing his theological mistakes (*The Retractions*).

Thielicke has some powerful things to say about the temptation to treat truth as a prideful possession. He calls the tendency to look down on those who don't know as much as we think we do "the disease of theologians." The cure is to love the truth more than our possession of it. You'll find this to be especially the case when it comes to theologians' preferred interpretations of Scripture.

That reminds me. Luther's adage has a part B: "The theologian is a perfectly free servant of all disciplines, subject to all." It's important in reading Scripture not to make theology a trump card for dismissing the work of biblical scholars and, for that matter, scientists. Augustine rightly rebukes those who interpret Scripture while ignoring the natural scientist's knowledge of the world: instead of embarrassing themselves and bringing disgrace on theology, they ought to shut up and listen.

I'm aware that I've only scratched the surface. To pursue these matters further, you should investigate, in addition to Thielicke, Karl Barth's *Evangelical Theology: An Introduction*, Mark McIntosh's *Divine Teaching*, Kelly Kapic's *A Little Book for New Theologians*, Avery Dulles's *The Craft of Theology*, and Ellen Charry's *By the Renewing of Your Minds*.[4] (You asked for summer reading recommendations.)

So there you have *believing* and *behaving* as a theologian. Let me conclude with a few words about *belonging*. The question is: Where and with whom are you most likely to flourish as a theologian? As to where, I've already mentioned some pitfalls of doing theology in and for the academy. You requested a "top ten" list of theological schools. That's tricky. I need to know more about your background, what you're looking for, and your future plans. I'll say this much: don't despise the MDiv degree just because it takes longer, often involves learning the biblical languages, and requires an internship. There is much to be said for reading Scripture in the original languages and for pastoral experience. It's erroneous to equate theological education with theological degrees—call it the sheepskin fallacy.

In one of his own letters to an aspiring theologian, C. S. Lewis warns, "Sacred things may become profane by becoming matters of the job."[5] It's a caution worth remembering. Lewis readily acknowledges that some are called to be theological teachers (Eph 4:11). And of course, on one level, all Christians should be biblically and theologically literate. Not everyone can be a doctor, but we should all know first aid. Would that all the Lord's people were theologians (Num 11:29)! The serious point is that whatever your location, your theology should build up the Church in the knowledge and love of God so that it can worship in spirit and truth (John 4:23–24). You can do this as either a pastor- or professor-theologian.

I'm struck by the parallel in Psalm 96:8–9: "Ascribe to the Lord the glory due his name. . . . Worship the Lord in holy splendor." *Ascribing* means setting forth in speech those joyful indicatives that describe God and his works, and this elicits worship. Sound doctrine prompts doxology.

Finally, *with whom* should you do theology? In the old days, most of my students identified with a particular confessional tradition. This is no longer the case. We often hear that millennials are more interested in spirituality than organized religion, hence the decline in denominationalism. I know you expressed interest in being a "free-range" theologian (that's my term, I know, but it's better than your "lone ranger," which I fear comes close to the way church historians often describe heretics). Recall what I said earlier about the importance of reading Scripture in communion with the saints.

I understand your consternation at being forced to act like a consumer in deciding which *particular* communion to join. But consider this: just as there was no contradiction between belonging to one of the twelve tribes and belonging to Israel, so there is no necessary contradiction between being local (or even confessional) and catholic. Jesus says, "In my Father's house there are many dwelling places" (John 14:2). There is much to be gained by inhabiting a particular theological tradition (a dwelling place), but confinement to a single room (or, as some translations have it, "mansion") can be suffocating. The important point is that whichever room you occupy, you should aspire to building up the whole house: preserving the integrity of its witness, orienting its worship, and increasing its wisdom.

Would that there were competent doctors in every house—in every place where the people of God dwell—in order to nourish them and keep them well.

Becoming a doctor of the Church involves more than not doing harm: our vocation is to speak the truth in love and love the truth (the way of Jesus Christ) we speak and those to whom we speak it. If I speak in the tongues of pastors and professors and have not love, I am a noisy guru, not a theologian. The Church is the theologian's natural habitat, its edification in truth and love their primary concern, its communion with the triune God their greatest prayer, hope, and joy.

I know you're concerned that you may not be intelligent enough to become a theologian. Well, God doesn't call people to do things without giving them the necessary equipment. You would do better to worry about avoiding the theologian's occupational hazards (blasphemy and heresy). Aspiring theologians, keep yourselves from idols (1 John 5:21)—and from what I call Feuerbachian slips, the convenient fiction that God is identical to our best thoughts about him.

A last exhortation: Why not approach the whole issue of whether and how to become a theologian (and where to go to study) theologically? Read Scripture, pray, and worship with other saints. As you do, keep an ear out for divine prompting. After all, one way for faith to seek understanding is to step out in faith. If you're reading between the lines, you'll realize that I view all of life as "a little exercise for young theologians."

Godspeed!
Kevin Vanhoozer

Notes

1 Helmut Thielicke, *A Little Exercise for Young Theologians* (Grand Rapids, MI: Eerdmans, 2016), 64.

2 John Webster, *Holiness* (Grand Rapids, MI: Eerdmans, 2003), 8.

3 Thielicke, *Little Exercise*, 67.

4 Karl Barth, *Evangelical Theology: An Introduction* (Grand Rapids, MI: William B. Eerdmans, 1963); Mark A. McIntosh, *Divine Teaching: An Introduction to Christian Theology* (Oxford: Wiley-Blackwell, 2007); Kelly M. Kapic, *A Little Book for New Theologians: Why and How to Study Theology* (Downers Grove, IL: InterVarsity, 2012); Avery Dulles, *The Craft of Theology: From Symbol to System* (Freiburg, Germany: Herder & Herder, 1995); Ellen Charry, *By the Renewing of Your Minds: The Pastoral Function of Christian Doctrine* (Oxford: Oxford University Press, 1999).

5 C. S. Lewis, *The Collected Letters of C. S. Lewis*, vol. 3, *Narnia, Cambridge, and Joy, 1950–1963*, ed. Walter Hooper (New York: HarperCollins, 2007), 82–83.

17

Bram van de Beek

Congratulations on your decision to enrol in theology! It is the most challenging study of all. It concerns the highest and deepest reality—the ultimate. All other disciplines deal with topics limited by space and time. Theology is about the infinite. The sciences investigate the depth of the universe, yet even a postulated theory about the entire expanding universe is limited.

Human sciences deal with human thought and behaviour. Human thought is immensely creative. It can conjure up that which may never occur in physical reality. However, these sciences are the products of the human mind, of carbon and phosphor, and the higher their speculative and metaphysical flight, the less impact they have on everyday life.

Theology concerns that which transcends this limited reality. It is not about a specific part of the universe or a particular property—not even about the universe as a whole or the full composition of all its characteristics—but about its ultimate ground and purpose. Thus indeed it concerns every moment of daily life, every human being, and every creature. Theology seeks to establish that which defines humanity—that is, its origin and purpose. So it is the most relevant study for humankind, not only for its final destination, but also for any act and any reaction in daily life and, consequently, for society and ecology. This is the challenge you have decided to accept. It will give you undreamt of joy and inconceivable freedom.

The Real God

The real God is not the result of arguments. He is not the rational conclusion of complicated evidential discourses. He is because He is. We speak about Him because He is present. He was bodily present in human history in Jesus of Nazareth, as bodily as a human body can be. He was a child in a manger, not in a stable, but beside the well on the square of Bethlehem, where travelling merchants fed their donkeys. He was the son of a homeless young woman. He cried like any baby, and his mother also changed his nappies. Theology speaks about this God. It speaks about a young man in distress, kneeling on the ground because he fears the coming day will be unbearable for him—the day when he will die crying, "My God, my God why have You forsaken Me?" Theology is about Mary's encounter in the garden when, in a moment of ecstasy, she wanted to grasp Him, but He disappeared, like the glory on the mountain disappeared when Peter wanted to make a dwelling for the divine glory. Theology is a continuous exegesis of the earliest Christian hymn about God in Philippians 2:6–11. It is *Jesus* who is the beginning and the end. It is the paradox that Paul summarised: they "crucified the Lord of glory" (1 Cor 2:8). Theology is nothing else than thinking about the meaning and the impact of this lapidary sentence. Such a theology is not a theory; it is a life. As the very ground of my being, my life is borne by Him. God is where the homeless mother has no other place for her baby than the street. God is where a young man follows his calling, not because this is a challenge, but because it is the will of God for salvation. God is where nothing is left for a human being but the cry "Why?" No answer or explanation follows. He is the answer Himself. God is where a man is executed, rightly executed for being responsible for human atrocity.

Be well aware that the position of a theologian is not an easy one. It is difficult to have to say what people do not like to hear. It is much worse, however, to abandon your integrity. As a scholar, you are expected to search for the truth. This truth may involve the correctness of physical theories. It may stress the best diagnoses and cures in health care. It may be the truth about human behaviour. A scholar publishes and says not what people want to hear but the truth—as far as they know for the moment. This is also appropriate for theologians: they focus on truth, even the Truth, whatever the consequences may be. When you start negotiating about truth, you lose your academic independence and also your freedom.

Sources

It is time to write about the sources for your theological research. There is no other theologian than a Christian theologian, for Jesus is the true God, and there is no other God. Thus the basic sources for a Christian theologian are the writings we find in the Bible. Theology is, first of all, the study of the Bible. The best understanding of the Bible is gained by reading it in the original languages. You can never trust a translation. John writes, "No one has ever seen God, the only-begotten God who is at the Father's side, He has made Him known" (my translation). Most translations change this text. They leave out that He was "begotten" or replace "the only-begotten God" with "the only-begotten Son," though the original has "the only-begotten God." This does not correspond with the idea of the eternal unmoved Mover in the philosophical concept of God. Therefore, translators changed the text. They can even call on text traditions that have "Son" instead of "God." Of course they can, for copyists were confronted with the same problem. However, when the normal procedure of text criticism is followed, it is clear: John writes "the only-begotten God." You must be able to read the Greek yourself and be acquainted with the text tradition to be able to check the translation—and to discover the challenging core message of the Christian faith. It is God Himself who came to us in this suffering and executed Man.

Because the Bible is the basic source of theology, you must use it in its entirety. Many Christians only use a selection of favourite texts. They prefer a theology of security and have a collection of texts to support this, with fine meditations in the biblical diaries as its summum. It is a predictable theology and does not need an academic study to propagate it. It only selects those Bible verses that suit this system. The mighty will not be shaken from their pedestal, and the poor will be kept silent so that nothing changes. Such a theology is only a confirmation that religion is opium for the people.

When you read the Bible, and not only the pleasing verses, you will time and again be amazed. When I was a young minister in my first congregation, I chose for my sermon Isaiah 63:9 (ESV). It is a beautiful verse: "In all their affliction he was afflicted, and the angel of his presence saved them; in his love and in his pity he redeemed them; he lifted them up and carried them all the days of old." When doing my exegesis, I discovered that the chapter is more complicated.

I decided not to preach about this text that Sunday. I chose another one. But the chapter challenged me, and thinking about it, I discovered that biblical texts are not everlasting information about God but express the living companionship of God and His people, with interactions, conflicts, reconciliation, anger, conversion—not only of the people but also of God. The Bible is the book of the living God with living people. That makes it such a challenging book, full of surprises.

When I was a young professor in Leiden, I was appointed for dogmatics. However, I also had to teach biblical theology, because my colleagues from the departments of the Old and New Testaments claimed to teach only old Semitic and early Christian literature, investigating what people said about God but without committing themselves to these beliefs. I am still grateful that I was given this task, though I was not at all prepared for it as a systematic theologian. I learned to read the Bible, together with students who often knew more than I did. So do not be too impressed by your professors; always check what they say yourself, and a good professor will also challenge you to do so.

Interaction

Your professors! Most of them will be more acquainted with their field of teaching than I was when I started teaching biblical theology. They will train you in various methods. That is most important, for methods are instruments of investigation. Even those professors who are from a different tradition than yours can often train you even better because you learn to see what their convictions are, for methods, too, are never free of prejudice. You need a set of tools before you can start your critical research. You also need a tradition as a screen for distinguishing your own position. Where do you agree with and where do your opinions diverge from what is taught? And why do they differ? Is this because you thought so? Or is it because you found other information? Such divergencies are eye-openers for study. *Am I wrong? Or does the professor need to review his investigations? Or does she have a different approach in mind?* And of course, ask the professor to discuss the topic, preferably in the classroom, so that all students can benefit from it.

And after the classes and all discussions, after all reading of the sources, take your time to think. My supervisor once said, "You must write your doctoral thesis while cycling." "Dare to think," as another supervisor advised one of my doctoral students. Do not take things for granted. Not in the classroom, not in your papers, and not in your sermon. Nothing is so boring as that which is taken for granted—no surprise, always more of the same.

At university, there is a community of professors and students. A theologian also always has another community: the church. Theologians can operate freely, but within and on behalf of this community. This requires loyalty to her—to her traditions, liturgy, teachings, and doctrines. This does not imply that you accept everything without any critique—if this would ever be possible in such a diverse community with so many subcultures and ideas. This loyalty is to the church, which means to the whole body of Christ. Do not enclose yourself in a subgroup of like-minded people. Inbreeding is deadly, not only in nature, but also in the life of the church and in living theology.

Christians are—like all people—inclined to keep to their own group, claiming absolute truth. Theologians know that Truth is always greater than my truth. I write this not to make everything relative but as a challenge to you and others for deeper understanding.

Resourcing

The church is a dynamic community and so is theology. Theology changes with the dynamics of history. We live in a different context than our predecessors in the sixteenth century, and you start your study in a different context than I did. You should be well aware of this. I do not say this in order to warn you against conservatism only, but also because theology is part of the flux of time and culture. Some theologians are inclined to follow culture without criticism, like other theologians who easily keep to the old tracks of conservatism. This can also be the ease of following a subculture that is seemingly critical of mainstream developments while taking its own ideas as absolute certainties. It is always easy not to need to think! It does not matter if this is a liberal, conservative, or alternative ease.

Theologians must not follow the flow of culture. They must be critical and orientate themselves on the fundamental message of the church. The best help for this is not to try to read all recently published books (if this could ever be possible!). Just read some so that you are aware of current trends in this field. Study the classics, such as the works of Thomas Aquinas and John Calvin. Even better guides are the writings of theologians of the first centuries (up to about 350 CE), when theology was dominated not by a state-bound church but by the teaching of a small minority, often persecuted and always considered subversive to the ideology of the state. They were not revolutionaries (they were loyal to the state), but they did not follow its ideas. They did not try to change the political institutions by force, but they prayed for those who were in power. They were pacifists, because power perverts, and human lives are holy. They just followed their Lord. These theologians were dedicated to express who He is, a suffering man who is the Lord of glory.

These early theologians open perspectives that make many present-day discussions irrelevant. Why should you discuss what a just war is if you reject war as such? When I read their writings, there is always a surprise—what Origen writes about the historicity of biblical stories or Hilary of Poitiers about theological language, the fascinating lessons of Cyril of Jerusalem for young Christians, making them aware of the beauty of nature and the glory of the Eucharist. And if it is about ease, you can find them all on the internet!

Correctness

Do not try to be politically correct. Theologians who wanted to be politically correct supported the most awful systems and societies, such as the German Christians (Deutsche Christen) in the time of Hitler or the theologians of apartheid in South Africa. Jeremiah was not politically correct when he called for surrender to the Babylonian army. The political leaders blamed him for undermining the morale of the people and thus supporting the fall of Jerusalem. Elijah was not politically correct; neither was Habakkuk. Jesus was not politically correct when he dined with tax collectors or proclaimed the fall of Jerusalem. Theology is not about political correctness but about truth—not the truth of political ideology or opposition but the truth of God, who transcends all political claims and conflicts. He is not bound to a party or a system but demands justice and mercy. As a theologian, *you* must do so too.

Also, do not try to be culturally correct. By being culturally correct, the message becomes blunt. Amos was not culturally correct when he called the rich ladies of Samaria "cows of Basan." Judas, the brother of Jesus, was not culturally correct when he likened his opponents to waterless clouds and waves with foam of shame. His other brother, James, was not culturally correct in his philippic against the rich. Neither was Jesus when He called the religious leaders whitewashed graves. His words were not kind. Hearing Him and His brothers, I suppose that sometimes in mother Mary's house, the gloves were off! Christians are not softies. Yes, they were called softies in those early centuries, but that was not because they adapted to culture but because they had soft hearts for broken people, for the poor and excluded, for people infected by deadly diseases, even for criminals. For that kind of softness, much courage is required, and to make it effective, many "incorrect" words are sometimes needed!

Do not even try to be theologically correct. The friends of Job were theologically correct. They blamed Job because he said God was unjust. With a correct theology, you can say the worst things and be merciless toward your fellow Christians or hide evil that should be eradicated. In the time of Jesus, it was correct theology that a man could simply send his wife away. It was written in the law. Jesus mopped the floor with their way of thinking. Correct theology was used to benefit the hard-hearted men at the expense of weak women.

Keep to the Core

You can spend much time in all kinds of discussions in which theologians abound. Take note of these, but on your part, keep to the core: God's coming in Christ—the wonderful paradox of the almighty, glorious God of whom the prophets speak and the psalms sing, who was executed like a slave—on our behalf. Keep to His calling for justice and faithfulness and to His mercy by taking responsibility for unjust and unfaithful human beings.

Do not waste your time on debates about whether the snake had actually spoken, whether Balaam's donkey talked, or whether Jonah really was in the fish. Rather, be interested in the message of these stories. This does not mean that historicity is not important for theology. The historical liberation of Israel from Egypt is fundamental for the faith of Israel and the praise of their God, whom Christians adore. The hardness of the nails of the cross has no meaning for a spiritual message if it is only fiction. The biblical story is as concrete as land, death, and social relations. It is physical—as physical as a body can be, even a dead body. But you must always distinguish the genre and the way a story is applied. A mere reading of biblical texts with historical claims leads to absurdities. According to Chronicles, King Ahaziah was two years old when his father was born. The Chronicler should have checked his data and corrected the text before publishing his book. But he was not interested in the age of kings and the date of their birth. His only interest was whether they served the Lord and kept His temple holy. The writer of Kings was not interested in the economic success of the reign of Jeroboam II but focused on the social injustice on which the economy of the country flourished. That is the true story of that time, not the statistics of economic growth published by political leaders. That is God's story with His people, and that should be the focus of theologians.

Libraries have been filled with books, and innumerable symposia and conferences have been held about the relation between faith and science, with the focus on the historicity of the story of creation in Genesis 1–3. Many people claim you cannot be a Christian if you are not a creationist. As if the Bible would be interested in evolution, in geology or biology. The biblical authors just followed the scientific ideas common to their time. They were interested not in correcting science with divine information but in teaching people about the One who is the Creator and about the calling of human beings. The confession that the Lord who called Israel is the creator of the earth is presented in the language of creation discourses of that time, and the biblical writers borrowed from these contexts what they thought was useful. Consequently, we find diverse creation concepts in the Bible. The imaginations and scientific constructions are not relevant, but the Lord who created this world is. Genesis 1–3 gives information not about the year 4000 BCE but about the world in which we live. Not about a couple who lived six thousand years ago but about the human condition. Who is their Lord? What is their calling? How do they behave? It is concentrated in this probing question: "Adam, where are you?" (Mankind, where are you?) That is a more difficult question than the debate about creationism and evolution. And *that* is the question Genesis raises.

There are many other topics that let emotions run high, especially on ethical issues. People often select a single verse or a few verses from the Bible. They make these absolute, neglecting any context whatsoever. Questions concerning gender and sexuality sometimes seem to be touchstones for orthodoxy. Here, too, the adage is due: keep to the core. The core is what the church confesses in her Creed—about God, about Christ, about the Spirit and the church. It is not about homosexuality or the position of women. These may be a matter for ethical discussion, as any human behaviour is, but they are not more than the debate about fasting or the Sabbath.

What is necessary in Christian ethics is not a set of rules but the basic rule of being in Christ—He who humiliated Himself on behalf of humankind. Living in Christ is counting others more important than yourself, the life of the other more important than your own life.

The Attitude of a Theologian

As a theologian, you must not be afraid. You are free in Christ. Your life is His life. Even if you have to die for your faith, your life is secure in Him. I am sure you will not take your study lightly. You see it as your calling. As a theologian, you will not become rich. You will not be honoured by prestigious rewards. The highest reward is the gratitude of people who heard a voice of understanding without empty promises, heard a voice sharing their sufferings, and found a person who embodied this voice. Even if you fall short of your original ideals—and perhaps you will—theology is not about *you* but about Christ. Keep to your calling not only as a theologian but as a Christian: provide care and love for those who are in need and oppose the egoistic indifference of the powerful. When you follow the ideal of the imitation of Christ and are confronted with your own weakness, you will understand the weakness of those who are not able to raise their lives from the slums and mire in which they are trapped.

Theologians have failures just like other people. One disease, however, is typical for theologians: the messiah complex. They think they must be excellent Christians. When they are successful, they become unimpeachable. When they fail, they become frustrated and disappointed and lose confidence. For a theologian, it is enough to have confidence in the Lord. It is your task to tell fallible people about Him who, as the ground of their being, was not successful but died unmarried, in the prime of His life, when other people start their successful careers.

Theologians are not better Christians than other Christians. Their faith is no less contested. On the contrary, when you start your studies, it will soon become clear that things are more complicated than you thought. Only the naive can remain unshaken. Your study will do away with your naivete. When reading the Bible, you will come across texts you do not understand. That should not frustrate or disappoint you. It should rather make you modest—not the modesty that all opinions are equal but the modesty that is required when we think about the incomprehensible acts of God. Origen suggests that God may have written texts in the Bible that we are not able to understand so that we will always be aware that it is God's book, not ours.

You will be confronted with texts and experiences that will shake your life and your faith. Do not give up in such situations. Perhaps you will not find an answer, but you will learn to live with unanswered questions and with experiences that will never fit neatly in a theological system. They will deepen your faith, enrich your life with God, and make a theological concept more theological—more about God.

Continue teaching the love of Christ and what this love means: He saves failed lives. This is what you share with all other Christians and what you celebrate in the Eucharist: eternal life in the remembrance of His death on our behalf. Dying with Him and rising in Him is imperishable life. The early Christian theologian Hilary of Poitiers says that we should not do theology at all, but we are compelled to do so because of the nonsense or malevolent things people utter about God and that we must refute. Actually, we should just live and celebrate being in Christ. I must add, we also do theology for a deeper understanding of this life and celebration. This is a wonderful experience. The more I think, the deeper and higher it becomes. Christ gave me a foundation through His life, and I think about Him and about living in Him. Celebrating His passion and resurrection, ever-wider perspectives unfold. New aspects always appear on the horizon. Theology is open, open beyond the borders of the universe—beyond the borders of my earthly life, beyond the sorrows and troubles of history. Theology is about God, who created this world and its history and loves her even in her failure. Theology is speaking about Him as a loving Person as expressed by the earliest Christian hymn in Philippians 2.

I wish you much joy and freedom in this work and, most of all, that your work may serve those who are in need of salvation, whatever their troubles may be, to the glory of our God who came to serve such people.

Bram (A.) van de Beek

18

Daniel Migliore

Let me begin by welcoming you to the always challenging and often joyous activity called theology. In some ways, I wish I could be in your position rather than finding myself being asked to offer you a little advice about the adventure you have entered. Doing Christian theology requires the humility of being ready to begin again and again in the quest for deeper understanding of the reality and purpose of God and of all things in relation to God. In that sense, I hope I will always want to be as much a beginner in theology as you may now consider yourself. You will be cutting your theological teeth at a time of enormous challenges confronting church and world, and the time cries out for extraordinary courage and lively hope. Maybe this is one of the reasons you have chosen to become part of the company of theologians.

Since all theology is marked, in part, by life experiences, let me tell you a little about my own decision many years ago to enter the path you are now walking. My father arrived in the United States from Sicily at the age of twelve, accompanied by his parents and his two younger siblings. Eventually, he would become the pastor of a modest-sized congregation of Italian immigrants in Pittsburgh, Pennsylvania. Mostly poor folk with little formal education, members of the congregation were eager to hear the gospel and to find their way in a strange new land. To the end of the Second World War, worship services were held in both Italian and English. My father's primary responsibilities as a pastor were the usual: preaching the Word, administering the sacraments, leading Bible studies, and making pastoral visits. Other tasks, however, were also important, including giving employment and legal advice, offering lessons in civic responsibilities, and helping the new immigrants navigate through the ethnic biases they frequently encountered.

Experiencing this sort of ministry as a youth proved formative in my own faith journey and in my choice of vocation. When I became a student of theology and later a member of a theological faculty, I focused on the classics of the theological tradition but also learned much from the liberation movements that shook up the theological world in the latter half of the twentieth century, especially the Black, Latin American, Latino/a, Asian American, and feminist theologians. In large part, they moved me because I heard in their prophetic voices echoes of indispensable aspects of the biblical message always in danger of being forgotten by a complacent church, but also in part because these voices resonated with my own experience as a young boy in that congregation of immigrants where ministry was not simply verbal or theoretical but concrete and practical, affirming the dignity of all God's children, welcoming the stranger, standing on the side of the poor, and in the words of the prophet Micah, being engaged in justice making, loving mercy, and walking humbly with God (Mic 6:8).

This personal story gives me the occasion for my first bit of friendly advice, which has two apparently contradictory aspects. As some of you may discover soon enough, your theological studies will sometimes clash sharply with your previous learnings and rustle some of your cherished convictions. This may cause deep personal struggles. Count on being wounded by theology. The Christian gospel continually disrupts our preconceptions and prejudices, causing a veritable shaking of the foundations on which we were once convinced we could firmly stand, awakening us to the fact that God is always greater than what we are inclined to imagine. Should this happen, do not be dismayed or discouraged. You are being offered an opportunity for personal and theological growth. In the Gospels, the disciples are often portrayed as shocked and dumbfounded by the new things Jesus teaches them and what they see him do.

On the other hand, you may also discover that some of what you bring to your studies from your earlier life experience contributes in important and surprising ways to what you are learning from your theological readings, class discussions, and your own teaching and writing. Be thankful for these moments in which formative events of your past now strike you as fragments and anticipations of larger and deeper truths. All this is to say that what you bring to the study of theology is like clay out of which the greatest of potters can mold something genuinely new.

But now first and foremost, as you press ahead in your theological studies, I urge you to become a lover of Scripture. Maybe that goes without saying, but I think it is worth saying anyway. Discover the Bible as an inexhaustible source of your devotional life, your emerging theological perspective, and your ethical commitments. I doubt that it will surprise you if I say that in your studies, you will encounter a vast array of theologies, some boring, some immensely stimulating. Some may even have the power to cast an enchanting spell over you. At one point in my own theological development, I was mesmerized by a theologian—no need to mention the name here—who seemed to me to offer a brilliant and intellectually satisfying account of the whole of reality. In time, I came to realize that the great system, which sailed so impressively in the rarefied stratosphere, failed ever to touch down on earth, where it would have to wrestle with the messy realities of human life with all its struggles, doubts, and hopes. I also noticed that this great theologian seldom lingered long over a passage of Scripture. A pity, because it is precisely the witness to God at work in the messiness of life that you find in the Bible.

But I want to add at once that loving the Bible does not mean reading it naively and uncritically. Said differently, loving the Bible does not mean biblicism. It means allowing the Bible the freedom to engage you again and again in startling ways with its rich array of witnesses and its manifold genres. To be sure, their witness is marked by limitations common to every human effort to speak of God, needing to be grasped in its own historical context, understood within Scripture's overarching story of the judging and redeeming work of God in the world, and then proclaimed and faithfully lived out in courageous ways in the here and now. You will be greatly helped in this endeavor if you eschew a loner's approach to biblical study and resolve to attend carefully to the voices of other readers of the Bible in times and places different from your own. Theology is at its best not in solitude but in community. Love the Bible, then, not because it is a collection of disconnected infallible dicta but because it is the foundational witness of the Christian community that at its center tells the good news of the decisive activity of God in the life, death, and resurrection of Jesus for the redemption of the world, including theologians like you and me.

It goes along with loving the Bible that you never need to be afraid to change your mind. I do not mean that in your theological studies, you should be tossed from one cultural or theological fad to another, like a leaf blown in the autumn winds. If you read the Bible under the guidance of the Spirit of Christ and with the help of the confession of the church universal, you will be in touch with a reliable and firm direction for your thinking and acting. If you allow the gospel of God's grace attested in

Scripture to be your theological GPS, you will have a steady guide as you travel through what may seem, at times, like an impenetrable thicket. The study of theology, indeed the whole of Christian life, is a journey, and in every journey, course changes are to be expected. You will read about dramatic changes in the lives of people like the apostle Paul, Augustine, Luther, Julian of Norwich, Barth, and many others, not only at the beginning of their faith journey, but on later occasions as well. Like them, you too will experience times when you find yourself hastening down a seemingly promising path only to discover it is a cul-de-sac. Another way of saying this is that Christian life—and with it, theological study—involves risk. Mistakes will be made. But if you stay close to the treasure in the earthen vessel of the Bible, you will not be led far astray. Even if you do not have a precise map of the terrain before you, you will always have the north star of the central biblical message of God's holy and steadfast love.

Then, too, keep your theological studies in dynamic relationship with your life of prayer and common worship. Doesn't it strike you as odd to want to talk so freely about God (third-person language) but never think it important to engage in prayer to and worship of God (the subject of theological study being not an impersonal "It" but a "You" who invites our trust and calls us to responsibility)? Anselm, you will remember, was not embarrassed to set his famous proof of the existence of God in the context of a prayer, and Thomas Aquinas and Karl Barth began their dogmatic treatises with a prayer for God's assistance. In the final three years of my teaching theology, among the courses I offered was one for beginners called Credo. It was basically an introductory study of the Lord's Prayer, the Apostles' Creed, and the Love Commandment. Reading this, some of you may notice that the course followed the pattern of the old catechisms, and today most of us find the method of neat questions and answers used in these old documents as unattractive. But while the old method no longer appeals, the idea of holding together the practice of prayer, the search for understanding, and the call to do justice and love God and neighbor seems to me an exemplary agenda for all theological study. I recommend that as a young theologian, you move back and forth between the lecture hall and the chapel with some regularity.

While the witness of Scripture has a central place in theological study, this does not mean closing your eyes to the grace and judgment of God present both in the world of nature and in the turmoil of human history. In our time, the world is faced with an unprecedented environmental crisis. A critical and constructive theology of creation has become one of the most important items on the theological agenda. A personal confession is in order here. I and many other theologians of my generation were so impressed by the theological revolution of the early part of the twentieth century, which set the revelation of God in the biblical narrative so sharply over against what could be known of God in the natural world, that we often skipped past or dealt only marginally with the witness of creation. Given the context in which that theological revolution occurred, it was a necessary course correction, and I am far from suggesting that we go back to the idea of two completely independent channels of revelation, one from "the book of the Bible" and the other from "the book of nature." Instead, perhaps you will find a more promising approach in starting with the radiance of God's triune activity culminating in Christ that not only is able to illuminate our personal and social worlds but also enables us to see the beauty and wonder of all of God's creatures, calling us to responsible care for the environment and all its strange inhabitants rather than viewing them as a field for human domination and exploitation. It will be a major task of your generation to explore further what a course correction of this sort means not only for the doctrine of creation but for all loci of theology and, equally important, for the witness and ministry of the church.

Likewise, I hope a critical and courageous engagement between theology and the public world will be a constant in your own theological reflection and activity. A robust theology cannot avoid the world of politics where issues like social justice, the quest for peace, and compassion for the poor are addressed for weal or woe. As Karl Barth once put it, theology needs to have the Bible in one hand and the newspaper in the other. One corollary of this truth is that every responsible theologian will take with utmost seriousness the need to respect, love, and learn from neighbors near and far, from people who may be different in many ways, whether by race, ethnicity, class, gender, or religious commitment. In the words of one of my favorite lines from the *Brief Statement of Faith* of the Presbyterian Church (USA), this will mean allowing the Spirit of God, who breaks down walls and builds new community, to enable us "to listen to voices long silent."

Of all the topics about theological responsibility in the public domain, those of racial injustice and the vast gulf between the rich and the poor stand out. They will certainly be pervasive features of the world in which your theological work will be done. The church in South Africa knows this well, since it has had to wrestle long and bravely with the crisis in racial relationships in both church and state during the era of apartheid and its aftermath. The United States—a nation in which racial injustice has been present from its beginnings and which endured a horrific civil war over the institution of slavery—is again deeply divided over its embedded racism. And in recent years, the challenge of otherness has been further intensified by the migration of peoples happening worldwide, a phenomenon most likely to increase in the years ahead. If I am not mistaken, the recent marches protesting racial injustices and the ever-expanding chasm between the rich and the poor portend difficult struggles ahead for both church and society, and theology will be an important arena of this struggle. You will be asked by your theological, nontheological, and antitheological friends and strangers how your emerging theology, voluminous reading, hearing of many lectures, published articles, and soon-to-be-published books have any bearing on the realities of injustice and poverty that crush the lives of so many people today. However uncomfortable it may be, as a responsible theologian, you will not want to avoid such questions as you explore Scripture, ponder the central tenets of the Christian faith, and listen to voices of the excluded and oppressed.

Then there is the matter of the terrible pandemic that, as I write, is making deep and perhaps long-lasting changes to life around the globe. In the United States, people of color have been disproportionately affected by Covid-19, exacerbating the racial divide and the widening gap between the rich and the poor. Although some South American countries have been experiencing improvements in their living standards in recent decades, they now face a deadly illness that threatens to undo much of this progress and push millions once again into deep poverty and poor health. What will be the response of the theologians and the churches to this crisis? Will the theologians of the new generation see their task as engaging in intramural controversies, or perhaps devising novel theodicies to justify the ways of God to humanity? Or will they seek guidance from the Old Testament prophetic tradition and from the New Testament proclamation of the strange power of the weakness of the crucified and risen Christ that continues in the activity of the Spirit who brings new life? Will they speak of the indomitable hope of resurrection that is not confined to life after death but includes life before death as well? Will the strategy of the churches be to turn inward and seek to protect their members and possessions as much as possible from the ravages of the virus scourge and from concurrent threats like climate change and widespread food insecurity? Or will they find new inspiration for mission and ministry in the love commandments and in Jesus's reminder that in attending to the needs of "the least of these who are members of my family" (Matt 25:40), it is the Lord himself who is being served? If you are committed to doing serious theology, these too are questions you will not be able to avoid.

I hope the previous paragraphs do not come across as a politicization of the gospel and of the theological vocation. This is not my intention. A sharp and crucial distinction must be made between a theology with a prophetic dimension and a politicized theology. You know as well as I that our world needs to hear—loud and clear—the proclamation of forgiveness and reconciliation and communion rooted in the astonishing grace of God. When true to its task, theology exists to test and assist the proclamation of the good news of the gospel by fresh study of Scripture and the church's central doctrines, by asking how these speak to our present existential crises, and by encouraging the practices of Christian service that work to build and support communities of human life, which, while never identical with, may, by the grace of God, become parables and foretastes of the coming Kingdom of God. The gospel gives us reason to hope that by God's grace, not only can personal lives can be transformed, but the social orders we construct can become more just, more equitable, more peaceful than they are today. But please, no reduction of Christian faith and hope to the latest ideology, whether to the right, the left, or the all-too-comfortable center. There is no greater danger in the political and religious domains than a nationalism or racialism infused with distorted religious zeal. If theology should not seek to absent itself from the prophetic critique of present injustices, it must also remain ever mindful that it is not within human capacity to bring about a time when it will no longer be necessary to pray, "Thy kingdom come!" I hope the new generation of theologians will not let the church or the world forget that.

My parting words: I do not want anything I have written to leave you with a heavy heart and a spirit of doom and hopelessness. The gospel is good news! God is making all things new! Amid human confusion as far as the eye can see, the Lord nevertheless reigns! Just for these reasons, the study of theology can be an exciting undertaking. It will urge you not only to face the depths of human need without flinching but also to keep alive the hope of a reconciled humanity and a renewed world. The study of theology has gone awry if, for all our doubts and moments of despair, it does not ignite in us a spirit of hope and thanksgiving in our own and our world's darkest hours, maybe even permitting us at times to discover the work of theology as a precious—can we also say a beautiful?—undertaking that in its own way may offer a very faint and flawed reminder of the beauty of the gracious God who is its subject.

Daniel L. Migliore
Princeton, New Jersey

19

Wolfgang Huber

A dvice to others is usually just a disguised way of putting one's own life experience in perspective. But no one can avoid having their own experiences. They are not always individual. There are also experiences that are characteristic of entire generations. Those who, like me, began studying theology sixty years ago should therefore be particularly careful with advice. The most important thing they can pass on is that theology can still be exciting and challenging even after sixty years. I have never regretted the decision to take this path.

Of course, I have also experienced crises. Yes, my studies began with a crisis. I studied not in a theological seminary but in Heidelberg at a state university. At the age of seventeen, I found accommodation in a student dormitory. We were a colourful mix, especially in terms of the subjects we studied. All faculties were represented in our dormitory.

A mathematics student was the first person I got into conversation with. When he heard about my field of study, he said, "What, you are studying theology? Yet I thought you were quite a reasonable person." The idea that one had to be unreasonable to study theology was alien to me. I did not come from a family of theologians and was the only one among my siblings who chose theology as a subject of study. But that I, the youngest of five brothers, was just as sensible as the others was the least I had taken away from this childhood upbringing. I probably answered the mathematician that belief in God and the use of reason were not mutually exclusive. It could not be otherwise, because God had not accidentally created us as rational beings. The question of the relationship between faith and reason accompanied me from the beginning.

Later I got to know the Anglican principle that Scripture, tradition, and reason are to be considered as sources of theology; I also came across the Methodist extension, which speaks of a quadrilateral of Scripture, tradition, experience, and reason. When studying at a German-speaking theological faculty, it was not easy to deal with this proposal. For to simply place Scripture and tradition side by side violated the Reformation principle of "Scripture alone." It was already drilled into us by the fact that the first semesters of theology studies were focused on biblical languages and basic courses in biblical subjects.

Yet the reference to the special position of sacred Scripture does not mean indifference to other sources of faith; it points to how clarification can take place when these sources come into tension with one another. Such tensions, even contradictions, also exist in the biblical sources themselves. This is why the reformer Martin Luther already specified the principle of Scripture to the effect that this does not simply mean that the biblical texts must be dealt with according to the question of what "Christum treibet"—that is, what promotes the understanding of God who promotes Himself in Christ.

The biblical orientation of Protestant theology did not prevent me from appreciating the high value of the Christian tradition very early on. In my studies, the experience of crisis was joined by the experience of happiness. I immersed myself in sources from the time of early Christianity. The appropriation and interpretation of the Christian faith in the first Christian centuries, together with the course set for the church tradition, stimulated my curiosity. I was able to investigate this through the development of the Easter festival and the content of Christian Easter sermons in the first Christian centuries. I researched the old sermons, marvelling at the fact that they had survived the millennia at all, and made sense of them. This exemplary approach to the emergence of Christian tradition was at the same time connected with the experience that theology is dependent on reason; it is a science that proceeds in a methodically controlled manner and must meet historical-critical standards.

A fortunate turn of my life led me into the realm of experience. I married early, and my wife wanted to join me in gaining experience in Christian communities. We did this with youthful recklessness; above all, we realised that people without theological training were far ahead of us in terms of faith experience and that we could learn from them. I learned Christianity in action from a master baker: hardworking in his profession, with a keen eye for people in need, firmly rooted in a faith in God that found support and orientation in Jesus. Since then, I have repeatedly experienced that as theologians, we are dependent not only on theological teachers but on people whose faith has matured in experience.

Of course, these can also be theologians—possibly even theologians whom we have never met in person. For me, Dietrich Bonhoeffer has become such a role model. What concerned me most about him was the unity of faith and life, the indissoluble connection between theology and existence. As sharply as he thought as a theologian, he was, at the same time, hungry for experience. The most impressive and, in a special way, tragic example of this is his unfulfilled longing for an experience of his very own kind. For years, he planned a trip to India—which was anything but a matter of course ninety years ago—to seek out Gandhi, to live with him in his ashram, and to understand not only the political methods of nonviolent resistance but also the secrets of his spirituality.

Bonhoeffer's plans to travel to India had been known for a long time. We also know from a reply letter from Gandhi that he asked Gandhi in autumn 1934 whether it would be possible to visit him. Gandhi replied laconically that Bonhoeffer was welcome to come if he brought enough money for the return journey. He could also participate in Gandhi's life as long as he was not travelling or in prison. But the letter to which Gandhi responded so practically and openly was unknown until now. Only recently has a Gandhi biographer tracked it down in New Delhi. The Bonhoeffer researcher Clifford Green has published the English original; I have made it accessible in a German translation. In my many years of involvement with the legacy of Dietrich Bonhoeffer, this was a particularly moving experience.

Bonhoeffer had decided to study theology at a very young age and had already begun his studies at the age of seventeen. Nevertheless, he claimed that he only became a theologian comparatively late—namely, after a renewed, intensive study of the Sermon on the Mount in 1932 (i.e., at the age of twenty-six). In the following year, when he had experienced and suffered the first storms of the church struggle after the transfer of power to Hitler, he decided to take up a pastorate abroad in London. He took up this post on October 17, 1933; he had to interrupt his teaching at the faculty of theology at Humboldt University in Berlin for an uncertain period. He was already in London when his essay "What Should a Student of Theology Do Today?" was published in Berlin. It is a brusque text that has always caused me personally great problems. Bonhoeffer only recognises an inner right to study theology for those who are convinced that they cannot study anything else. Why nothing else comes into question must be shown by the fact that one convinced of this "comes upon the cross in the midst of his questioning and searching" and "recognises the end of all his passions in the suffering of God under the hand of man."[1]

But a year later, in October 1934, Bonhoeffer writes an agitated and stirring letter to Mahatma Gandhi, with Bonhoeffer asking whether he himself can remain a theologian. For he finds no role model in his own church, or even in the larger framework of Western Christianity, who is able to show the way to a new Christian life in uncompromising agreement with the Sermon on the Mount. Only if such a path is shown and followed can a "becoming real of faith" be achieved. But this is the task for which one is a theologian—at least, that is how Bonhoeffer sees it. I am convinced that he hits the mark. Wherever we live and work as theologians, it is always about faith becoming reality.

Bonhoeffer left behind the idea of an uncompromising conformity to the Sermon on the Mount in the years that followed. The longer, the clearer he saw the crucial question not in how Christians can "heroically get out of the way" but in how future generations can live. The longer, the more clearly he saw that our lives and actions remain fragmentary. But his wish was that we could see how the whole was meant. So he did not follow a path that dispensed with sensible weighing for the sake of supposed uncompromisingness.

Bonhoeffer's example shows how indispensable Scripture, tradition, experience, and reason are for a theological existence. When, after many years of theological research and teaching, I took on a church leadership role as a bishop, this became clear to me once again in completely new dimensions. The role of the Bible in the daily and weekly rhythm of life gained importance. The formative role of traditions for the profile and shape of congregations and churches became clear to me day by day. I encountered the Christian faith in people's life stories. But I also learned about the inhibiting significance of well-rehearsed patterns of faith, unreflectively adopted traditions, and constricting experiences for a change in the church. I had to realise how difficult it can sometimes be to use reasonable arguments to fight against such stable patterns of behaviour. Reforming the church is also difficult in the churches of the Reformation.

In all the countries and continents I have visited in the course of time, Scripture and tradition, experience and reason play a major role in the life of the churches. In all my travels, I have also experienced that the Christian faith has lost its self-evidence for many people. It is not the biblical message that is to blame for the fact that many people are strangers to the Christian faith; it is much more the traditionalism of the churches and the strangeness of their language. In order to overcome this strangeness, one has to know and understand the tradition. One must take people's experiences seriously. In order to bring the word of the Bible close to them, one has to meet them with reason and love.

There is no country have I visited more often over the course of many decades than South Africa. I found a second theological home there. I got to know the country even during the apartheid era. I met Beyers Naudé, who was called the South African Bonhoeffer, as well as Desmond Tutu. The Belhar Confession became as important a document to me as the Barmen Declaration. Part of my theological existence is the encounter with sisters and brothers who live in conditions very different from those with which I am familiar. From their struggles, we also learn for our own struggles. From their example, we can learn how faith gains reality today.

To every reader: blessings for your theological journey!
Wolfgang Huber

Note

1 Author's translation from Dietrich Bonhoeffer, "What Should a Student of Theology Do Today?," in *Berlin: 1932–1933; Dietrich Bonhoeffer Works*, English ed., ed. Larry Rasmussen, trans. Isabelle Best and David Higgins (Minneapolis: Fortress, 2009), 433.

On Flourishing, Blossoming, Liberating

20

Miroslav Volf (III)

In my first letters, I invited you to love theology—even, in a certain sense, to lose yourself in it. But why? Why theology, when you could love and lose yourself in so many other endeavors? To answer the question, I first need to say something about theology as a discipline.

As the word itself says, theology is about God. You can take this in two ways. One is straightforward and was dominant through theology's two-thousand-year history: theology is talk about God. Thomas Aquinas, one of theology's most accomplished practitioners, puts it this way: the subject matter of theology is "God and everything in relation to God."[1] But you can take the statement that theology is about God in an altered sense: it is not a disciplined kind of talk about God but *talk about* talk about God. In this case, human discourse about God, and not God directly, would be the subject matter of theology. I am a proponent of the first definition, which, of course, doesn't exclude what the second definition says that theologians should be doing. To talk well about God, you'd be foolish not to engage also in the talk about the talk about God. After all, lots of very smart and dedicated people have talked about God, and you'd want to know and critically sift through what they have said.

So the subject matter of theology is God. At the end of one of my letters, referencing Jeremiah, I implied that God can be a *reason* for doing theology—at least that was and still is so in many cases. God "enticed" Jeremiah and "prevailed" over him (Jer 20:7), lit the fire that burned "in [his] bones" (20:9) and made it impossible for him not to speak even when he knew that speaking would land him in the stocks. Jürgen Moltmann, my doctoral supervisor, puts the Jeremiah-like experience of theologians this way: "It is simple, but true, to say that theology has only one single problem: God. We are theologians for the sake of God. God is our dignity. God is our agony. God is our hope."[2] I am with Moltmann here. The motivating reason for doing theology and the subject matter of theology are one and the same: God. We are theologians for the sake of God.

What does this being a theologian "for the sake of God" mean? Why does God light the fire? Why should you love theology and devote your life to it? Some will say that the *purpose* of theology is the same as the subject matter and the reason for theology—God—and in a certain sense, that's surely the right answer. God created all things "to" God, as the apostle Paul famously says in Romans 11: "From God and through God and to God are all things. To God be the glory forever" (my translation). It is important, though, to understand rightly what it means that all things, including theology, are "to God." For the truth of the matter is that theologians aren't of much benefit to God; neither are the prophets. The reason is simple: God has no needs that any humans can satisfy, just as God has no interests of God's own to realize at any creatures' expense! When it comes to creation, the "need" and the "interest" of God are the good of all God's creatures, the flourishing of each individually and of all of them jointly. God created them out of love to thrive as objects of God's delight. Here's what that means for theology. Though theology is *about* God, theology isn't *for* God; theology is for what God is after. The purpose of theology is furthering God's purpose for creation: the flourishing of creation in the life-giving presence of God. The dignity, the agony, the hope, and the delight of theologians lie in their role within that *grand purpose* of God. I find this an exhilarating thought.

Some people can't get quite as excited about the orientation of theology toward flourishing life as I do, and you may be among them. The opinion is widespread that everybody knows, more or less, what the content of flourishing life is. Some say that we all feel it in our gut; others think that the careful observation of human behavior can tell us what makes us flourish. Our pressing need, both groups believe, isn't formulating a compelling vision of flourishing but securing the effective means for all human beings actually to live a flourishing life. I disagree. The idea that securing the means to flourishing is all that matters is, I believe, one of the great misconceptions of the present cultural moment; you might even call it an ideology, in the pejorative sense. Neither our inchoate feelings nor the results of very articulate sciences can tell us what the purpose of our life is, the content of a truly flourishing life. For this isn't a factual question that we can answer by registering feelings and paying attention to our behaviors but a *normative* question. It's not about what we aspire to, not even what we aspire to in the hidden depths of our being; it's about what we *ought* to aspire to if we want to live a life worthy of our humanity.[3]

Don't misunderstand me: I am *not* putting down science. It would be a fool's errand to try to elevate the importance of theology by denigrating science. Modern science is extraordinary in its ability to describe reality and to foster technological innovation, helping us orient ourselves in the world and negotiate our way in it with increasing ease. It can tell us how best to get from point A to any point B we choose. But what it cannot tell us, and what its clearest-thinking advocates do not pretend that it can tell us, is which point B is worthy of our humanity. Now, it can tell us which point B we need to reach if we want to get to C, and which C if we aim at D. Notice all the *if*s in previous sentences. Science is about means, not about the goal that is good in itself.

Great philosophies and religions have grappled for centuries with this question of our human purpose, with the content of flourishing life, each in its own way. They have also argued with one another about their disagreements. Christian faith has a distinctive answer of its own—or rather, a family of distinctive answers. That's where theology has to come in, at least theology that is doing what it seems to me theology should be doing. Its purpose is to discern, articulate, and commend visions of flourishing life in the light of God's self-revelation in Jesus Christ. That's what excites me about theology. That's why I have been studying it for almost half of a century with undiminished enthusiasm. That's why I haven't regretted even for a single hour that theology became my vocation, not even when I had to raise my own support to be able to continue with the work.[4]

Now, it won't help you much to know the purpose of theology if you don't know how to *do* theology to achieve that purpose. At the time I was unceremoniously declared a "doctor of theology"—a mere handshake with two professors present—I knew how to write a dissertation, but I wasn't confident that I knew how to go about doing theology. You might think that writing a dissertation just *is* learning to do theology, and that may be true for some students. But it wasn't for me. So I went to Moltmann for advice. I have always admired how alive his theology is, a bit like the gospel itself, full of promise for the world. "What do I do now?" I asked him. I'll never forget what he said: "Identify what moves people and shine the light of the gospel on it."

I couldn't have said it better myself, I thought self-mockingly at hearing his simple but profound answer. It wasn't long before I realized that doing this kind of theology required disciplined work and what my friend and fellow doctoral student in Tübingen, Siegfried Zimmer, called *Mut zur Unvollkommenheit*, courage for imperfection. For following Moltmann's advice required that (1) I knew what the gospel and its light, reaching from the first century into the present, are; that (2) I could understand adequately what moves people; and that (3) I could figure out what kind of bearing the gospel has on the matter. Getting a handle on each of these three and all of them together is the heart of the exciting but difficult work of theological improvisation.

Doing theology is a challenge. But don't let the difficulty of it blind you to the adventure that it represents. Moltmann's advice helped me realize that surrounding me on all sides is a cornucopia of themes, sufficient to keep my theological appetite alive as long as I live. Never a dull moment! In my experience, those who consider theology boring and useless have never really gotten to know the real thing—or have ceased believing that God matters much to life in the world.

These letters have grown long. And there is so much more to say about being a theologian—about the need for wonder, attentiveness, curiosity; about how firmly or loosely we ought to hold to our convictions; about theological virtues like courage, gratitude, humility, and faithfulness (in its interplay with creativity); about the centrality of the Bible in theological work and the challenge its serious reading presents; about the need for solitude, communion with the likeminded, and friendship with those who think very differently from you (including non-Christians); about admiring and learning from theologians whose lives were in some regards appalling (which experience I most vividly have in relation to one of my heroes, Martin Luther); about the importance of sensitivity to those who suffer, especially those who aren't even capable of expressing their pain except through tears and sighs, let alone of protesting against it as the righteous Job did.

More could be added to the list of important things about which I could write you as well. But these three letters should get you going.

Yours,
Miroslav

Notes

1 I am paraphrasing Aquinas's answer to the question of whether God is the object of theology in *Summa Theologiae* I, q. 1, a. 7.

2 Jürgen Moltmann, *Theology and the Future of the Modern World* (Pittsburgh: ATS, 1995), 1.

3 See Miroslav Volf, Matthew Croasmun, and Ryan McAnnally-Linz, "Meaning and Dimensions of Flourishing: A Programmatic Sketch," in *Religion and Human Flourishing*, ed. Adam Cohen (Waco, TX: Baylor University Press, 2020), 7–18.

4 If you want to explore this vision of theology's purpose, take a look at the book I wrote with my colleague Matthew Croasmun at the Yale Center for Faith & Culture: *For the Life of the World: Theology That Makes a Difference* (Grand Rapids, MI: Brazos, 2019). It sketches a research program for theology of the kind I have just described.

21

Robert Vosloo

Writing a letter like this holds the temptation to universalize the particular. One can easily assume that your experiences and observations are valid for everybody, that your advice is wisdom for all. This is obviously not the case, so therefore, this letter should be read with a pinch of hermeneutical salt. This being said, writing these kinds of letters holds the opportunity for the author thereof to remember and to renarrate—to think back on what one has received and to discern what is worthy to pass on. And in reading about the particular experiences and perspectives of other theologians, the little miracle can even happen that one recognizes in another theologian's words something that transcends that theologian's concrete historical and social location and speaks to one's own intuitions and questions. It is in this spirit, and with this hope, that this "letter to a young theologian" is presented.

I started my theological studies in 1985 at Stellenbosch University. The group of theological students of which I was part consisted almost entirely of white, male, Afrikaans-speaking students who were preparing for ministry in the Dutch Reformed Church. In our smaller circle of friends and classmates, we debated passionately theological topics such as the Reformed doctrine of election and the question of infant versus adult baptism. Although these are not unimportant topics (and I later came to appreciate the deep significance of doctrinal topics for public life), with the gain of hindsight, it is clear that our conversations at the time happened in a vacuum, disconnected from the broader sociopolitical and economic realities of apartheid South Africa. This was the time when the apartheid government declared a state of emergency, but our theological discussions were not really informed by the injustices and violence that millions of South Africans experienced. In the following years, however, for some theological students, ecumenical encounters across racial and cultural barriers increasingly unmasked the limitations and dangers of a type of theology and piety that takes refuge in an ahistoric, acontextual, and apolitical stance, often unconscious of how such a position underwrites the status quo from which one benefits. For me, and others of my generation, the conviction grew that a timeless theology based on supratemporal principles will not do. Therefore, it resonated with my experience when Professor Jaap Durand, a systematic theologian from the University of the Western Cape, later spoke at a conference on "how [his] mind has changed" about his theological journey "from eternal truths to contextualized metaphors."

Although I realize that over the years, I might not have faithfully embodied this emphasis on the historical and contextual character of the theological task, I still believe that this is a crucial insight for theological thought and practice. In a very particular way, we are historical and storied beings; we are situated within history and narrative contexts. To understand ourselves, our convictions, our actions, our gestures, our histories—as well as that of others—we need to be conscious of larger interpretative frameworks. In my doctoral studies on narrative theology and ethics, I came to appreciate how this insight was expressed in the thought of the moral philosopher Alasdair MacIntyre and the theologian Stanley Hauerwas. MacIntyre would claim, for instance, in his book *After Virtue* that "the concept of an action is a more fundamental concept than that of an action as such."[1] Actions and ideas are, therefore, not to be abstracted from the narrative frameworks that give them meaning. Therefore, if I may for a moment in this letter succumb to the temptation to universalize my particular experience, I would reiterate the point that one should not seek refuge in abstract and ahistorical theologizing; one should not show disdain for what is concrete, historical, time bound, earthly, and embodied. This is said not to limit the scope and reach of the theological task but rather to connect theology to the fullness of life.

In my own theological journey, the specter of apartheid theology (the type of theology that justified the logic and policy of separation and segregation) looms large. Much can be said in this regard, but one can conclude that at its heart, this type of theologizing is guided by a posture of isolation and insulation. This basic mindset—an attitude that is, of course, a perennial temptation for theology—is one of being fearful of what is unknown and perceived as being strange. Other conversation partners, including critical voices, are not welcomed. Otherness is ostracized; the strange is strangled. One's position is not so much to be refined or enlarged through encounter and conversation but to be defended against what is seen as foreign and other. When I was a theological student, another theological student once walked into my room and looked at the book that I was reading at that moment. I was quite excited about the book and started enthusiastically to speak about it. But the fellow student interrupted my explanation of the argument of the book, saying, "Yes, but just tell me, is the author a heretic or not?" This is an insignificant episode, but in many ways, it became indicative for me of a closed and unattractive approach to theology—and life in general.

We should certainly evaluate what we hear, see, or read. We are not to be eclectic consumers of ideas (even great theological ideas) for the sake of their novelty or popularity. We need to evaluate, integrate, and at times resist ideas, arguments, and practices from the perspective of our own received but also dynamic theological frameworks. But openness and curiosity—maybe one can even speak of holy curiosity—remain, in my view, central theological virtues. Or stated in another way, hospitality not only is a virtue for the moral life in general but also belongs to the heart of what it means to do theology. This implies that in addition to the key role of well-established spiritual practices, theologians should also cultivate habits that expose us to what is strange and other. This will find different expressions for different personalities. In this regard, I can mention two practices that, in my case, proved to be quite significant. The first is the engagement with the medium of film, especially movies that stretch the heart and the imagination. By taking one to places that one doesn't often go, also in one's own psyche, cinema (and the conversations and actions that it can birth) can be formative as it fosters understanding and empathy. In this sense, it can be an aid as we grapple with what it means to embody the gospel in our world today. The second practice that proved to be theologically productive is that of city walking. One can, of course, point to the value of hiking in nature too, but I have often been surprised about what comes to mind when exposed to the sights, sounds, and smells associated with the complexity, plurality, and messiness of urban life. Especially when the goal of one's walk is not some commercial or productive activity. These are random examples, and the point is not to propagate these specific activities for everyone but rather to underline the value of cultivating in one's life and ministry—given one's personality and passions—those practices that help one pay attention to those persons, things, and ideas our minds and hearts are often closed to.

The hospitable openness that I see at the heart of the theological enterprise stands over against an attitude of enclosed isolation. In my engagement with theology, I was attracted to the person and work of those theologians who did not view their faith or denominational tradition in an insulated way but sought connection and conversation with others. This is not to say that they did not take their particular theological traditions seriously. In fact, they motivated and practiced their broader intellectual and social engagement by emphasizing and drawing on their own particular faith identity. Thus, for instance, they would say that they are ecumenical because they are Reformed. Or as archbishop emeritus Desmond Tutu often said, "I am ecumenical, because I am a good Anglican." Looking back, I can say that I am grateful for the example of those theologians who combined the knowledge and love for their own traditions with an openness to other voices; their concern for the church with a concern for public life; their commitment to the discipline of theology with an emphasis on the value of other knowledge resources and interdisciplinarity. A hospitable openness to what is other and even strange is, of course, not an unqualified good. Wise discernment is always needed. But a theology that is unwilling to be tested and transformed by otherness and strangeness, a theology that is averse to rooted risk-taking or traditioned creativity, ends up being stale, mute, and joyless.

These emphases on the importance of historical embeddedness and hospitable openness for doing theology expressed so far in this letter are motivated by my own experiences of the poverty of and the harm being done by a theology marked by the pretense of ahistorical, timeless truths and the mindset of enclosed identity. And maybe even more formative for my understanding of theology was the experience of the vitality of the lives and thought of South African theologians who managed to embody an alternative to such a stuffy mindset—theologians who, in their diverse ways, witnessed and still witness to the fact that theology matters. Therefore, it is a gift to young theologians if one can spend time with theologians who exhibit the theological traits mentioned previously, theologians for whom conversation partners are not mere recipients of their wisdom but vital for an encounter that can midwife something profound (and often unexpected) in a way that thinking in isolation could not. To this we can add that it is a gift to keep company with living theologians for whom theology matters, and we should also expose ourselves to the discipline and joy of reading the works of theologians who, through the centuries, grappled honestly and passionately with the subject matter of theology.

In our engagements with these theologians, we are called not to mere repetition of their work and witness but to be guided and informed by our questions and sensibilities. I have always been struck by Dietrich Bonhoeffer's comment—in his essay "What Should a Student of Theology Do Today?"—that one may bring to theological studies one's own zeal and passions, that one can enter theology with one's whole self. Without these very passions, we will be poor theologians. I think Bonhoeffer's comment is also to the point when he adds to this insight: "But theological students must then learn and know that the driving force in their lives and thinking, as theologians, can only come from the passion of Jesus Christ, our Crucified Lord." The study of theology, Bonhoeffer continues, cannot be conquered by the vitality of one's own passion; rather, the real study of theology "begins when, in the midst of questioning and seeking, human beings encounter the cross." Therefore, his crucial observation: "Theological study no longer means revealing the passions of one's own ego; it is no longer a monologue; no longer religious self-fulfillment. Rather, it is about responsible study and listening, becoming attentive to the Word of God, which has been revealed right here in this world."[2]

Writing this text in the turbulent 1930s in the light of the threat of the Nazification of Germany and the German church, Bonhoeffer is clear about what is at stake. Theology matters. In this context, Bonhoeffer links theology to confession: "One must learn to recognize where and when the church of Christ reaches its hour of decision, when it is time for confession."[3] What I take from Bonhoeffer's remark is that theology is not about abstractly acquiring interesting or novel insights about God and the spiritual life; rather, in the midst of life, theology is in search and service of the gospel of Christ and its meaning for us today. This, of course, raises new questions about what the gospel entails and what it means to serve the gospel in truth in love. I have found two guiding questions to be of vital importance in this regard. The first is to ask, Is our theological thinking and practice in service of justice? And as a second question, Is it marked by grace? Admittedly, when applied concretely to real-life situations, these two questions often lead to heightened tension and seeming contradictions.

But it is my experience that it is exactly this tension that makes theology productive and life giving—in short, what makes it *theological.*

At the beginning of this letter, I mentioned that I started my theological studies in the mid-1980s and that in many ways, my fellow students and I were isolated from the realities of apartheid South Africa. But it was also at this time that the then Dutch Reformed Mission Church accepted a confession known as the Belhar Confession (in draft form in 1982 and officially in 1986). This Reformed confession should be situated within the broader confessional movement in church and ecumenical circles at the time that sought to bring the gospel to bear on the reality of injustice and separation in apartheid South Africa and to challenge the underlying theology that justified and kept the logic and ethos of apartheid in place. This (continuing) theological trajectory that one can associate with the Belhar Confession stands in my mind as an exemplification and reminder of a theology that is timely, historical, and concrete, and as such, it is often experienced as being able to speak to others (in other places and times) in a way that helps them make sense of and respond to their own concrete realities of disunity, separation, and injustice in a deeply theological way.

Looking back on my engagement with theology over the last few decades, I am grateful that the type of timeless and defensive theology that was dominant at the beginning of my theological studies was not the only option. The exposure to a theology that is deeply historical and marked by hospitable openness (not despite but because it aimed at being deeply theological—that is to say, deeply christological) provided the sources and support that sustained my theological journey. And the last few years, I also became increasingly aware of how younger theologians and students—with their own questions, passions, and convictions—provide creative and, at times, alternative modes and resources for doing theology today. Therefore, this letter is not merely one that conveys something of my own experiences and observations but also an opportunity to express to younger theologians a word of thanks—and an invitation to further conversation.

Robert Vosloo

Notes

1 Alasdair MacIntyre, *After Virtue: A Study in Moral Theory* (Notre Dame, IN: University of Notre Dame Press, 1984), 209.

2 Dietrich Bonhoeffer, "What Should a Student of Theology Do Today?," in *Berlin: 1932–1933; Dietrich Bonhoeffer Works*, English ed., ed. Larry Rasmussen, trans. Isabelle Best and David Higgins (Minneapolis: Fortress, 2009), 433.

3 Bonhoeffer, 434.

22

Ellen T. Charry

When I was a young theology student, my husband of blessed memory had a sweatshirt made for me that read "Junior Theologian." When I began my teaching career, he had another made. It read "Serious Theologian."

I confess that I miss you young theologians terribly. You have always been the strength of my life. Here I share with you some things that I have learned from teaching students just like you—eager, impassioned, and hopefully, a bit daunted.

Theology is sustained intellectual work that helps people know, love, and enjoy God and the things of God better for their own flourishing and for the common good. There are two corollaries to this definition. Because theology forms people for a fine life—a holy life with God, creation, and other people—it is a spiritual practice. At the same time, it is a public and political practice. This requires some unpacking. First, consider theology as a spiritual practice, then as a public and political practice designed to promote the flourishing of the larger communities in which religious people participate.

As a spiritual practice, theology seeks to help people know, love, and enjoy God better by shaping them for an excellent life. Like all learning, it requires a set of virtues, and one does well to prepare for it. Begin with Psalm 119:33–35: "Teach me, O Lord, the way of Your laws; I will observe them to the utmost. Give me understanding, that I may observe Your teaching and keep it wholeheartedly. Lead me in the path of Your commandments, for that is my concern" (my translation). Try eating a piece of candy and praying: "Holy and gracious Father, you have brought us safely together for a new course of study and service that we may flourish in your light. Bless us as we learn together. Empower us to build one another up in your truth. May our study together be sweet in our mouths to invigorate and nurture our souls. Amen."

The tasks of knowing, loving, and enjoying come from Augustine of Hippo. Salutary communities need virtuous citizens who support the greater good and tend to their social responsibilities for the moral health of the community, although a foolish streak in us pulls us back to perceived personal short-term advantage. How to deal with this divided self is a theological question that Augustine struggled with throughout his life. He proposed the three tools—knowing, loving, and enjoying God—to help us. Now turn with me to knowing God.

Christianity and Judaism are persuaded that they know the one God, maker of heaven and earth, even as they generally admit that this knowledge eludes human grasp so that we know yet do not know the God we know. Those who admit this perplexity gain theological humility by bowing before God's ungraspable reality.

At the same time, we believe that we know God through Scripture. That can be very tricky. We cannot be good readers of the Bible without good tools to guide us. These are hermeneutical principles for exegeting texts that make us pause or should make us pause if we read both to understand what the various writers meant when they wrote those words and to (only later, perhaps much later) ask what to make of those words in our context. We do a disservice to the writers, including those we disagree with, unless we read on both levels. Reading texts only for what we want them to be saying to us is simply rude.

Yet we are not alone when we read these ancient writers. We are in the presence of a cornucopia of interpreters who enable us to expand our interpretation of the texts. They are our companions on the way. Hold hands when you go out in traffic.

Christians and Jews also know God through creation. Psalms 8, 19, and 104 are quite clear on that. Other psalms also point to God's authority over nature. Judaism reminds people that nature does not stand on its own but depends on the providence of God. There are individual blessings when seeing the wonders of nature, experiencing a thunderstorm, seeing a rainbow, seeing the ocean, seeing trees blossom as winter ends, experiencing striking natural beauty, seeing unusual creatures, donning new clothes, seeing snow for the first time that year, seeing a friend recently recovered from severe illness, eating new foods, waking in the morning and being able to prepare for the day. All have specific blessings that praise

God for each event and experience. Fittingly worded morning and evening prayers thank God for the cycle of day and night: "Let everything that breathes praise the Lord!" (Ps 150:6).

As you seek to know God better, the heritage itself will accompany you. We each live in a tributary of that flowing stream. We want to swim in it even in rough winds, not simply be carried by the current. There may be rocks under the surface. Great creeds and councils of the church are buoys to guide us. Now, let us consider loving God.

Loving God is commanded by Deuteronomy 6:5: "You shall love the Lord your God whole-heartedly, thoroughly, and with all the strength that is in you" (my translation). The passage also tells us how to keep that responsibility foremost in our lives. Surround yourself with these words wherever you are and whatever you do. Matthew reports that Jesus took the command seriously as "the greatest and first commandment" (Matt 22:38). Paul proclaimed love as the highest virtue.

Saint Augustine also took this commandment seriously, teaching that love is the key hermeneutical principle for interpreting Scripture. His definitive work on hermeneutics, *De doctrina Christiana* (ca. 397), spells that out in a cautious note: "So if it seems to you that you have understood the divine scriptures, or any part of them, in such a way that . . . you do not build up this twin love of God and neighbor, then you have not yet understood them" (my translation). Reading Scripture is a spiritual practice. Knowing that love cannot be forced, Saint Augustine also taught that loving God and neighbor are gifts from God.

In the first half of the eleventh century, Saint Bernard of Clairvaux, abbot of the great monastery at Clairvaux, wrote the devotional classic *On Loving God* for his monks. He distinguishes four degrees of love. The lowest is self-love because one benefits from it. The second degree is loving God because one benefits from that too. There is then a big jump to loving God because it benefits God. Yet the highest level of love is to completely lose yourself in loving God in what positive psychology today calls "a state of flow."

Enjoying God is a widespread theme in the Older Testament, where singing and rejoicing in God in response to his wondrous works on Israel's behalf are prevalent.[1] There are even two verses that celebrate God rejoicing in us (Isa 62:5 and Zeph 3:17).

The Psalter begins and ends with the joy that comes from loving obedience to God. It begins by praising the righteous who delight in God's teaching:

Happy are those
who do not follow the advice of the wicked,
or take the path that sinners tread,
or sit in the seat of scoffers;
but their delight is in the law of the Lord,
and on his law they meditate day and night. (Ps 1:1–2)

One of the clearest examples of enjoying God is Psalm 30's conclusion:

You turned my lament into dancing,
You undid my sackcloth and girded me with joy,
that my whole being might sing hymns to You endlessly;
O Lord my God, I will praise You forever. (30:11–12; my translation)

And it crescendos with the last five great "halleluyah poems" that celebrate enjoying God to the hilt, concluding,

Praise the Lord!
Praise God in his sanctuary;
   praise him in his mighty firmament!
Praise him for his mighty deeds;
   praise him according to his surpassing greatness!

Praise him with trumpet sound;
   praise him with lute and harp!
Praise him with tambourine and dance;
   praise him with strings and pipe!
Praise him with clanging cymbals;
   praise him with loud clashing cymbals!
Let everything that breathes praise the Lord!
Praise the Lord! (Ps 150)

Finally, loving God is the gift that brings us joy.

The Younger Testament speaks of enjoying God indirectly. Many passages focus on people's joy in accepting the gospel, experiencing or anticipating the reign of God, and believing that Jesus of Nazareth is God's next anointed one. Paul also points to enjoying God, or receiving the Holy Spirit, the Spirit of God, through particular charisms that contribute to the well-being of the community (1 Cor 12:1–11). In other passages, enduring suffering and persecution on account of the new way is also a means of enjoying God, "for during a severe ordeal of affliction, their abundant joy and their extreme poverty have overflowed in a wealth of generosity on their part" (2 Cor 8:2). The last privilege (blessing) in the Sermon on the Mount speaks of enjoying God even in suffering: "Blessed are you when people revile you and persecute you and utter all kinds of evil against you falsely on my account. Rejoice and be glad, for your reward is great in heaven, for in the same way they persecuted the prophets who were before you" (Matt 5:11–12). It calls forth encouragement to endure affliction for the sake of the gospel, but the writers also promise hope that the suffering will eventually turn to triumphant joy. As you meditate on how you enjoy God, keep in mind those Christians who are currently suffering for their faith.

Sometimes Christian piety falls into solipsism, thinking that one's relationship with God is all that matters. Keep in mind that while theology is a spiritual practice, it is also a public practice because it ultimately aims at the well-being of society by forming people to be excellent contributors to the communities that claim them. We all live in several communities at once, and these ramify around the globe. A volcanic explosion, a wildfire, a tsunami, a hurricane, and so on affect climes, dollars, and people far removed from the immediate events. As you think theologically, it is not easy to keep in mind the far-reaching effects of disposable diapers, plastic, carbon, and sex even as you grow in knowing, loving, and enjoying God. Actually, the two lists are deeply interconnected. Theology is public because it reminds us simply that whether we intend to or not, whether we appreciate it or not, whoever and however we interact with others affects their ability to know, love, and enjoy God truly and contribute to society's well-being.

From decades of cogitating on these things, I conclude that theology is a subversive activity because it destabilizes the status quo with truths that emerge in the interaction between the heritage and the culture. Destabilization drops the bottom out of treasured assumptions about reality and where one belongs in it. It is then responded to by reconstructing what was lost on different terms that render life and one's location in it sensible again. The dynamic of destabilization followed by reconstruction characterizes the western intellectual tradition. Destabilization is divisive and threatening, but it keeps the traditions awake and aware, lest they become complacent breathing their own carbon dioxide and perhaps using accumulated power badly. Taken in its broadest sense, the destabilization-reconstruction cycle is theology at work.

When new ideas or unanticipated events crash in, destabilizing society, theology's task is to make sense of God, the world, and ourselves. But the reverse is also true. When new ideas and unanticipated events crash theological assumptions, they may help theology reconstruct the heritage on new terms. For example, after the destruction of the temple in Jerusalem, proto-Judaism had to reconstruct itself, and that process resulted in both Christianity and Judaism. Upon encountering Neoplatonism, the early church fathers used it to construct Christianity as we know it. Maimonides and Thomas Aquinas did that again upon encountering Arab philosophy and Aristotle in the twelfth and thirteenth centuries. In the sixteenth century, Protestantism upended medieval scholasticism, but it produced Protestant scholasticism in the seventeenth century, its own go at rationalism. At about the same time, modernity quite destabilized Aristotelian and Neoplatonic theology and classical science, and the Christian understanding of truth itself was undermined and had to be reconstructed using a different set of intellectual tools. Immanuel Kant reconstructed Christianity using "practical reason." To this, Hegel added the notion of progress and launched modern theological rationalism. That in turn was chastened by Kierkegaard. At the same time, Feuerbach, Nietzsche, Freud, and Marx destabilized Christianity from other directions in the nineteenth century, and Christian theologians used them to reconstruct Christianity in the twentieth. Existentialist philosophers (Sartre, Camus) and playwrights (Theatre of the Absurd: Sartre, Genet, Ionesco, Beckett, Pinter) along with composers (Schoenberg and more recently John Cage), artists (cubism, pointillism, expressionism, et al.), architects (Frank Lloyd Wright), poets (e. e. cummings), choreographers (Martha Graham), and so on deconstructed the stability of western civilization, and theology is still recovering. Critical theory destabilizes the very meaning of language. This is a tedious list, but the point is that each destabilization is responded to by reconstructing the heritage, which is sometimes recast using the very framework that destabilized it.

From the foregoing, it becomes evident that theology is about the health and acuity of religious heritages on two fronts. One is the need to remain awake and aware of itself and the changing world within which it finds itself, lest it become un-self-critical and unable to repair itself. The other is that religious heritages want to tend to the healthy formation of people who seek an excellent life guided by God and the wisdom of the ages. As society changes, theology's strategy is to partake of society's strengths, seek shelter from its deforming elements, and criticize it appropriately, as do the Vatican's statements regarding ethics in advertising (1997). Theology invites the heritage to view itself from the perspective of the wider culture and to view the culture in terms of its tested wisdom.

My prayer for you is that all that you think, plan, and do in theological study will contribute a tiny bit to Christianity's ability to form believers in a beautiful life in love with God. And not merely, "May the Lord bless you and keep you; the Lord deal kindly and graciously with you; the Lord bestow his favor upon you and grant you peace!" (Num 6:24–26; my translation).

Go in peace to love and serve the Lord.
Ellen T. Charry
Princeton Theological Seminary

Note

1 Exod 15:1, 21; Judg 5:3; Pss 13:6; 96:1; 98:1; 104:33; 147:7; 149:1; Isa 42:10; and 1 Chr 16:23 all lift up this theme.

23

Emmanuel Katongole

It is a beautiful Saturday morning here in South Bend, Indiana. It is the last weekend in October, and it is a lovely fall day. The sun is out, the air is chilly but crisp, and the tree leaves have turned brown and red. Normally, I would not be in my office at the University of Notre Dame. I would be working around my house, raking leaves in my compound and enjoying the beautiful weather. However, I came in today in order to write this letter to you. I am very happy to learn that you are soon beginning your journey of theological education. When I think of you, I cannot but think of my own journey—a journey that has brought me from my native village of Malube in Uganda to the University of Notre Dame, where I serve as a professor of theology and peace studies. It has been a long and extraordinary journey, with many steps along the way, and so I thought I would share a few reflections about that journey, what it is that I am trying to realize as a theologian, how I go about it, and why I think theology matters for the life of the church.

I must, however, note at the very outset that I became a theologian accidentally (sort of), which is to say, I was not trained as an academic theologian. My PhD research was in moral and political philosophy. It was in the context of that research in philosophy that I discovered the work of Stanley Hauerwas, a theologian, which I ended up working on for my PhD in philosophy. Looking back, I realize there are a number of reasons why I found myself drawn to Hauerwas's work, and why his work has continued to shape the way I understand what my task as a theologian is, and how I go about it. I note this because what I share is nothing but my convictions about theology, which may not be shared by other theologians, whose backgrounds are different and who may understand and do theology differently. It also means that as you embark on your theological journey, you will encounter many authors, ideas, and approaches to theology, all of which might be confusing. All the more reason for one to have a good sense of the big picture of what theology is about and why it matters for the life of the church. Here I can only share a few "matters"—convictions that have come to matter deeply and that I now think are essential for nurturing, shaping, and sustaining a lively theological engagement.

First, story matters. It was the emphasis on "story" as a central category that first drew me to Hauerwas's work. God, the World, the self—everything is constituted through story and becomes intelligible only through story. This also means that there is no better way to argue for the significance of story than through stories. Accordingly, Hauerwas writes narratively and in the process also tells many stories. As a philosophy student, I found myself drawn to the accessible narrative style of his work, which I also found interesting. Even without explicitly saying so at that time, I found myself thinking that where much of theology has become "academic," which is to say "jargon filled and esoteric," we need to recover the beauty and simplicity of theology as the explication of the story—the interesting story—of God's journey with creation. This requires learning to think well and to write simply (without much abstraction). It also requires constantly remembering the broad audience (beyond the academy, beyond the guild) to which a theologian's work is directed.

Second, church matters. The other thing that I found attractive about Hauerwas's work was his attention to the church and why the church matters for the life of the world. It may be that I become attracted to Hauerwas's theology because I was already a priest, and as a Catholic priest, I instinctively knew what it meant for the church to be the center of the Christian's life. What Hauerwas helped me understand is the church as a distinct community shaped by a distinct story, a community that is the church to the extent that it lives true to that memory. Accordingly, the church is not so much an institution as a story, an event, a movement—God's new people in the world whose unique calling is to receive, remember, relieve, and reenact the story of God's self-sacrificing love for the world. Moreover, the church's calling is not simply for herself but for the life of the world. Theology not only grows out of the church; it is shaped by and in turn helps shape the life of the church. This is what makes all theology a form of ecclesiology. Its aim is to explicate the nature, calling, and mission of the church in its theoretical, historical, and practical dimensions. But theology must do so in a way that does not obscure (make invisible) the reality of the church or the reality of the world in which she stands as a unique gift and presence. This is what makes the theological task interesting: it involves both critique and invitation directed not only to the world but equally to the church, constantly pressing her to live more fully into the church's calling as the memory of God's self-sacrificing love for the world.

Third, Scripture matters. What I also learnt from Hauerwas is the centrality of Scripture to the theological project. In the seminary, while I enjoyed and passed well all my courses, Scripture was my favorite subject. I had wanted to study Scripture; instead, I was asked to study philosophy by my bishop. In hindsight, I now see that I have always been a passionate and ongoing student of Scripture, and that it is this love for the Scripture that shapes and drives my theological vision. From Hauerwas, I learnt to appreciate Scripture as a story or set of stories all centered on God's life and God's relationship with His creation. From this point of view, one can understand Scripture (following Sam Wells) as a drama in five acts. In act 1, we encounter God in creation, of which Genesis 1–11 gives an account. Act 2 is the story of Israel—God's election of a people, the covenant, and God's journey with Israel (which is principally the story of the Old Testament). Act 3 is the incarnation (God's work in and through the life, death, and resurrection of Christ), which the Gospels narrate. Act 4 (from Pentecost on) is God's journey with the church, moving toward act 5, the *eschaton*—the end of times. This means that Scripture is both a witness to this story of God and an invitation into the story so that we learn to see God, the world, ourselves, and indeed, the whole of creation through the biblical lens. Thus Scripture not only shapes our imagination; a lively scriptural imagination is at the heart of any theological enterprise in that its goal is to constantly invite us to see the world truthfully, which is to say in the same way that God sees the world.

Fourth, reconciliation matters. While it is important to understand Scripture as a story or the drama of God's journey with creation, it is even more important to understand the central plot of the story that Scripture is. Scripture is the story of God's reconciling love. I discovered this crucial conviction in the process of my work as a founding codirector of the Duke Center for Reconciliation. Reconciliation, I came to discover, is not simply mechanism, technique, or event; it is a story and a journey. It is not our story in the first place but God's story and journey with creation. God, Paul writes, "has been reconciling the world" (2 Cor 5:18 PHILLIPS). For Paul, this journey of God with the creation has come to a definite climax in the Christ event, but it is what God has been doing all along. And so the entire journey of Scripture bears witness to this voyage of God's reconciliation (the drama in five acts). Reconciliation is both a gift ("all this is from God" [2 Cor 5:18]) and an invitation into this drama. Keeping this central plot of Scripture is important because without it, the approach to Scripture becomes either merely technical or randomly selective, focusing only on those texts one likes or finds useful while overlooking or dismissing the rest. With reconciliation as the central motif of Scripture, one is able to appreciate God's ongoing journey with creation, with its ups and downs, while allowing the "toward what"—the new creation made possible by God's reconciling love—to shape and drive one's theological journey.

Fifth, theology matters. I describe myself using the "three Ps"—priest, professor, and pilgrim. What the threefold designation seeks to get at are the intersections at which my life is located. Even though each of us is not simply one story but a set of stories, of many loyalties and fragments, there is the constant "danger of a single story"—that of reducing everything to a solitary narrative that claims to cover everything.[1] We need to learn not to be afraid of fragments and intersections. To be a theologian is to be called into a story of intersections. The church itself is such an intersection of many stories (God-world, here-beyond, sacred-mundane, one-many, holy-sinful). The vocation of a theologian standing within these intersections is to learn to name the fragments while pointing to the whole that is greater than the sum total of its parts. The study of theology is meant to equip one for these tasks. The naming of fragments is at the same time the exposing of lies and various forms of idolatry, stories that would seek to dominate and exclusively claim our lives—and thus turn our worship away from the true God. That is why the study of theology can never be in isolation but must be in constant conversation and engagement with other accounts of reality: sociology, political theory, economics, psychology. In engaging with other disciplines, the student of theology remembers that the task of theology, as the British theologian John Milbank reminds us, is not apologetic or even argument; it is to tell again the truth of the Christian story, explicate its inner logic, and inspire Christian praxis in a manner that restores the freshness and originality of the Christian story.

Sixth, hope matters. Another way to say what Milbank says is to note that Christian theology is about hope. Peter's invitation to "always be willing to give an account of the hope" (1 Pet 3:15; my translation) provides a good summary statement of what theology ought to be about: an account of hope. This hope cannot but be grounded in the lived reality of a community, of a people, of history. This lived reality is often filled with the pain of injustice, violence, poverty, and all forms of suffering. This means that the theologian's vocation is born out of and always connected to a cry—the cry of lament, the cry of suffering humanity—that they learn to attend to within the context of another cry, that of the crucified God. It is this memory, what the German theologian John Baptist Metz describes as "dangerous memory," that makes the cross the point of reference for all Christian theology but also turns theology into a form of political theology. For God's suffering drives the theologian not into a life of quietism or simply into further theoretical exploration but into engagement on behalf of and with others, especially the forgotten and marginal ones in history. For as the father of Latin American liberation theology, Gustavo Gutiérrez, reminds us, "If theological reflection does not vitalize the action of the Christian community in the world by making its commitment to charity fuller and more radical . . . then this theological reflection will have been of little value."[2] In this role of vitalizing the action of the Christian community, the theologian assumes the role of prophet, *denouncing* false and shallow promises of hope—the kind that "heal lightly the wounds of my people, saying peace, peace when there is no peace" (Jer 6:14; my translation)—while *announcing* and pointing to, through stories and other encounters, genuine signs of hope in a suffering world.

Finally, Africa matters. As a young African student embarking on theological education, you could not find yourself in a more exciting context to study and do theology. The challenging social, political, economic, and ecological conditions in which the majority of African peoples find themselves raise theological questions that press for answers. At the same time, the unprecedented growth of Christianity in much of Africa, which has contributed to the shift in Christianity's center of gravity from the Global North to the Global South, creates great opportunities both for world Christianity and for theology going forward. As Christianity makes its home on the African continent, it is encountering new questions from Christians who are negotiating multiple sets of challenges—not only challenges emerging from their inherited cultural and spiritual heritage but also challenges of health, political instability, violence, and poverty. In a word, they face uncertainty within their postcolonial history. That is why we find ourselves, theologically at least, in unchartered waters. It is a moment that calls for intellectual attentiveness and theological innovativeness, for ongoing engagement with the inherited Christian tradition and fresh theological reformulation and experimentation. The way African theologians like yourself are able to engage these tasks and provide helpful guidelines for a way forward will become a gift not only to African Christians but to global Christians as well as non-Christians elsewhere who may be wondering whether there is any more need for theology in a rapidly changing world.

Just in case you are wondering from all I have said about why and how theology matters, my own sense is that theology is not only all the more needed for our world today; there is something urgent about the theological task. That is why I am both excited and hopeful when I see a brilliant young scholar like yourself committing oneself to the study of theology. Remain, therefore, assured of my prayers, well wishes, and support on your theological journey.

Yours,
Emmanuel Katongole
University of Notre Dame

Notes

1 Chimamanda Ngozi Adichie, "The Danger of a Single Story," TED-Global, July 2009, https://www.ted.com/talks/chimamanda_ngozi _adichie_the_danger_of_a_single_story?language=en.

2 Gustavo Gutiérrez, *A Theology of Liberation* (New York: Orbis, 1988), 174.

24

Mitzi Smith

Welcome to the contested space of biblical studies. It is a space where the presence of black and brown people is questioned. As in other disciplines, it is often presumed that we have arrived in the academy by the accident of affirmative action or the lowering of standards of whiteness or Eurocentrism and, consequently, have displaced more-qualified white people. Some would have you believe that you entered this contested space because you are exceptional, that you are among the Du Boisian "talented tenth," that the masses of black people are inherently incapable of earning a terminal degree in biblical studies or religion, and that those who have been rejected are precluded because they were never as talented or resilient as you. This logic of exceptionalism can bamboozle you into a comfortability with and apologetics for the paucity or absence of black and brown scholars in the field. This logic of exceptionalism encourages a "crabs-in-the-barrel" mentality—a grappling for the crumbs that whiteness tosses at us—and discourages our collaboration. It feeds an incredulity by black and brown people admitted to the field toward other black and brown peoples' horror stories (e.g., racism, sexism, elitism) in the academy, at least until one accumulates one's own testimonies of terror. If you became a biblical scholar because you believe you are exceptional, you will find it difficult to support and mentor other black and brown biblical scholars and/or graduate students. Conversely, know that you are no imposter. You belong and are needed in this space. Do not allow impostor syndrome to stifle your creativity, productivity, and voice. You are only an impostor if you claim perfection and invulnerability and, by doing so, render innocuous the pretentious dominant elitist gaze of superiority and infallibility. Never forget that there have been others as capable and worthy as you who stood on the threshold but for whom the gates were shut and bolted by racism, sexism, classism, and/or political, institutionalized idiosyncrasies.

My dear "young" colleagues, I have received your emails expressing discouragement or seeking advice about writing and publishing an academic presentation or your dissertation topic. I have gladly shared with you samples of syllabi and successful grant applications. You have also expressed curiosity about my journey. You have been mostly black and brown women, but this letter is for whoever reads it. Race, gender, and class still matter and should not be ignored when doing biblical interpretation. The Du Boisian "color line" of race/racism persists, even as white scholars clamor to read works that black and brown scholars produce and/or produce their own volumes on whiteness and race/racism; perhaps it is a type of performative allyship void of risk and sacrifice.

Speaking of the "color line" and thinking about the importance of context, I am writing to you from Decatur, Georgia, where we are in a pivotal fight of our lifetime for democracy, human decency, equity, and equality and against racism and white supremacist nationalism. As a historically "red" state, Georgia has turned blue, or purple. I voted weeks ago. As African Americans, we were already struggling to breathe in the streets, in our homes, and in hospitals where we are disproportionately afflicted and dying from Covid-19. What are we doing as biblical scholars as the bodies of Casey Goodson Jr., Breonna Taylor, Ahmaud Arbery, George Floyd, and many other black and brown women, men, and children pile up? Race, gender, class, sexuality, and other socially constructed categories that impact how we exist, move, or survive within a web of interconnected power structures and systems still matter. This is the world, the context, in which we do our work; the academy, our students, and readers are not unscathed.

In Howard Thurman's *Jesus and the Disinherited*, he asks what the religion of Jesus has to say to black people "who stand daily with their backs against the wall."[1] The masses of black people function in "barely-scraping-by" or survival mode. My dear colleagues, I grew up "barely scraping by." This path or vocation is not what I imagined for myself. It was not part of the sociocultural or religious imaginary constructed for me because of the gender politics of the church and the racism and poverty that enveloped me as a poor black girl living on the "wrong side" of the railroad tracks. The railroad tracks, less than a mile from the housing projects where we lived, separated my world from a mostly white, privileged world. We seldom entered that world, but when we did, it was only briefly. I could count on my fingers the number of times we crossed the tracks to downtown Columbus, Ohio, before I graduated from high school, when my mom took us to see the *Ten Commandments* debut at the RKO Palace, to shop at Woolworth's, or to transfer to another public bus.

My mother, Flora Ophelia Carson Smith, relied on public transportation—or her feet when money was scarce—to get to work. A few times when it was too cold to walk miles to work, she stood at the bus stop praying for a miracle—a free ride or something. On one such occasion, God showed compassion on her when a dollar, like a magic carpet, road the wind and landed at her feet just before the bus arrived. Another time, she arrived at work practically frostbitten and was fired for her late arrival before she could explain. I wonder, Where was God that day?

Dear colleagues, my mother, whom I recognize as my earliest mentor, incarnated the perennial presence of God—or Goddess, I should say—in our home. Her wisdom, ways of knowing, skillful improvisation, unremitting hope, and prayers shaped and sometimes shielded us. She encouraged and fortified us through her stories, prayers, inspirational Scriptures, and determination to never stop "putting one foot in front of the other," even after she was confined to a wheelchair. My mother articulated an indefatigable hope in God for "making ends meet," survival, healing, and restoration. She encouraged me to recite Bible passages and to trust God without question, as she had been raised. Her favorite text for me, an extremely shy teenager, was "Greater is he that is in you, than he that is in the world" (1 John 4:4 KJV). Although I learned to love and be inspired by Scripture, I struggled with texts like "I not seen the righteous forsaken, nor his seed begging bread" (Ps 37:25b KJV) because of the dissonance between the writer's testimony and my own. I still hold this theodical tension in my body and in my critical engagement with Scripture. When I became a biblical scholar, I registered my dissent; the psalmist's testimony does not represent the masses of black people who stand daily with their backs against the wall. As inspired as his testimony might be, it is not universally applicable or objective. God still inspires people, and black people are no exception.

I was the first in my immediate family to earn a bachelor's and master's degree. It was not my idea, not initially, to pursue a PhD. My mother first imagined and nudged me, often, to pursue a law degree (I was a formally trained, experienced legal secretary and paralegal) or a PhD in something. In retrospect, I wish I had pursued a joint degree in law and religion (it's not too late). My mother was convinced that I could and should earn a terminal degree before I imagined it. Even when we can envision what we might be or do, we cannot underestimate the impact of encouragement from trusted others, which is particularly important for poor black and brown peoples who are often bombarded by implicit and explicit racism and discouragement, by people telling us what we cannot do or, as someone once said to me, "That's a tall order." To which I told myself, "God specializes in tall orders."

You arrive in the academy, my dear colleagues, at a time when the numbers of black and brown biblical scholars are greater than they were twenty years ago. I had never set eyes upon a black biblical scholar or theologian before enrolling at Howard University School of Divinity (HUSD)—a historically black school—to earn an MDiv. I had purchased Cain Hope Felder's *Troubling Biblical Waters: Race, Class, and Family*, but I found it a difficult read.[2] I understood it well enough through my reading and hearing others discuss it to appreciate its significance for the black church community; I wanted to learn more from him. Sitting in Felder's classes, consuming and admiring his brilliance and excitement for biblical interpretation and justice, inspired me. Felder was the second person to suggest I should pursue a PhD. Just as race and gender still matter, so does representation. My dear friend, your presence and voice as a black or brown scholar or graduate student matter. My mother planted seeds; Felder and other professors at HUSD—Michael Newheart, Gene Rice, Kelly Brown Douglas, Alice Bellis, Cheryl Sanders—planted more seeds and nurtured the soil; my hard work watered and nurtured the seeds as well.

The seeds planted in us will not go unchallenged by internal and external forces. Transitioning to Harvard University and Cambridge, Massachusetts, was not easy; I knew it would not be. I was warned about the isolation, especially for a black woman. Some of us have left the academy because of isolation. I immediately joined an organization for black graduate students across schools and disciplines. They advised entering cohorts to create and live a balanced life, to practice self-care and participate in extracurricular activities—see a movie, exercise, eat healthy, attend social events, and so on. Initially, I attended a few social events, including an apple-picking trip to Maine! But soon I was inundated with acclimating to a new space and place (one demographically and culturally different from the DC metro area); stress and feelings of isolation overwhelmed me. One day I sat in my dorm room starring at words on a page, seeing and recognizing symbols but hearing or understanding nothing. I hadn't turned the page in the book I was reading for a while. Eventually, I believe I heard the Spirit whisper to me, "I am the same God who was with you before you arrived at Harvard; pull yourself together." That voice energized me. It sounded like something my mother would say (she had a major stroke the year I was accepted at Harvard; I almost did not go). My mother never let me cry or pray too long about a problem; she'd insist I dry my eyes, get up, and figure something out—find, call, ask . . . somebody. "Now, what you gonna do?" she'd ask. She is from the generation that had to keep it moving, be resourceful, and improvise to survive. I decided that night to reclaim my life. I began walking for exercise, eating healthier, and searching for somebody I could confide in and dialogue with. I enrolled in a speed-reading course. I also moved into a studio apartment because of the thin-walled dorm rooms. The journey is stressful. The stress does not diminish after you earn your degree, obtain your first academic job, or write your first book; it morphs. As a doctoral student, I approached a black woman scholar about mentoring me. She agreed to but said she first needed to take time off in the summer to address her health. Sadly, she died that summer. Typically, we are the only black woman scholar in our entering cohorts and in the institutions where we work. Be intentional about reflecting, reassessing, and maintaining a balanced life. As bell hooks declares in *Sisters of the Yam*, for black women, self-care is a radical political act of resistance.[3] Black and brown women are all too often expected to be everybody's caregivers. Work smartly. Set boundaries and respect others' boundaries. Say no when necessary for health. Identify accountability partners; take a day off weekly from everything. Black life is already precarious. I have always been encouraged by the life of Dr. Morton-Finney; look him up—you too will be inspired by his extraordinary life of learning, excellence, and balance.

Concerning writing, my dear colleagues, do not allow the subject of your dissertation to delimit future intellectual projects. Feed your spirit of creativity by engaging a diversity of trans- and interdisciplinary voices and genres, including fictional works. Learn to recognize and listen to your divine inner voice and trust it; intuition is divine and is often a neglected force of insight, wisdom, and creativity. My dissertation advisor, François Bovon, valued intuition. Assume that you always have something valuable to contribute. Be open to change or to learning new ways of reading or approaches to reading texts. In her *Parable of the Sower*, Octavia Butler insists that "God is change."[4]

Writing is performance and performative; it can facilitate change and freedom. And it's hard work! Learn how to write more concisely and clearly and in a way that is accessible to a broader audience beyond the academic specialists and scholars. William Zinsser's *On Writing Well: The Classic Guide to Writing Nonfiction* and Claire Cook's *Line by Line: How to Edit Your Own Writing* are great resources.[5]

My dear friends, do not allow publishers to dictate your writing projects or to discourage the work you feel compelled to produce. When my coauthor and I sought publishers for *Toward Decentering the New Testament*, one publisher told us what we proposed was not an introductory text; I disagreed.[6] When seeking a publisher for *I Found God in Me: A Womanist Biblical Hermeneutics Reader*, a woman of color editor at a very reputable and elite press told me that they do not publish womanist books, just feminist![7] Do not allow those publishing houses that center whiteness and marginalize blackness to devalue your work. The pressure exists to conform to the performance of whiteness in your writing, to privilege the voices of white scholars and exclude or marginalize the voices of black and brown scholars. I implore you to engage the scholarship of black and brown peoples; our scholarship is often ignored—and often by those white scholars and others who insist that we cite their work. I encourage you to remain true to your passions and commitments. Don't wait for white scholars to invite you to write or squander your time on writing projects for which you have little interest or passion.

In closing, I encourage you to re-member and identify your communities of support, formation, and accountability and your roots in and commitments to them. What do you care deeply about and what difference does it make that *you* care? What makes the difference in your writing that you care? What difference will you make because you care? Care and hope are interconnected. Despite the precarity of blackness in the academy, we must garner hope in the face of black precarity to do our work. Conversely, our work will engender hope. We and our work can be a hope no longer deferred. We are the hope of the ancestors who died resisting and persisting. Dear colleagues, I wish I could tell you that persistence is key to your success (it is one factor). But our persistence does not guarantee survival or thriving in the face of oppressive systems and structures responsible for black precarity. There is a mutuality between persistence and survival. There is no survival without persistence; we cannot persist unless we survive. Yet persistence does not guarantee survival. This is the dilemma of persistence that the masses face. Many who persisted did not survive and never experienced freedom. As womanist theologian Delores Williams argues in her text *Sisters in the Wilderness*, God is not always a liberator God but quite often is a God of survival and quality of life.[8] Perhaps it is hope that gives quality of life to black precarity. Persistence is often evidence of hope, hope that our persistence produces a better today and tomorrow. Unjust systems and structures that must be destroyed are often threatened by our persistence and protest. So in spite of them, I encourage you to persist while we work to destroy systems and structures of oppression in society, in the academy, and in sacred texts. Persist despite the rejections, the presumptions of incompetence, the silencing of your voice, the refusals to read and acknowledge your work, the misrepresentation of your work, and the commodification of our presence and scholarship. You matter; your voice matters. You belong and are needed in this contested space.

Mitzi J. Smith
Decatur, Georgia

Notes

1 Howard Thurman, *Jesus and the Disinherited* (Boston: Beacon, 1976), 13.
2 Cain Hope Felder, *Troubling Biblical Waters: Race, Class, and Family* (New York: Orbis, 1990).
3 bell hooks, *Sisters of the Yam: Black Women and Self-Recovery*, 2nd ed. (London: Routledge, 2014).
4 Octavia E. Butler, *Parable of the Sower: A Powerful Tale of a Dark and Dystopian Future* (London: Headline, 2019).
5 William Zinsser, *On Writing Well: The Classic Guide to Writing Nonfiction*, 30th anniversary ed. (New York: Harper Perennial, 2016); Claire Kehrwald Cook, *Line by Line: How to Edit Your Own Writing* (Boston: Houghton Mifflin Harcourt, 1985).

6 Mitzi J. Smith and Yung Suk Kim, *Toward Decentering the New Testament: A Reintroduction* (Eugene, OR: Cascade, 2018).

7 Mitzi J. Smith, *I Found God in Me: A Womanist Biblical Hermeneutics Reader* (Eugene, OR: Cascade, 2015).

8 Delores S. Williams, *Sisters in the Wilderness: The Challenge of Womanist God-Talk* (New York: Orbis, 1993).

25

Traci C. West

You are seeking. Good. The courage, integrity, and unsettledness that you will need for a Christian social ethics that disrupts racial, gender, and sexual norms that idolize patterns of domination have to begin with seeking. Those societal norms, likely wrapped in the language of supposedly universal Christian theological ideas and rituals of communal practices, morally discipline you to become complacent and then indifferent to your complacency. They enable you to sink ever deeper into a comfortable tolerance of both the deleterious consequences for the most vulnerable who are harmed as well as to unjust benefits that accrue for those systemically advantaged.

A reflexive reliance on universalized expressions of Christian theology and ethics that rejects critical consideration or even notice of the particular sociopolitical contextual lenses that you bring exemplifies this inculcation of indifference. It stifles reflectiveness and thus closes off the possibility that you will recognize the prevalent impacts of those patterns of domination and the need to disrupt them. As I write to you—a nascent intellectual taking time to reflect on the process of developing this theological field—I am reminded of the span of intellectuals in other fields who have corresponded in a similar manner and how social particularities are so formative for learning from them. For instance, Rainer Maria Rilke's social particularities as a white European male author hold relevance to classic considerations. His complex relationship to gender norms and his context of a multiethnic and multilinguistic community in the nineteenth-century Austrian Empire deeply informed his letters to a young poet and other writings. Or, in this early twenty-first-century moment, African American studies scholar Imani Perry's explicit analysis of her own social identities vitally infuses her excavation of historical dynamics of and scholarly writings about gender, race, and class in her letter to her sons.[1] So too, your particular social context, identities, and status matter for the quality of theological seeking that you do.

Now I am not suggesting an individualistic, solitary path for this intellectual work. Our relatedness, yours and mine, centers on our shared commitment to seeking knowledge and insights about Christian theology and ethics. This quest must serve a social purpose beyond the gratification of our self-interests and neediness for intellectual affirmation from others. Yet it cannot be untethered from the elevated social status that allows us access to public spaces that nurture this seeking and provide platforms to articulate its aims and vision. In venues that steeped in long-established institutional patterns of sociopolitical subjugation, how does one commit to the crafting of Christian social ethics and theology that insists on disruption? The willful indifference to and explicit catechisms of deference to the insatiable greed in Christian traditions for power and status based on gender, race, nation, and sexuality can too easily subsume your theological imagination. For me, my students have played a pivotal role in such commitments within my own intellectual formation as a black feminist liberationist ethicist. For sustenance of the sense of call to ongoing struggle challenging harmful social norms in Christian ethics and theology, I am indebted to all of the Asian, white, Latinx, African, and especially black American students who have challenged me. I have been schooled by their sharp questions that so often arose from the naming of their contextual starting points that differed from those reflected in my own US-American blackness. These exchanges have consistently reignited my capacity to perceive how our communal choices about unrecalled cultural histories of Christian traditions can hide structural exclusions and shaming hierarchies so often related to social definitions of human embodiedness.

Claiming the theological significance of Christian traditions related to Scripture, ordination, communion, mission, or other Christian ideas and practices always involves what you remember. Or more precisely, they require you to decide what you feel you must remember for the sake of preserving it. In most traditional theological settings in the church and academy when this memory work occurs, you will feel pressure to choose the center as distinct from the periphery or margins. Your moral compass will be shaped by particular gender, racial, national, sexual, and other cultural assumptions that guide you to protect the positioning of historically centralized Christian theological and ethical truths, communal habits, and voices as more essential to remember than marginal others. The questions that you choose to ask about this inherently political process of remembering can provide basic equipment for seeking theo-ethical ideas and practices that refuse indifference to the harms of Christian heteropatriarchal domination and racist hypocrisies.

I know that powerful temptations encourage you to avoid, delay, or at best, temper any such questions. Routine incentives threaten the viability of such an intellectual trajectory before you even start to embark on it. Your understanding of intellectual success may be tied to measuring your ability to reiterate what is considered the best theology and ethics and becoming identified with it by citing it. A standard sense of achievement weights studious efforts to hide how your social and political vantage point shapes the interpretive lens that you bring to what you seek to preserve with your assertions. The very criteria for classifying what is most valuable in the tradition, for which you will be academically and culturally rewarded or penalized, usually also demands that you disconnect the implications of where those traditions live from their truth value. This means, at best, you may find some merit in attributing ancillary significance to the communal contextual settings of empire, rape, slavery, genocide, and colonization, in which those Christian theological and ethical ideas and practices were birthed, became serviceable, and created legacies of such brutal consequences for the dominated. Most often, you will reap few standard rewards by placing at the center of the history and meaning of Christian theology and ethics either these realities or the communal thriving and leadership that occurs in spite of and deeply informed by one's identification by Christians as innately subordinate or of lesser human worth and dignity. And it may appear to you too onerous to find another way to incorporate their centrality in your work other than the generally accepted method of citing these voices and sociopolitical locations as merely examples of key concepts supposedly acontextually and singularly produced by individual great male Christian thinkers.

But the separation of concepts from social practices in locating the primary sources of Christian theology and ethics forms another major impediment for the kind of seeking that intentionally interrupts Christian traditions of subjugation. When defining the core traditions of Christian theology and ethics, you will be tempted to count only what individual Christian leaders write about certain concepts while discounting and treating dismissively what Christians do, both individually and collectively, in their leadership of social practices. Note, for instance, how impactfully and explicitly the leaders asserted Christian theology within European Christian pogroms, witch hunts, genocidal campaigns against Indigenous nations, the transatlantic slave trade, global colonization, or lynchings by white US Protestants. Yet seemingly none count key expressions of European and Euro-American Christian theology and ethics in most classic representations.

I urge you to craft an alternative method that listens for and to such influential theory-practice forms of harm at the center of this tradition instead of conceding to the temptations and incentives to hide them. For it is the method—the design of the inquiry—that allows any yield of creative and vitally expansive understandings of theology and ethics. I encourage you to embrace knowledge production that revels in conceptual configurations discovered in bold and interactive listening to communal life and practices. Find the disruptively conceptual and theoretical, for instance, in the conventionally marked-off as spaces of immutable binaries, marginal transgender and nonbinary, and other gender expressions in communities of faith. Analytically include interactions that may occur as a result of your own intersectional queerness or textual histories in ancient Christian negotiations of gender status and relationality. Finally, there are few more compelling reasons for your commitment to this seeking, nor riskier for dismissal as something related to a discussion of practical rather than conceptual or systematic theology, than including attention to harmful intimate actions of gender-based abuse and violence by Christians such as sexual assault, domestic violence and abuse, and sexual harassment. Such intimate forms of gendered torment and brutality are meaningful for defining essential principles of Christian theology and ethics precisely because they reveal abuse of power so comprehensively leveraged to exploit the emotional, spiritual, physical, and social worth and dignity of another person.

Finally, please remember how grateful I am that you are considering this endeavor. Indeed, we must rely on one another to find multiple and varied methods for seeking to disrupt entrenched patterns of subjugation in Christian theology and ethics because it is just too costly when they are left intact.

In solidarity in disruptive, justice-seeking theo-ethics,
Traci C. West

Note

1 Imani Perry, *Breathe: A Letter to My Sons* (Boston: Beacon, 2019).

26

Allan Boesak

What a wonderful privilege to be able to write this letter to you, to engage your precious young mind, to speak to your heart, and to feel the connection with your spirit. Welcome, congratulations, and buckle up! As a student of Black liberation theology, you are entering a wonderful and exhilarating but contested and stormy world. It is a revolutionary endeavor. As womanist theologian Katie Cannon writes, you will have to keep one ear to the mouth of the people and the other to the mouth of God.

Black theology is, so to speak, one of a set of historic triplets: Black consciousness, Black theology, and Black power. Black consciousness, that powerful philosophy and movement from the 1970s led by Steve Biko, gave us the power to expose and overcome the toxic falsities of "race" and ethnicized thinking, reject the deliberately divisive labels forced on us by colonialism and apartheid, and come together as the Black oppressed, fighting side by side for our freedom, our dignity, and the return of our land. *Black*, despite the nefarious and unconstitutional racial recategorization of the African National Congress (ANC) and its strategists, includes all Black Africans, whether they be labeled "Black," "Coloured," or "Indian." One of the truly wonderful things today is the scholarly effort by our own historians to retell, reinterpret, and rectify South Africa's history and shed new light on its "foundational peoples" and on the meaning of "Africanness" for all Black South Africans, as people's historian and heritage activist Patric Tariq Mellet does in his meticulous and fascinating work *The Lie of 1652: A Decolonised History of Land*.[1]

In the euphoric aftermath of 1994, many theologians—most of them white, but some Black—rushed to declare Black theology "irrelevant" and "passé." It was no longer necessary, they argued, because "freedom" had come, our people had voted the ANC into power, "Marxism" (which they confused with liberation theology) was dead, and we should move on to more "constructive" things. The struggle was over. All of a sudden, the "de-racialization of capital" (for the chosen few) replaced the deracialization of society. The struggle slogan *Sekunjalo!* (Now is the time!) was replaced by "Rome was not built in one day." "Incrementalism" was the new code for "revolution." "Power to the people!" (that famous *Amandla a Wethu!*) was set aside for "ANC Rules!" meaning the rule of the new Black aristocratic elite by permission of, and in collusion with, the old white capitalist elite. The celebrity icon Nelson Mandela replaced Jesus, the revolutionary Black Messiah. But the people knew better. Black theology, like Black consciousness, remained resilient, relevant, and vital.

We should perhaps begin with Latin American liberation theologian Jon Sobrino. "The first task of Christian liberation theology," he writes, "is to try to attempt honesty toward reality." It is a difficult task, he says, because not only is our world characterized by institutions, systems of injustice, and violence; it is also characterized by systems of concealment of injustice and violence. This makes it extremely difficult for us to be honest about our reality. I agree. Why? Because the forces of imperialism, oppression, racism, patriarchy, white supremacy, and enslavement benefit from both the violence and the injustices as well as the concealment thereof.

South Africa post-1994 has not changed much for the vast majority of our people. The new Black political aristocracy has made common cause with the white apartheid capitalist class. It is "an elite conspiracy," as Sampie Terreblanche, one of our foremost progressive economists, calls it. Too greedy to test new ways of thinking about economics and economic policies, they embraced with uncritical and unseemly haste the death trap of neoliberal capitalism, entrenching and exacerbating the old apartheid inequalities, making South Africa the most unequal society in the world today. Instead of fighting for that promised "better life" for all our people, they revel in greed, corruption, and entitlement, enriching themselves at the cost of the poor and powerless, dooming the vast majority of our people to depressingly downward cycles of impoverishment. Our politics post-'94 is a far cry from the ideal of the politics of integrity, honesty, decency, and courage our people fought and sacrificed so much for.

The world is in the grip of a global apartheid, every bit as vicious, exploitative, oppressive, and death dealing as South African apartheid was then and Zionist-Israeli apartheid is now. The general reference to "global apartheid" today is the division of the world between the so-called

1 percent and the 99 percent, made crystal clear in Oxfam's annual reports: In January 2017, Oxfam reported that just 8 white men own as much wealth as half the world's population. One in 9 people do not have enough to eat, and more than 1 billion people live on less than $1.25 a day.[2] In 2019, Oxfam reported that billionaire fortunes grew by $2.5 billion *a day* while the 3.8 billion of the poorest half of humanity saw their wealth decline by 11 percent.[3] During the pandemic, and profiting shamelessly from it, the already rich have more than tripled their wealth.

Across the world, what I have called "the politics of vulgarity" seems to have taken firm hold. New forms of fascism and reinvigorated ethnic nationalism are shaping politics in the United States, Brazil, India, and a growing number of countries in Europe. In Africa, where corruption and the hunger for power allow presidents to claim six terms in succession, as in Uganda recently, and election fraud is as common as elephant dung, our people, despite the astounding mineral wealth of this continent, remain among the poorest populations on earth—things are no different. Homophobia, transphobia, religious intolerance, especially Islamophobia, patriarchy, and a malignant masculinity, all intoxicated by divine sanctification, seem inseparable from these vile forms of politics. Violence, in all its forms—physical, structural, psychological, and deeply systemic—is always at its core. And the issue here is not that these are merely present in society, or tolerated, but that they are invited, instigated, actively encouraged, and celebrated—deliberately garnered as political forces for political mobilization and political control. It remains quite astonishing how hard the reigning political classes, the intellectuals and instruments of the establishment, are trying to deny or conceal these realities.

For all these reasons, liberation theology, as a theology determined to speak truth about reality, is so relevant. For Steve Biko, Black theology is "a theology that seeks a fighting God who will not let the lie unchallenged." No hesitations, no equivocations, no prevarications. No compromises with a white, blue-eyed, sweet and gentle Jesus whose innocent blood saves our souls but who cannot save us from white oppressors, whose hands are dripping with the blood of the innocent. James Cone speaks of the Black theologian as an "exegete of Scripture and of life." Reading Scripture without knowing, understanding, and interpreting its meaning for the life and real lived experiences and faith of the oppressed is meaningless. For that very reason, I titled my dissertation *Farewell to Innocence*.[4] All of us understood that living in a hostile, white-controlled world, Black people cannot afford to ignore the realities of what we came to call "the condition of blackness."

That is the condition of a deliberately designed, insidious, persistent series of pandemics brought on by a history of imperialism, colonialism, enslavement, genocide, epistemicide, land theft, oppression, economic exploitation, and dehumanization. It is what Frantz Fanon calls "a virtual Apocalypse." Black theology insisted that whites should not be able to claim the innocence of this history and their agency in it and that Black people should not be allowed to feign innocence while the struggle for freedom, dignity, and life was going on. That is why studies as that of Dr. Joy DeGruy on "Post-traumatic Slave Syndrome," studying the aftermath of histories of slavery and its intergenerational impact on Blacks today, are so crucial.

The times in which you will study have brought a new crisis, challenge, and condition. It is called the novel coronavirus, and it has already claimed victims by the millions. But for us, here is the important thing: the coronavirus has itself destroyed the myth that the pandemic is "the great equalizer." It has not only exposed the criminal inequalities in health care; it has exposed all the entrenched structural, institutional, and systemic economic, social, and political inequalities and the incessant, comprehensive war against the poor and vulnerable, globally and nationally. Whether we are talking about people of color in the United States, United Kingdom, and Europe or Native Americans in the United States, Canada, Bolivia, Brazil, or Chile, the racial element in all this, nationally and globally, is now undeniable. Experts say that poverty, hunger, diseases, and violence exacerbated by the pandemic, including gender-based violence, may dwarf the number of those dying of the virus itself.

In the search for a vaccine we hope will stem the tide and even turn the forward rush of the virus, the rich have already secured their own safety. The United States has cornered the market for the vaccine by securing contracts worth almost $7 billion with four pharmaceutical companies for four hundred million doses of these vaccines. Other rich countries, like the United Kingdom and the European Union, are doing the same. Poor countries are not only way down the line; they are completely out of sight. Now that some vaccines are indeed available, the World Health Organization is earnestly pleading against what it calls "vaccine nationalism." From experience, Black South Africans and African Americans know what that actually means for the rest of the (poor) world: "For Whites Only." Never before has the global apartheid been so glaring. All the subtlety and obfuscation are gone.

We are so insistent on this because Martinique's Aimé Césaire is correct when he speaks of "the singularity of blackness." Right from the outset, Black theology—as other expressions of liberation theology, feminist theologies, womanist theology, and more recently, queer theology—was defined and understood as a "contextual" theology. Unlike the claims of universality made by the dominant Eurocentric theologies, it grapples with the existential situations of Black, oppressed people engaged in life-and-death struggles for liberation and justice, refusing to give up their faith in Jesus, their liberator/Messiah. We embraced that Black experience in our struggle to embrace the Scriptures and the significance of Jesus of Nazareth not just for the human story in general but for the story of Black humanity in confrontation with white, Christian, racist domination, exploitation, and oppression.

And just as Black theology embraces the singularity of Blackness, so it embraces the singularity of gender and of Black womanhood in particular, the singularity of queerness, and the particularity of the Palestinian situation. A Black theology that understands the indivisibility of God's love and justice will welcome and learn from womanist and queer theologies in order to deepen the meaning of authentic singularity and embodied solidarity. So in essence, Black theology was trying to say what the Black Lives Matter movement made into such a strong rallying cry: Black lives matter!

Without doubt, the earliest expressions of Black liberation theology, historically, came into being within contexts of roiling revolutionary resistance. Dona Kimpa Vita from the Kongo was burned at the stake by the Portuguese as a revolutionary resister to colonialist oppression and the imperialist appropriation of the Christian faith by the Roman Catholic Church on July 2, 1706. It is she whose visions saw Jesus and his mother, Mary, as African, not as icons for meditative (or syncretistic missionary?) purposes, inspiring her to resistance to the foreign powers occupying her country. Hers was, as far as we know, the first explicit Black theology as an African expression of Black revolutionary resistance to imperialism. No wonder the present generation of young African activists acknowledges this Christian young woman as "the mother of the African revolution." She died a martyr of a revolutionary African faith.

And it was Bishop Henry McNeal Turner of the African Methodist Episcopal Church who visited South Africa in 1896 and stirred the embers of a militant Black theology of liberation there. It was that same Turner who first uttered the words "God is a Negro!"—words that would throw James Cone into a vortex of white fear, umbrage, and offended academic dignity when he dared to portray Jesus Christ as the Black Messiah in a work that caused such turmoil in white-controlled academia. *Black Theology and Black Power* remains a brilliant, unrelentingly challenging classic, laying the foundations for Black theology in its present form emphatically, clearly, and systematically.[5]

Birthed into, and within, the heat of struggles for justice, freedom, and dignity, Black theology in South Africa could not but be indelibly shaped, molded, and infused by those struggles. Being born into the literal flames of struggle in that decisive phase since the early seventies, baptized with fire, and nurtured by the suffering and the joys of fighting for truth, justice, and freedom endowed South African Black theology with a uniquely fashioned character. But it also brought with it a unique responsibility. From its inception, Black theology was held accountable, not so much to the rules and expectations of formal white-controlled academia, but to the expectations, sufferings, and hopes of the people. It is that connectivity with the struggles, hopes, and aspirations of the people that keeps Black theology rooted in the resilience and vitality of the faith of the people.

Black liberation theology is "a theology from the underside of history," declared the Ecumenical Association of Third World Theologians in 1976 when we gathered in Dar es Salaam. It is a theology "from below," seeing the realities of the world through the eyes of the oppressed, the suffering, and the destitute. As such, in my view, it is not so much a theology "from the margins" as it is a theology "of the marginalized." Jesus was from the margins, and the people he liberated and healed—like the woman suffering from hemorrhages, the man with the withered hand, or the Gerasene demoniac—were always taken from the margins and placed in the center, not just of attention, but of the liberating, humanizing, and empowering grace of God. And Jesus's resounding "in remembrance of her," speaking of the unknown and unnamed sister from Bethany (Matt 26:6–13), echoing his "in remembrance of me," speaking of himself in Luke 24:19, is perhaps the most astonishing illustration of this. It is a ringing affirmation of the conviction of a seventeenth-century African insurrectionist Khoe leader who insisted that "the gospel does not belong to white people" (even though they claimed sole ownership of it). Black theology is a theology of the marginalized, determined that the marginalized shall absolutely not remain on the margins forever but shall take their place at the center of God's revolutionary activity on the world.

The Dutch Reformed Mission Church, the church I was born, baptized, and ordained into, was established in 1881 as an apartheid church, created especially for people designated as "Coloured" in South Africa's racialized pigmentocracy. This church was the result of the white Dutch Reformed Church's racist, white supremacist–ideologized theology—the desire of the white colonizers of my country and my people to exert complete domination and full control over the colonized, in society and in the church. For three-quarters of a century, under the control of white missionaries and kept economically dependent on and theologically enslaved to the white church, my church did not utter one word of meaningful protest against colonization, imperialism, or apartheid. We were exactly what Steve Biko accused the Black church of: we were conniving with white Christians to keep Christianity the most effective instrument in the continued subjugation of our people. But our discovery of God as the God of liberation, of Jesus as the revolutionary Black Messiah from occupied Galilee, and of the Holy Spirit who transforms and empowers us as She moves among us changed all that profoundly. Black consciousness, Black theology, Black power, and the Soweto revolution in 1976 opened the door to that new understanding. We found our voice and mounted serious and more intense resistance to the regime and the church that provided apartheid's biblical, moral, and theological justification.

We debated and learned from experience, one another, and our endless studies. More and more, we understood the vital and, for us, deadly intertwinement of white Christianity, imperialism, colonialism, apartheid, and the white Dutch Reformed Church and her impact on us politically, socially, economically, ideologically, and theologically. Better and better, we understood what historian Hannes Adonis calls "the intertwinement of the Dutch Reformed Church's mission policy and the ideology of apartheid." We knew the struggle was not just for freedom from political oppression, economic exploitation, and psychological domination but also for freedom from an ideologized theological colonization.

We identified and exposed the fundamental and indispensable ideological power matrix that necessitated first a hierarchical, racist separation of people and of the church: a church for the colonizer and a church for the colonized. Second, we revealed the creation of a theology designed to justify, sanctify, and deify imperialist power—to protect, at all costs, white privilege, white supremacy, white innocence, and white victimhood.

Our white Christian rulers created a theology for civilized masters and slave owners and a theology for savages and slaves—

a theology for black heathens and a theology for white Christians,
a theology of justification that cancelled out a theology of justice,
a theology of subjugation and enslavement that eliminated a theology of freedom,
a theology of submission that rejected a theology of resistance,
a theology of pietistic quietism that left no room for a theology of prophetic, radical discipleship.

We should not forget the power of the theology of hymnology. We were given a hymnified theology of pious otherworldliness that denied our people a voice to sing of holy this-worldliness. It offered us only the kind of theology that made us sing longingly of the golden streets of the New Jerusalem while the white man was stealing our gold from underneath our soil, right beneath our feet here on earth.

They offered us a theology of imposed childishness but never a theology of dignified personhood.

In destroying that slave theology and creating that other theology, a theology of liberation, we discovered our freedom, rediscovered our childhood of God, reinvigorated our faith, and claimed the radical Reformed tradition as our rightful heritage.

You will no doubt have heard, or will read, that we call Black theology a prophetic theology, meaning a theology that seeks to stand in the prophetic tradition of Miriam, the eighth-century prophets of social justice, and Jesus of Nazareth. We also call it a people's theology. That means that we learn not only from books and debates among colleagues. We learn from the people's life experiences, and we take their wisdom seriously as a source for our doing theology. That is why James Cone was entirely correct when he described the Black theologian as "an exegete of Scripture and of life."

This is what I mean: In February 1968, I had just been ordained in the Immanuel Dutch Reformed Mission Church in Paarl, a picturesque town in the heart of the beautiful wine country in the Western Cape. At that time, the apartheid regime's Group Areas Act had reached our part of town. Whole areas were declared "white." All who were classified "nonwhite," specifically "colored," were to be forcibly removed. Homes where people had lived for generations were taken, land was stolen, whole communities were destroyed and scattered to their new designated areas. Everything those communities represented, historically and culturally, was shattered, their social cohesion shredded. Our church would be bulldozed. To this day, for millions of our Black population, the devastation and destruction remain traumatic. Nothing would ever be the same again.

I was doing my rounds as the new young pastor, introducing myself, when I met Aunt Meraai Arendse, one of those strong women the Black Church cannot do without and is so proud of. She welcomed me, bade me sit down, but did not waste time on small talk. "Reverend," she began, "you don't have to tell me about Jesus. I have known him much longer than you do. What I do want you to talk about is what is happening here. Our lands and houses are being stolen, our homes destroyed, our community broken up. By white people who call themselves Christians. I want to know what God is saying about this. Now on Sunday, I need you to preach about this."

It was an extraordinarily revealing moment, and it shifted my whole perspective. First, it is not that she rejected Jesus or thought that Jesus did not matter. I think now she meant that she wanted to hear no more about the Jesus she was taught about by the white missionaries. That blond, blue-eyed, European Jesus whose blood saved her soul but who could not save her, her family, or her community from this injustice. That Jesus who had blessed apartheid with his blood, and sanctified it with the blood of God's dark-skinned children, had nothing to do with her pain and suffering, could not rescue her from it, was too meek and mild for the raw, robust, racist power of the white Christians. It took me some years to say what I now know to be unquestionably true: "If you say Jesus, you have to say justice. And if you say justice, you have to say Jesus. The more you say Jesus, the more you have to say justice; and the more you say justice, the more you have to say Jesus, because without his mercy, grace, and empowering love, the struggle for justice would be too much for us." In those early days, though, I did not yet know how to say it.

Second, she revealed to me the total inadequacy of my theological training. Of course I preached that next Sunday, but I think my sermon fell hopelessly short. Nothing I learned in those five years in seminary prepared me for this confrontation with Aunt Meraai and the call for resistance. Those white Dutch Reformed missionaries sent by the white church to teach in our seminary—believers as they were in the theology of apartheid, in the supremacy of the white race, and in their chosenness as God's elect people—had no intention of teaching us anything else, let alone ways of preaching hope and resistance to a people whose suffering they caused and so handsomely profited from. How I needed a Black theology of liberation then! If I wanted to learn more, I knew, I had to look elsewhere. Today, I understand even better that the world of global imperialist oppression; free-market capitalism; fundamentalism; aggressive, never-ending militarism; and escalating authoritarianism is a highly complex world. Just as we could not take on apartheid without a proper intellectual understanding of what we were really faced with, we cannot take on global imperialism without intellectually preparing and arming ourselves for this struggle.

Third, that moment taught me the necessity of preaching. Aunt Meraai was not asking me to go lead a demonstration or go fight with the police or the people bulldozing the houses (all that would come later). What she did expect was a word of comfort and protest, a word of hope and resistance, a word that would make her survive this horrific moment and help her face her terrifying future. That is an unwavering reason why Black people come to church, to gather enough fire to take into the cold darkness of white hostility, white superiority, white control, and white power that awaits outside. Learn from the people!

Black theology is resistance against hopelessness. The hope that drives Black liberation theology is not what American journalist and social critic Chris Hedges calls "the childish mania for hope" that leaves us crippled, paralyzed, and disempowered—mystified by the hard realities of the world and confused by a groundless, mindless, endless optimism that leads us nowhere but to resignation. I am speaking of the hope the African church father Augustine taught us. He speaks of hope as a mother with two daughters. Their names are Anger and Courage. Anger about the things that are wrong around us and Courage to see that they do not remain the way they are. That is the hope that is empowering, transformative, life giving.

Right now, that hope has come to life in the millions of people gathered in revolutionary protest against empire across the world, under the banner of the Black Lives Matter movement. From New York to London, from Brussels to Berlin, and from Khartoum to New Delhi, they are there in their nonracial, intergenerational, international, intergender millions standing up for justice, equality, and dignity of life for all. It is kindled in the fire for prophetic ministry burning in you. You are here to help them make this revolution a success. And you can because of the grace of God, because of the choices you can make, and because, as Nina Simone sings, you are "young, gifted, and black."

God bless you richly as you prepare for
your studies and the ministry,
Allan Aubrey Boesak
Cape Town

Notes

1 Patric Tariq Mellet, *The Lie of 1652: A Decolonised History of Land* (Cape Town: Tafelberg, 2020).

2 Deborah Hardoon, *An Economy for the 99%: It's Time to Build a Human Economy That Benefits Everyone, Not Just the Privileged Few* (Oxford: Oxfam International, 2017).

3 Max Lawson et al., *Public Good or Private Wealth? Universal Health, Education and Other Public Services Reduce the Gap between Rich and Poor, and between Women and Men. Fairer Taxation of the Wealthiest Can Help Pay for Them* (Oxford: Oxfam International, 2019).

4 Allan A. Boesak, *Farewell to Innocence: A Socio-ethical Study on Black Theology and Black Power*, reissue ed. (Eugene, OR: Wipf & Stock, 2015).

5 James H. Cone, *Black Theology and Black Power*, 50th anniversary ed. (New York: Orbis, 2019).

27

Willie James Jennings

The first thing you must know if you wish to enter theological study is that choice comes later, after you realize that you have been involved with God for a while. You—wondering about the why of this or that thing beyond the mechanics to the reason for its very existence. You—responding to what you sense might be God's voice in this or that impression, event, or voice of another. You—talking in your mind or audibly to the luminous presence you sense around you. Any or all of these realizations mean that you are in the right frame of mind to become a theological student. That does not mean that if you don't have any of these realizations, you should stay away from theological study. Everyone interested in theological study does not have similar experiences or identical subjectivities. That would be impossible and certainly not desirable. You should, however, enter theological studies only if and when you realize that God is real and/or a real question for you.

To enter theological study is to step onto the uneven and rough terrain between God being real and God being a real question. This terrain feels exceptionally treacherous at this point in history because theological study is now being done in the aftermath of modern colonialism and the formation of a Christianity that is in large measure responsible for the shape of that colonialism. Modern western colonialism is not simply an event that occurred in the past, from 1492 when the new worlds began to be invaded by proto-Europeans. Modern western colonialism transformed the way many people understood the world and themselves. It formed the foundation of most of the problems we face today and, in so doing, offered up to us a very difficult task of thinking God as a reality and/or as a question. When I began my theological studies, no one told me what I just told you, and so I spent many years confused not about what I was learning but about what I was sensing with my learning. There was something else happening to me and around me as I was engaged in theological education, but no one could tell me what it was.

I was being brought into a struggle that was not presented to me as a struggle. It was a struggle between idolatry and exegesis. These are two concepts that are crucial to understand at the beginning of theological study because they give definitive shape to theological work. Idolatry as I define it here is the usurpation of God and God's life with the life of another, posturing itself as God and demanding our attention, our veneration, and our worship. Exegesis should be defined here as the slow opening up of the life of God and our lives with God. The struggle I was sensing was to overcome the idolatry I was being exposed to while engaging in the exegesis that I was being compelled to enter. That struggle opened up into three tasks that I have come to understand as crucial to theological study and that, I suggest, will determine both whether you are ready to traverse this terrain and whether you want to see yourself as a theologian. (I will return to this designation "theologian" near the end of this letter to offer a few thoughts on what it means to claim it for oneself.) These tasks, while listed separately, are intertwined, adding to their complexity and the challenging work of engaging each of them.

Confronting the White Self-Sufficient Man

The first task is to confront the white self-sufficient man, who is constantly trying to think himself through the world and think himself through you. As I note in my book *After Whiteness*, all western education is shaped toward one overarching pedagogical goal—that is, the goal of education itself, which is to form each of us and all of us into a thinking subject that embodies a self-sufficient white masculinist intellectual form that exhibits three abiding characteristics: possession, control, and mastery.[1] It does not matter your gender designation or sexual orientation; your cultural, ethnic, tribal, or national designation; your religious commitment or lack of commitment; your political allegiances or social alliances—all of us are presented in western education with this man as the goal of our cultivation, to show we have arrived at his state of being.

He emerged right from the beginning of colonial settler life inside the hopes and dreams of the master class, those men who looked out on their colonial holdings—their lands, their slaves, their animals, their crops and mineral deposits, their businesses, their power, money, and influence—and asked the crucial question of sustainability: Who will carry forward my legacy after I am gone? They asked that question as they looked at their sons and then asked another question that was decisive for the creation of western education: How must he (my son) be formed to handle the awesome responsibilities of carrying forward all that God has given into my hands? The colonial masters formed education in the new worlds and refashioned education in the old worlds of Europe to answer that question. Modern western education was formed in plantation desire—the desire of the masters to form their sons to handle power. Indeed, many masters donated the lands and resources that made possible a vast number of educational institutions. Many schools exist in the western world on the land of former plantations.

Theological education was central to this desire. Caught between the desires of old masters and the aspirations of young would-be masters, theological education focused its curricular imagination and its teaching energies toward forming elite faith instructors and faith instructors of the elites who could confirm that there were indeed men ready to handle power because each one of them possessed the knowledge necessary to address any task known or unknown, controlled their own emotions and passions and knew how to keep control of those under their charge, and had mastered the skills necessary to do those tasks that would translate into continued mastery of their environments and especially the colonial holdings of their fathers and grandfathers. These were men formed to enact their power—without apology or pride—for the common good. Even as societies shifted away from legal slavery and unabashed plantation life, the structural reality of western education remained not only intact but translatable and translated into every colonial site, embedding itself deeply into the institutional subconscious of the academy, especially the theological academy. What this means for you is that you must war against a spirit that haunts the theological academy, oftentimes driving people and processes in ways they are very reluctant to acknowledge or renounce.

I have called this the spirit of the *racial paterfamilias*—the rule of the father that seeks to establish itself in us. It shows itself most powerfully in two ways as I and so many others have experienced it. First, it is evident in the strong impulse to assimilate to a white masculinist intellectual posture in your comportment, your disposition, and your self-presentation, and your outlook on life. This reality of assimilation is not easy to pin down because it looks different in different places, schools, contexts, and moments, but it carries a similar affect. It draws you toward a strange calculation and negotiation of your adequacy or inadequacy to the social and physical space of the school. It brings a question to you wholly inappropriate for theological education: Do I fit here? There is a sense in which everyone in the academy might ask a question like that at some point in their educational journey, but the colonial impulse toward assimilation adds density to that question and makes it something else—torture. The question is inappropriate for theological education because (as I will explain in more detail later) theological study is about shared habitation and about worlds enfolding one another.

Do not confuse this colonial impulse to assimilate with taking on a particular style of dress or speech, or even learning a particular language, although it can work itself down into those decisions. This torturous assimilation turns your attention and affection toward all things white European and moves nonwhite cultural practices and cognitive structures to the periphery of intellectual focus and formation. To war against this spirit is to war against choosing the hierarchy formed of Eurocentrism. There is in theological studies, just like in every endeavor of study, an order of ideas, thinkers, movements—those things that should be encountered earlier than other things for reasons of instruction. And there is nothing inherently wrong with learning European cultural practices and cognitive structures or, for that matter, learning of and from European thinkers to help situate us in our current dilemmas. But the problem of assimilation that we are caught in has turned that order of instruction into a relentless white Europhilia. That white Europhilia foregrounds European or Euro-American thinkers relentlessly and relegates all other intellectuals to supportive roles, like embroidery framing a central picture.

Second, you must also war against a kind of evaluation that is poisonous, which grows out of the impulse to assimilate. This is not the practices of evaluation that are part of the academy and theological study but something that moves in, through, and around those practices, pressing on you a form of constant self-critique that makes you measure your thinking, your writing, your speaking, and your remembering against the ideal self-sufficient white man. This kind of evaluation turns the joy of not knowing something (which is part of the excitement of learning) into a sense of inadequacy and sometimes shame. This sense of inadequacy draws its life from colonial aspirations to show oneself finished, ready to be heard, and have one's voice taken seriously. But the finished state never comes once you are inside this sick reality of self-critique because you are forever measuring yourself against a phantasmic figure. Worst yet, this kind of evaluation narrows the way you might see your colleagues in study. You will find yourself measuring them against this ideal man and finding them either wanting or closer to that finished state than you and therefore ready to become objects of jealous contempt or admiration. There is something wonderful about being motivated to learn and work diligently at study because you have been honestly assessed regarding what you know and understand or what remains outside your grasp. Yet the motivation can become academy-sanctioned torture when touched by the hand of the white self-sufficient man.

What is at stake here is the gaining or losing of yourself in the work of theological study. The white self-sufficient man aims to have you think yourself inside thinking him and a world he seeks to claim as his own. This claiming has led to the damaging aspects of modernity, such as, for example, the objectification and commodification of so much of the world. An objectified and commodified world completes the dream of the colonial masters who saw the world in its potential—ready to be taken and used. That way of seeing the world is relentlessly reductive, shaving off stories, voices, and visions in order to hold it as a controllable thing. Theological study has always been inside the western academy's goal of the educated state—to form the one who knows how to take and use the world. There are many in and outside the academy and the theological academy who are pressing toward different ways of imagining the educated state, but they are yet to emerge as the majority in the western academy and the theological academy. Indeed, you will find that some of your professors and mentors are caught up in the quest to become the white self-sufficient man, and they will invite you into that quest with everything they say and do in their courses and classrooms. The task here is to identify the desires of colonial masters and the aspirations of their sons and to turn away from it, recognizing the idolatry at work in it, and to turn toward the exegesis that vivifies theological study. This is the second task of theological study.

Exegeting an Unfolding Life

Theological study is inside a Jewish story and Jewish hope for a changed world. There are, of course, other kinds of theological study besides Christian study, and these have great value, but theological study that claims to be Christian begins with the truth that it is inside the faith of another people, Israel. This means there is a scandalous weakness to Christian theological study that is inherent to it. Our intellectual work radiates out from a simple yes spoken by a Palestinian Jewish girl named Mary, who in faith and radical obedience to God gave birth to a child named Jesus. Jesus of Nazareth is the son of Mary and shares in her claim that he is the child of God. Christian thought builds from this unbelievable, scandalous truth: God has come into the world, entered fully into our weak flesh, and inhabits our world of pain and suffering, joy and sorrow, anger and hope.

Entering this work of exegesis positions you in the same place as all the disciples of Jesus (whether you are a believer or not) as someone grappling with two complex matters. On the one hand, you are trying to make sense of who God is as the identity of God is slowly opening to you through the story of this Jesus of Nazareth. Through that story, we learn that Jesus is exegeting God for us and inviting us into that exegesis with him through the Holy Spirit. This is challenging work because no one comes to theological study as a blank slate. Everyone comes with assumptions and ideas about who God is and what a god ought to be like. Yet by diligently attending to the contours of Jesus's life and ministry, we are being drawn to a careful and sometimes painful remapping of our ideas of divinity, allowing to crumble belief structures that have created a fantasy god instead of the God revealed in and through Jesus of Nazareth. Fantasy gods make sense because they carry forward a kind of logic that matches the particular configurations—social, cultural, political, economic, gendered—of the world that we have come to inhabit. They are hard to shake because they align so perfectly with how we understand power, imagine the good life, and calibrate our hopes for the future. The followers of Jesus have always struggled with fantasy gods, constantly needing to allow the life of Jesus to reshape their understanding of God.

Living now as we do on this side of colonial modernity, we have the added burden of the image of the white self-sufficient man who is often mapped across the life of Jesus as being one in the same. Jesus himself is often imagined as the finished man, the one in whom ultimate self-sufficiency—with complete possession, control, and mastery—resides fully realized. This Jesus is loved and worshipped because he is powerful, which means, in effect, that people are worshipping his completion and his power and not actually Jesus himself. The story of Jesus presents you and me with a different trajectory for life not aligned with the quest to become the white self-sufficient man. He aims your life toward communion (which we will consider later). Rethinking who God is in light of Jesus's life invites us into disciplined thought that is not easy to sustain. So much theological study goes offtrack because we fail to reckon with the human propensity to produce idols within our intellectual work. Even Jesus can be rendered an idol if aligned with the white self-sufficient man.

The second complexity to the work of exegesis is naming God in light of Israel's life. If, on the one hand, we are trying to make sense of who God is, then, on the other hand, we are trying to make sense of who we are in relation to the people of God, Israel. Jesus is the prophet of God to Israel. His life and ministry were aimed at Israel, for Israel's renewal. A conversation formed between Jesus and his people (Israel), a conversation that we (gentiles; those not Jewish) overheard. We were outsiders to this conversation and at the margin of consideration for those involved in it—that is, Jesus and his people. Remembering this dynamic of a conversation being overheard is crucial for theological study. Unfortunately, too much of Christian theology and Christian theological speech functions in deep denial of this history of being outsiders, choosing instead to believe that we Christians are the insiders, the authentic people of God, having replaced Israel according to the will of God.

There are many who believe that God rejected Israel and elected believing gentiles—that is, the church—to replace them as the people of God and thereby operate in a way of thinking that frames theological study in two tragic ways. First, it frames theological study inside pride rather than humility. It has been a powerful intoxicant to believe that we Christians are the chosen of God even if we also say to ourselves that God's choosing is based not on merit but on grace. God yet chose *us* becomes the inevitable conclusion. Divine grace, however, is mediated grace, having come to us through the life of Israel made known to us through the life of one of their own, Jesus, Mary's baby. Yet when grace is configured as clearing away Israel in order to be established in us, then we gentile Christians are left with a strange sense of focus—that God is focused primarily on us. Historically, that sense of divine focus worked itself down to ethnic groups and burgeoning nations, each of whom understood themselves to be Christians blessed by God with divinely sanctioned power and responsibility to convert those outside the faith. It was this sense of pride and divine focus that resourced the colonialists' sense of mission in the new worlds, allowing them to refashion those worlds into colonial holdings. This framing allowed each nation and the church within it to see itself as God's chosen vessel called to carry the gospel into the world. This framing has facilitated the idea that the gospel creates Christian peoples rather than a single Christian people in witness to and conversation with Israel about the victory of their God. It also solidified the idea that Israel was just another people (ethnic group or nation) who needed to accept the gospel.

Seeing Israel as just another group that needed to become Christian points to the other tragic way theological study has been framed—namely, without the dynamic of inclusion. We gentiles entered into a story that was not ours and a conversation that was not centered on us. How we did this is profoundly instructive for theological study. We entered as learners seeking to learn about the God of Israel, who, it turns out, is also our God. Historically, this position of learner entailed a posture of openness, adaptability, malleability, and flexibility as gentiles rethought their identities through a remapping of their cultural practices and beliefs. The Jewish followers of Jesus also found themselves in a rethinking of their lives in relation to the new identity and the new community being formed around the body of Jesus. The process of gentiles changing, adapting, and opening themselves was not just a historic event that made Christianity possible but the trajectory for performing the Christian faith. We were invited into lifelong learning with Israel about the God who joins us together in order to form the new human.

The term *gentile* designates many people, all of whom in this regard are caught up in the processes of opening and sharing, forming and reforming ways of life together with Israel and Israel's God. Yet this is a trajectory that gentile Christians abandoned early in favor of replacement ways of thinking. It is easier to imagine a God who replaces a people with another people than a God who creates a new people from the sinews of many peoples. The Christianity that formed through abandoning the work of joining is the one that you will have to confront through your theological education. That Christianity framed theological study not around learners listening to the ways of others and together seeking to follow the God of Israel but around teachers who enter with the purpose of correcting, changing, and eradicating ways of thinking and living that seem contrary to the faith. This correcting Christianity was in full display from the beginning of the colonial moment. It became our inheritance so that now, Christian instruction has been turned on its head.

A teaching faith is more legible to Christians than a learning faith, and the Christian life is first about getting others to change their lives, adapt their practices, and open themselves to Christian faith rather than presenting a faith that teaches first by showing itself to be a learner and a lover of peoples. The task of theological study here is to enter the work of exegesis that includes yourself. There is an unfolding of your life in and with the unfolding of the life of God that is at the heart of theological instruction. That unfolding is a sharing in and a sharing of your life with others, which brings me to the third task for you.

Aiming for Belonging

Theological study places you inside a drama—God claiming God's own creation as the site of divine love. That drama renders theological study a form of intellectual insurgency. Colonialist educators—missionaries and others—very often put the power of that insurgency to horrible use as they stripped indigenes of their lands and ways of life and attacked communal ways of knowing and thinking. They in turn bound indigenes together in forms of thinking that gloried in the individual as an autonomous unit of thought and decision-making, each person a lone thinking subject. The irony of the idea of the autonomous thinking subject is that it had to be made a shared project of western colonial education for it to take hold as fundamental to a vision of what an educated person looks like. Yet theological study promised a different insurgency with a different upending. Rather than undermining the communal in favor of the individual, its real promise shows itself in creating a new reality of belonging energized by God's claim on us.

We are inside the drama of God, and this story interfaces with the many other stories you are positioned inside of—of family, of people, of nation, of personal identity, and so forth. Yet this story, God's story, lifts those other stories. Like a rising tide that raises boats, making them movable and drawing them into the current, so too God's drama moves our stories in a new direction—toward God and toward one another. The western academy glories in the productive use of a fiction—that the thinking subject enabled by the academy itself lives in the suspension of story. It is as if the location—the grounds of a school, a college, or a university—supports the fiction of a suspension. There, away from one's families and communities, even if for only a few hours, you may think freely, choose freely, and live unencumbered by the dictates of your place of origin. There is something good about that fiction because it allows you to touch the edges of your own life in the world and your own agency. Of course, the suspension is a fiction because the modern western academy is itself inside the colonial story of tearing, separating, isolating, objectifying, classifying, and commodifying life.

You can make good use of the fiction if you remember it is a fiction. Yet the story of the western academy is not the story that grounds theological study or your life. This means that the aim of your education cannot be captured in becoming an autonomous thinking subject. Among the most important things that no one told me as I was moving through theological study was to aim for belonging. It is the goal of belonging rooted in God's desire to draw us together that should guide your work. Too many lose sight of belonging and forget exactly how revolutionary theological study is intended to be. It must give witness to the great overturning that God has done through Jesus and is doing in the world by the Spirit or it is not authentic theological study. You are in the midst of God crumbling from within this world order with its boundaries and borders, its systems of death and despair, and its violence and injustice. That overturning draws our intellectual work through the critique of existing social, political, economic, and cognitive structures and certainly through simply affirming or servicing them to envisioning the new that God is bringing that begins with new relationships and a new life together. We build intellectual life inside the overturning. This, of course, sounds contradictory, but it means that we sense the pull of our lives in and toward the gathering that God is creating.

Theological study offers one final gift that you should never take lightly, freedom. Yet it is freedom in weakness. Theological study looks weak in relation to the configurations of knowledge in the modern academy and in the deployments of knowledge in modern political economies. We who are engaged in this work have no powerful or compelling rationale for why we should be taken seriously. There is no intellectual shine on us. The most we can do in the court of public opinion is present ourselves as important for understanding a subset of religious people within the realities of religions. Or we can present ourselves as teachers of moralities we believe are necessary for the proper ordering of a nation-state or relations between nation-states or even corporations. Both these forms of presentation are indeed necessary, but only a foolish person thinks they are the reasons why you should take theological study seriously. You take theological study seriously because it offers freedom to think the life of God moving in and through the creation and moving in and through you, which means it offers real freedom to think your own life. That thinking points to the need of a world to be set free. To begin to see that freedom is also to see down into the depths of our captivities. Theological study is ultimately about chain breaking, especially for those who don't see their chains as chains. This does not mean theological types have full sight. It simply means we are slowly sensing a freedom that is there for us.

Anyone who stays with theological study comes finally to the choice—choosing to be a theologian or not. The designation *theologian* formally means to be a teacher of the church, one who opens to the faithful the anatomy of their beliefs and the anatomy of their lives as believers. In fact, no one can call themselves a theologian in this sense. It has to be given by the faithful over time (over decades and even over centuries). You could, however, take the designation in a less epic sense as someone who has come to the realization that being involved with God will fundamentally shape the contours of your life and your vocation, whatever it may be—pastor, teacher, mechanic, nurse, musician, writer, and so on—now and forever. Once you come to that realization, you will conclude that the choice came first, but in truth, it was not your choice.

Willie James Jennings

Note

1 Willie James Jennings, *After Whiteness: An Education in Belonging* (Grand Rapids, MI: Eerdmans, 2020).

28

Adam Neder

So then, how to begin this letter? Believe it or not, I am hesitant to give unsolicited theological advice. Does that surprise you? I can see why it might. We theologians are not known for our reticence. Nevertheless, responsible theological work is as likely to take the form of silence as to take the form of speech. God calls us to tell the truth, not to talk continuously, and when we have nothing helpful to say, we say nothing. That is especially true in our age of infinite information and endless digital noise. When Christian theologians are thinking clearly, we do not compulsively broadcast our opinions or envision ourselves as oracles. But as you must have noticed by now, we often lose our heads.

At our worst, we present ourselves as quasi-omniscient gurus. We aspire to duplicate ourselves inside your head. We interpret disagreement as disloyalty and teach as if being on our side is being on God's side. We exchange education for propaganda and develop elaborate theological explanations for doing so. We seek applause, market ourselves, and compete with one another as if we have never read the New Testament. True, none of this makes any sense if God is who Christians believe God is. Yes, this way of being turns us into embodied contradictions of the gospel of Jesus Christ. Of course, such posturing is sad and embarrassing and makes it harder for people to believe in God. But those facts are easy to ignore.

Why am I going on about all this? Because at the beginning of your theological education, you are especially susceptible to being duped by ideologues, and unfortunately, they are harder to resist than you might think.[1] The discipline of Christian theology can feel like a cluttered field of competing opinions, full of verbose scholars vying for attention and prestige. Theologians often write and speak as if those who disagree with them are benighted, malevolent, or hopelessly confused. Students new to theology often find this disorienting and unnerving. They know they are not competent to judge between competing experts, but they do not know who to trust. This often leads to various kinds of anxiety and insecurity that students are tempted to resolve by pledging exclusive fealty to one or another theologian or school of thought. I hope you don't make that mistake. If you do—if you exchange uncertainty for partisanship—you will temporarily alleviate your unsettledness and gain a sense of tribal belonging, but you will close yourself to the fullness of truth, which transcends every tradition and exceeds every theological framework. So remember: God is the only infallible theology teacher.

Even still, few things in life are better than finding a good teacher, as anyone who has ever had one should know. In fact, one helpful way to imagine your theological education is to envision it as a process of learning who to trust. At this point in your studies, you are searching for reliable guides, trustworthy mentors and conversation partners, teachers who know the terrain well enough to help you find your bearings and explore wisely. The most serious mistake you can make right now is to apprentice yourself to the wrong people. And so the pressing question becomes, How do I recognize a good teacher? The rest of this letter is an attempt to help you answer that question. And don't worry, I will not try to persuade you who to read, where to study, or which tradition to embrace. You have to decide for yourself who to trust. Instead, I just want to recommend a few qualities, beyond all the obvious ones, that you might not think to consider as you search for your theology teachers. So without further ado . . .

Good Teachers Are Disturbed to Find Themselves Talking about God

Anyone who does not find it strange that he or she should be the one to stand in front of a room full of people and talk about God is either foolish or has not thought very deeply about what is happening. Such people should not teach theology. Why? Because the subject matter of Christian theology is impossible to master, because everyone's life somehow contradicts what they say about God, because teaching theology is really hard to do well, because every teacher persuades people to believe things about God that are not true, but also and primarily, because God is God, and no one possesses the power to make God known. Since the truth is not something a teacher possesses, the truth is not something a teacher dispenses, no matter how gifted one happens to be. Good teachers speak with freedom, confidence, and joy precisely because they believe the success of their teaching depends not ultimately on themselves but on God's desire to be known and on God's willingness to enlist their instruction in that process.

Good Teachers Undermine Their Own Authority

Good teachers train you to think for yourself. Not by yourself, for yourself. To be sure, in the light of Scripture, within the communion of saints, and under the lordship of Christ, but on your own two feet. They know the difference between education and indoctrination. You may have noticed that theologians love to warn people about the dangers of individualism. They make an important point. But very often, the implicit conclusion embedded in these warnings is "Therefore, let us do your thinking for you." That paternalistic mindset should not be confused with real theological education. Life is full of challenges, and many students respond to them by looking for teachers who will tell them exactly how to think and live. Good teachers are alert to this inclination and resist it by intentionally undermining their own authority. They do not inflate their importance and indispensability. They do not want students to remain dependent upon them. They are not threatened by disagreement. They do not pretend to pronounce the final word. Instead of all that, good teachers aspire to become transparent to the subject matter. Their goal is to get out of the way—to disappear as they point away from themselves to God.

Good Teachers Do Not Create Safe Classrooms

We hear a lot these days about making classrooms safe for students. In many ways, this guidance is obviously sound. As you know, people do not tend to learn in environments where they feel demeaned, threatened, ignored, coerced, or exploited. Most students close themselves to teachers who do not respect them, take them seriously, listen to them, care about them, or give them the freedom to formulate their own ideas as they explore the mysteries of faith. You should flee from such people. But that does not mean you should seek teachers who create cozy classrooms where everyone always feels settled, secure, and undisturbed. Such classrooms are not conducive to theological education either. If you never feel challenged, if you never sense that your basic commitments are being probed and called into question, if you never find yourself fighting for your life, then the atmosphere of the classroom belies the subject matter of the discipline. Christian theology emerges from encounter with the God whose healing love tears us away from many of our default patterns of thinking and living. In the light of that love, we find ourselves challenged and exposed. Theology classrooms that do not reflect at least something of the spirit of that struggle—classrooms that provide sanctuary from the threats inherent in Christian existence and the risks involved with believing in God—will mislead you about what Christianity is.

Good Teachers Know Who You Are Because They Know Who Jesus Christ Is

Every pedagogy assumes an anthropology, and as Christian theologians, your teachers should know that whatever else turns out to be true about you, the fundamental fact of your life, the essential truth of your identity, is that you are loved by God in Christ. Jesus Christ sets you at peace with God and calls you to live at peace with God, your neighbors, and yourself. In one way or another, good theological education trains you to receive and respond to the love of God and, in so doing, to become who you already are in Christ. As Dietrich Bonhoeffer once put it, "Christian education begins where all other education ceases: What is essential has already happened."[2]

Good Teachers Know the Difference between Ideas and Existence

It is impossible to teach Christian theology seriously, responsibly, or professionally without attempting to clarify what Christianity is. And as every honest reader of the Gospels knows, Christianity cannot be reduced to thinking the right thoughts about God. Jesus Christ seeks disciples, not dilettantes. He desires people who follow him, not people who agree that following him is a good idea. "The truth, if it is there, is a being, a *life*," Kierkegaard writes—indeed, the truth is only known "when it becomes a life in me."[3] Thus your aim as a student of theology is not merely to understand but to live in what you understand. Teachers only tell the truth about Christianity when they make it clear that knowledge of God is a matter of existence, not merely a matter of ideas.

Good Teachers Pray

Seek professors who pray—not as a public or private demonstration of piety but simply because theology without prayer makes no sense. No matter how intelligent, well-read, eloquent, or wise a teacher happens to be, there is no guarantee that their classes will amount to anything more than wasted time. Knowledge of God is a gift of divine grace and thus depends ultimately on the presence and activity of the Holy Spirit. There are no foolproof rhetorical or pedagogical strategies for guaranteeing the success of theological education. What Kierkegaard says about the Christian life is also true about theology: "To need God is our highest perfection."[4] Therefore, theology teachers pray.

OK, that's plenty—probably too much. Thanks for reading. Let me know what you make of all this . . .

Adam

Notes

1 The thing about being duped is that it doesn't feel like you're being duped. Especially when the one duping you says a lot of things that are true.

2 Dietrich Bonhoeffer, "'Catechesis' (1935–1936 Student Notes)," in *Theological Education at Finkenwalde: 1935–1937; Dietrich Bonhoeffer Works*, English ed., ed. H. Gaylon Bobert-Stützel, Dirk Schulz, and Ilse Tödt, trans. Douglas W. Stott (Minneapolis: Fortress, 2013), 538.

3 Søren Kierkegaard, *Practice in Christianity*, ed. and trans. Howard V. Hong and Edna H. Hong (Princeton, NJ: Princeton University Press, 1991), 206.

4 Søren Kierkegaard, *Eighteen Upbuilding Discourses*, ed. and trans. Howard V. Hong and Edna H. Hong (1990; repr., Princeton, NJ: Princeton University Press, 1992), 312.

On Healing, Wholeness, Dignity

29

Rachel Muers

It is a strange honour and a privilege to be asked to put together some words of advice for people beginning the study of theology, particularly as these words are to be included in a collection including letters by people from whom I would gladly take advice myself. Writing this in the condition of "lockdown" required by Covid-19, I miss our students; I especially miss the sense of shared excitement about a project. My theological location is in the academy, and I address myself especially to the situation of academic theology.

I want to start the words of encouragement with a word about the specific vocation of academic theology. As theologians, our subject matter could, literally, not be greater. In my experience, this can lead to impatience with the constraints of academic spaces and academic style. Theologians want to speak in large and impressive terms, which might begin to convey something of the scale and importance and urgency of what we are saying. I want to suggest that although much ink has been spilled on the subject of theology's precarious place in the academy, it is really similar to other academic subjects, in this respect at least: a small solid advance is worth making and much more likely to endure than a giant leap that fails to land.

What constitutes a "solid advance"? At least in academic writing, we are not exempt from any of the rules of good scholarship. We need to persuade with reasons, give a fair hearing to all the arguments, follow up the sources, read the texts carefully, know what we mean when we say it, and say no more than we mean.[1] Of course, this academic style is not the only way to write theology, and one of the features of our discipline—as with literary studies—is that many of the texts we study are nothing like the texts we write. This can be troubling, especially for those who are also producing theological work in other genres—in sermons, for example, or in devotional texts. Whatever your other callings, I invite you, respectfully, not to denigrate or neglect the specific demands of an academic vocation or its particular goods. Academic norms are not merely something sent to try us. There are good theological and ethical reasons for wanting to do this well.

People whose vocation is academic work care passionately about truth, and about the careful reception of what we have been given, and about that aspect of the love of one's neighbour that involves careful and charitable listening and clear communication. We do not want to betray either our subject matter or our audiences by saying something that sounds good or edifying but might not be quite true, or might not really make sense. As one of my teachers, the late Nicholas Lash, used to say, as theologians, we watch our language in the presence of God. Alongside and not apart from this, we watch our language in the presence of our friends and colleagues, and we accord them the respect of reflecting critically on what they say. Doing theology in a critical space can be particularly challenging. Ideally, in the academy we nurture an environment, very rare in the contemporary world, where correction can be accepted as a gift. I need you to show me when I get something wrong, because it matters much less that I should be right than that the name of God should be honoured.

Talking about responsibilities within the academic community brings me onto difficult territory, though, because "success" in an academic space is not just about the search for truth. The world of academic theology has plenty of unspoken rules. This is a world of theological "guilds" and "schools" with hard-to-determine membership criteria, of genealogies and pedigrees (whose student are you, whose work do you cite or not cite, who do you praise, and who do you denigrate)—all the complexities and power struggles that senior theologians sometimes have the privilege of *not* seeing and those starting out can rarely ignore. Theology, as it intersects with ecclesial spaces with their own power structures and their own judgements of orthodoxy, is perhaps more beset by these issues than are other academic subjects.[2]

Aware of all this, I want to say to new theologians, "Don't let it get to you"—or, more positively, "Trust your vocation; the one who calls you is faithful" (see 1 Thess 5:24). And this is easy to say in general terms and in the abstract, but it carries different weight for each person.

For example, I remember one of my first students telling me how anxious she felt about putting onto paper her critical reflections about the texts and questions she was studying. What does it matter, she asked me, what *I* think, when all these superintelligent people have already said it? She was the first person in her family to go to university, and she was excited by the theology and intimidated by the institution; I was not sure, in fact, whether her anxiety was more about the scholars on the page or the fellow students in the lecture room. Of course I told her, "You have as much right to be here as anyone else, you have as much right to speak as anyone else"—meaning both in the contemporary university and in the great ongoing intergenerational conversation to which we often compare theology. But I knew that it was not that easy, because she did *not* fit the pattern, she did not "look like a theologian," she would need to get used to the sound of her theological voice because it sounded different. I wanted to say it more urgently and to say it to anybody starting out in theology: Whoever they are, don't let them get to you. Whichever voices are telling you that you can't do what you are doing, don't stop for too long to listen to them. The work is what matters. The work needs your voice as well. Let us hear your voice.

For another example, I have a very vivid memory of going into my first graduate-level theology research seminar. There is a long room with a long table, men sitting around the table (I think there must have been a few other women there, but in my mind, as I enter the room, I see a group of men), and large portraits on the walls of large men in large gowns, looking down at me benevolently but rather puzzled: What is this person doing here? Is she really going to sit at our table? In a theology faculty where, not so long ago, she was several versions of impossible (she is, after all, a nonconformist and a layperson and a woman, and we are an ancient institution). *Friends, I know you weren't expecting me*, I said in my mind to the large benevolent men in the portraits. *It turns out it was possible after all—how about that? So I'm here now; let's talk.*

Academic theology has its shibboleths (Judg 12:6)—those little features of the academic voice that can secure or bar admission, names that you drop into your texts to prove that you belong to this grouping and not that one, phrases possibly in Latin or German that mark you out as a "real" theologian for some context or some purpose. When I reflect on what this means for new theologians, I want to say first that, insofar as it is a problem, it is not *your* problem. Those who hold power in the contexts where theology is done have the responsibility to broaden their own perspectives, to resist the temptation to reproduce theologians in their own likeness, to subject their criteria of judgement to its own judgement. If you, as a newer scholar, find that in order to succeed you are required to work in ways that betray the truths you find—the truths you find as you reason through your experience with Scripture in intergenerational company—I can only apologise. We should not be asking you to distort your own accent beyond recognition in order to have an academic voice, and you, as a new theologian, should not be expected to bear the burden of changing the academy (or, for that matter, the churches). In order to help us change things over time, I encourage you, if at all possible, not to narrow your own horizons. You should read and listen widely, test everything and hold fast to what is good, and in due course—although I have not always succeeded in this myself—take whatever risks your position allows you to take. As the opportunity arises, raise a neglected concern, point to a road not taken, amplify a voice that has not been heard.

Perhaps most importantly, however much you come to love the language of academic theology—with all the gifts it can bring—I ask you not to forget your own first languages, the languages in which you have been comfortable speaking with and of God. Stay connected with all your sources of spiritual strength. There will always be things you can only say in your first languages—and you may find, as you progress in theology, that less and less gets lost in translation. It is also always important to remain connected with different contexts in which theological thought and speech happen—to maintain the habit of hearing and recognising theology in different genres and forms.

When I think about the process of doing theology, I often come back to thinking about the medieval English theologian Julian of Norwich. Although she is writing in a very different idiom and context, she deserves some attention from the new theologian because she shows her work. We can almost watch her working out how to do theology as she writes and rewrites her account of her "visions of divine love."[3] In successive revisions, Julian writes herself *out* of her text, so that we know very little about who she was or what kind of life she had; but at the same time, she writes herself *into* it, finding a distinctive voice with which the text resounds. The end result is that she is not talking about herself; she is talking about God, and God's ways with the world, *as* herself. Her insights are unquestionably her own and also never limited to or by her own experience and context. She has no recognised position of authority from which to speak, so she cannot disappear into a role or an office. She offers her work to her fellow Christians as a gift that she, Julian, was given and does not yet fully understand—and that is not completed when she stops writing, because it needs to be heard and tested and put into practice.

Julian makes no attempt to conceal how difficult she finds it to reconcile the tensions and conflicts around her central vision of the God who "makes all things well." We see her asking urgent questions of God and not letting go until she finds an answer, circling back round to issues she thought she had resolved, testing out her findings on specific cases, frequently stopping in bafflement or wonder. Julian engages in "faith seeking understanding" not as a paper exercise but as an exercise of the whole heart and mind; she asks about what she *needs* to understand—not in order to win an argument but in order to live at the heart of a suffering city, in order to listen to her neighbours, in order to pray and praise. To use the title of the book edited by Virginia Fabella and Mercy Amba Oduyoye, Julian does theology "with passion and compassion." In all of this, moreover, she holds to the revelation of God given to her, she seeks understanding, she puts her mind to work.

Rather than finish with one contextual example of theological practice, however, it seems appropriate to offer a biblical image. Various theologians and biblical scholars have used the story of Jacob wrestling with the angel to illustrate "wrestling" with difficult or puzzling texts and conversation partners. I see it as an image of theological work in a broader sense, and I focus on the idea of claiming a promised blessing. Our work is a struggle that confidently expects a blessing and holds on, a struggle that involves the whole person, a combination of audacity and humility. I keep hold of this strange tradition, these strange texts, and I demand the blessing that I was promised and that I cannot bestow upon myself. If God calls me to be here, I am staying here, and I am not messing around; I am putting into this everything I have. Theology proceeds on the basis that reading and rereading Scripture, reading and rereading the writings and lives of our predecessors, will allow a blessing to emerge that is specific to the present moment. There might be other places to look, but this is where we find ourselves. It is a risk because we do not yet have what we need. It is not enough simply to repeat what has already been done in the same terms, and it is not even enough to point out the problems or deficiencies in what has already been done. There is something here worth striving for. There is, after all, supposed to be good news here. Sometimes, I say, it really is that simple; if we are giving an account of Christianity that is *not* good news to the people who most need good news, we can be absolutely sure we have got something wrong.

There is, however, one important caveat to both of these images, Julian writing her book and Jacob wrestling the angel: both of them are alone, and theology is a companionable enterprise. I can confidently promise you good company in your work, and I hope you will want to continue the journey.

Rachel Muers
University of Leeds

Notes

1 It was difficult to bring myself to write this letter without endnotes. You'll see that I didn't quite manage it.
2 I've learned a lot about this from the pioneering Black British theologian Anthony Reddie.
3 Julian of Norwich, *Revelations of Divine Love* (Oxford: Oxford University Press, 2015).

30

Denise Ackermann

You may not be young in years. I was not young when I started study-ing theology. I understand "young" as including anyone who has re-cently embarked on the study of theology and who would like to exchange ideas and explore different themes and contexts. It is to you that I write this letter. A letter is not a treatise. I write from the heart in an attempt to share a few insights with you that have played a role in my theology.

Our world is in dire need of healing. This is nothing new. However, I confess to a deep sense of urgency that challenges us as theologians to engage with current issues from our particular contexts. The theological themes that I deal with in this letter reflect, in some way or other, my de-sire for a more humane world.

When I started studying theology, I hoped I would find answers to some of life's intractable questions. Questions such as "How can I reconcile sci-entific discoveries with a creator God?" "How can a loving God allow the innocent to suffer?" "What about the contradictions in the Scriptures?" I found few ready answers. I certainly found new questions. And I found much more. Perhaps this will be your experience.

Nearly twenty years ago, I wrote a book of letters (*After the Locusts: Letters from a Landscape of Faith*) in an effort to explain how faith makes life worth living.[1] Looking back on what I wrote, certain themes remain central to my theological thinking, such as the desire for justice and the affirmation of human worth (*Menschenwürde*). Most of my life, I lived under apartheid and in a society that was and still is patriarchal. I was angry. I longed for a more just society, one in which after the locusts of apartheid, not only our sons but also our daughters would prophesy (Joel 2:25; 2:28)—one in which our shared human worth would be respected. Theology offered me a language of resistance and hope. My longing for a just world is, of course, utopian. This does not, however, exonerate us theologians today from pursuing hope for a better, kinder world.

Anselm's classic definition of theology as "faith seeking understanding" is well known. Moreover, I found that the search for understanding was also driven by a deep longing—in my case, not only a longing for justice. I longed for a deeper understanding of our relationship with God. In the process of finding my theological voice, I learnt to rely on my longing and found it a reliable guide. Identifying that inner longing is vital for our task.

As I wrestled with many questions, I found no easy answers. In lines attributed to him, Augustine warns us, "Let neither of us pretend to have found truth; let us seek it as something unknown to both of us." Life is unpredictable and is both ordered and disjointed. Contradictions do not disappear. My pursuit of theology became, in Thomas Merton's words, more like traveling "in the belly of a paradox . . . a whale of a ride." Uncertainty and the inexplicable abounded. "Faith seeking understanding" does not promise a charter of certainties.

A theologian must learn to embrace contradiction and paradox. Paradox, unlike contradiction, promises that an apparent contradiction can express a possible truth. "Either/or" and "both/and" are woven into the fabric of life: light and dark, head and heart, life and death. It is not always easy, but discovering the promise in paradox is decidedly liberating. Our very faith rests on a paradox—a child born in a stable to a young unmarried Jewish woman who, as a man, dies like a common criminal on a cross is the ascended Christ, our Liberator. If theology lies in the tension between certainty and uncertainty, you may well wonder whether there are any certainties. My certainties are a matter of faith and are simple. God is both knowable and unknowable. God is loving, just, merciful, and compassionate, and God in Christ defines what love is. Jesus—through his life, teaching, and death—is our friend, our tutor for life and the way to salvation. The ever-present Holy Spirit is our guide, our interpreter, and our comforter.

My context as a South African woman underlies my theological concerns, hence the theme of contextuality. As I write, my country—and indeed, the world—is gripped by a viral pandemic and its consequences. At the same time, gender-based violence in my country has reached lamentable proportions. Pandemics are not new; neither are misogyny, racism, violence, suffering, corruption, or poverty. Today, tragedy stalks our streets as our economy melts down, exacerbated by shameless political profiteering. The inequalities in our society are stark. The consequences of Covid-19 will be with us for many years.

Christians are taught to share, to feed the poor and hungry, to welcome the stranger, and to stand with those who suffer. Thankfully, there is much evidence at present that these injunctions are being taken seriously by many believers in my country. But what does the present reality ask of us as theologians?

How do we address femicide and sexism? How do we respond to the despair, anger, suffering, deprivation, and inequalities of our context? As a person of privilege, I never cease to wrestle with this simple question: "When is enough, enough?"

The "enough" question is without doubt related to another: What is humanity's greatest challenge since the beginning of our existence? Our wastefulness, greed, and thoughtlessness are destroying our natural world at a rate previously unequalled. Our very existence is threatened. At the creation of our world, God saw that it was "good." Every day, what God considered "good" is being destroyed by our rapaciousness. I cannot conceive of contemporary theology that does not give urgent attention to the destruction of our natural world and the survival of humanity. The survival of our species—and indeed, our planet—calls for prioritising justice-centred actions, an equitable sharing of our resources, and care for one another.

The inequalities in our world raise the question of difference and otherness and the pressing need for theological reflection on this reality. My country is multiracial, multicultural, multilingual, and religiously pluralistic and has known democracy only since 1994. The most tragic difference in our society is the deep chasm that separates the "haves" from the "have-nots." I wonder about yours. Surely, difference is not limited to my context; it is a worldwide reality that has taken a prominent place in philosophy, law, theological ethics, and anthropology as well as our reflections on our religious practices. There is a dire need for dealing honestly with our differences and the barriers they create between people.

What do I mean by difference and otherness? To speak of "difference" is to speak of boundaries, our bodies, cultures, traditions, ideologies, and beliefs. To speak of the "other" is to speak of that other human being whom I may mistakenly have assumed to be just like me but who, in fact, is not like me at all. To speak of the "other" is to be open to otherness within myself, to the possibility of a foreigner within my own unconscious self.

To speak of the "other" is to speak of poverty and injustice, sexuality and gender, race and class. To speak of the "other" is to acknowledge that difference is problematic—often threatening, even alienating—and that we do not always live easily or well with it.

To speak about difference and otherness is to speak about the nature of the church, the body of many parts called to be one in Jesus Christ. To speak of the Other is to speak about God, the One who is Wholly Other and yet Wholly Related. The reality of difference will not go away, neither should it. It is who we are. But here is a fundamental paradox: human beings have countless differences, yet we all have equal worth and dignity because we are all created in the image and likeness of God. We are called to live in the fullness of our humanity within the reality of difference and otherness. Contemporary theologians will hopefully explore an ethic of relationship both among people and with our natural world.

What do I mean by "relationship"? Alienation or apathy, isolation or separation are clearly inconsistent with being in relationship. Relationship is what connects us to one another and to creation. Relationship is like the strands of a web, spinning out in ever-widening circles, fragile and easily damaged yet filled with tensile strength. Relationships that are mutual shape us as individuals and as members of our communities. We are not made to live alone.

Martin Buber, the Jewish philosopher, says, "In the beginning was relation." Our triune God is a God-in-relation. We worship a Trinity that is in a mutual self-giving relationship. Each one of the divine persons of the Trinity relates to and expresses the presence of the other. In turn, our Trinitarian God desires reciprocal relationship with each one of us, with faith communities, and with the whole of creation. God's desire for relationship offers us the possibility of being-in-relationship with God, ourselves, each other, and all that God has made. This understanding of God-in-relation with humanity permeates the stories in our Scriptures. With the injunction "to love your neighbour as yourself," Jesus teaches us that our neighbour is often the radically other who is also the radically related. Our neighbour has inviolable claims on us to be welcomed as Christ has welcomed us. Perhaps this requires an epiphany?

Hopefully, an epiphany will help us understand that mutual relationship is not just an abstract theological truth. Mutual relationship is practised with our entire being—our bodies, our emotions, and our minds—in what we see, hear, say, and do. The practice of relationship is both profoundly simple and formidably demanding. We are innately relational beings. We are also congenitally antagonistic. Difference becomes threatening and a cause for conflict. The practice of mutual relationship comes when I turn my gaze from myself and "look" into the face of the other. It is you and I, they and we, seeing and being seen. I see the "other" as an authentic human being. We both reflect something of the image of God. The practice of relationship means that I acknowledge that I am not complete unto myself. I am not fully me until I can see "me" in your face. We mirror each other. In my context, the African concept *ubuntu* believes that a solitary human being is a contradiction in terms. As Desmond Tutu says, "We are made for complementarity."

At the moment of truly seeing the other and being seen, surprised, and illuminated, I am converted to relatedness, and I hope that the other chooses to be in relationship with me. Then, and only then, do I begin to fathom the claims of justice and love that are made on me by the hungry child, the abused woman, the refugee on a dusty road, those whose race or gender or sexuality differ from mine, whose ideologies are not mine, whose religion is not mine, whose community is at odds with mine. Relationship needs to be reciprocal for the healing we seek.

The phrase "being fully human" sounds like a pipe dream, something unattainable. And in a certain sense, it is. Not one of us will achieve our full humanity in this life. Only Jesus Christ was fully and perfectly human. But, and this is a big *but*, we are called by the Spirit of God to dedicate ourselves in all we believe, do, and pray to become what God intends us to be—fully human. One of my favourite theologians, Karl Rahner, reminds us that every statement about God is a statement about humanity. He believes that in essence, the call to live towards our full humanity is a call to be bearers of the image of our God. So here is my plea: Can "young" theologians reflect afresh on how relationship is necessary for human flourishing—and indeed, for the healing of our world?

Theologians are called to engage with the nature of hope. Francine Cardman, friend and church historian, writes, "Hope is an elusive virtue, whether theological or practical. It calls us, draws us on, fades into shadows, dies. It bears us up and lets us down. It disappoints and it emboldens."[2] Hope is an enigma. It is a theological challenge we dare not ignore.

First of all, hope is not optimism or wish fulfilment. Theologically speaking, we hope in things not seen and yet to come. Hope is a matter of faith. Practically, it is to grasp and then act on the belief that where there is despair or injustice, circumstances can be transformed. It is to hold a vision of what is possible. Hope is both creative and expectant. So we act in such a way that what we hope for may just come about. There is no way of escaping the truth that the way we hope should be the way we live. As Brazilian theologian and philosopher Ruben Alves says, "Hope is hearing the melody of the future. Faith is to dance it." The dance is now.

Second, to hope is to risk. There are no guarantees. We will not achieve peace, right relationships, or the ability to live fruitfully with difference if we are not prepared to risk. We will risk failure, having doors shut in our faces, rejection, and even ridicule when we try to cross boundaries. We may risk having to face difficult truths about ourselves, such as a lack of courage when we encounter opposition. Voluntary risk is the opposite of fatalism, apathy, resignation, and acceptance of things as they are, but we trust that somewhere in the deepest recesses of the human spirit is the capacity to hope in the face of daunting circumstances. Finding our way through disappointments requires discernment (*diakrisis*), that intentional and self-reflective process that probes both our theological understanding and our innermost longing. Practising discernment teaches us to trust in the power of the Holy Spirit who accompanies us on our journey of faith. Being prepared to wait expectantly is to resist a world that wants instant answers.

Third, given its risky nature, hope requires patience and endurance. As Paul reminds us in his letter to the Romans, "But if we hope for what we do not see, we wait for it with patience" (8:36 ESV). When we risk for God's sake, for love of neighbour, and in the cause of justice, we take a calculated risk that requires patience. When the void of hopelessness threatens to overwhelm us, we need endurance, the power to continue despite setbacks. We may well be surprised and sustained by a "passion for the possible."

Fourth, our spirituality is our most precious tool for holding on to hope. I do not want to impose my spirituality in this letter. I shall assume that we share the desire to see the values of the kingdom of God come on earth "as it is in heaven." I have, however, found that our relationship with our God, our membership of our faith communities, and how we live in prayer and engagement with the Word are the grounds of our hope. We cannot avoid sharing in the suffering of the world, and we will know joy when we are embraced undeservedly by love.

Finally, I cannot resist sharing a few favourite lines by American poet Emily Dickinson:

Hope is the thing with feathers
That perches on the soul,
And sings the tune without the word,
And never stops at all.[3]

May your hope for your theological endeavours, in your world and in your voice, be blessed.

Denise Ackermann

Notes

1 Denise Ackermann, *After the Locusts: Letters from a Landscape of Faith* (Grand Rapids, MI: Eerdmans, 2003).
2 Francine Cardman, "Practicing Hope," in *Healing God's People: Theological and Pastoral Approaches; A Reconciliation Reader*, ed. Thomas A. Kane (New York: Paulist Press, 2013), 215.
3 Emily Dickinson, "'Hope' Is the Thing with Feathers," in *The Poems of Emily Dickinson*, ed. R. W. Franklin (Cambridge, MA: Harvard University Press, 1999).

31

Catherine Keller

It feels like the right time to write this letter. Theology comes into its own in times of crisis: it has resources for any scale and variety of apocalypse. I have always been grateful to work with a public discourse that can rise to the occasion in crises local or global, personal or collective. As I write, a global pandemic surges amid crises of democracy, white supremacism, immigration, and destitution. As you read, the endlessly larger global health crisis of climate change descends upon us. Theology, unlike so many other disciplines, does not mute itself out of a sense of irrelevance. Lively and critical forms of theology meet these menaces with a discourse of responsible meaning and action. But before we can think about theology's responsiveness to crisis, don't we need to pause, pivot, and respond to the crisis of theology itself?

Oh, that.

I tend to want to get on with the creative work, with its meditative and timely demands, and not worry about the long-term viability of theology itself. I have dedicated a life to theology—that is, to a very live practice, to a discourse that surges and moves with waves of social change, with currents of transdisciplinarity. A discourse that makes waves of its own, sweeping up from the depths. The depths of all that is. I have been endlessly surprised by the fresh gifts of ancient metaphors. The vibrancy of theology—pastoral and prophetic—in its resistance to stale orthodoxies and aggressive certitudes has, over and over, taken me off guard, taken me into its mystical darkness as well as its polydox potentiality. I wish that for my students. I wish that for you.

This work, this vibrancy, has presumed a world, a community, in which theology has a home. Once on this journey, I was always able to find a version of church and of academy in which theology is understood to be a necessary voice. So there has been institutional support in some continuity with the ancient history of church-related academies. The engagement of theology in many secular institutions committed to the study of religion also continues to bear fruit. Yet religion departments—nervous about confessional bias, uncritical belief, or offense to secularist sensibility—can rarely provide a home for theologians. As a live process and not just an object of analysis, theology has continued to depend on institutions widely varying but with historic roots in the education of clergy.

There is, at this time, no way to be confident in the future of such theologically hospitable institutions. One cannot altogether avoid the statistical trends: decade after decade, the stately processional of established religions toward demise marches on. The richly endowed elite of theological schools may persist indefinitely, as may the most reactionary: these do not provide any likelihood of livelihood for any young theologian reading this letter. This murky prospect of professional insecurity must be spoken. I have tried to remind myself to say it to prospective PhD students in theology for many years—not to advise against the study of theology but to encourage them to undertake it with mindfulness of the professional improvisation such uncertainty may entail, to cultivate flexibility in formal self-descriptions (you may be a theologian, a philosopher, and/or a scholar of religion, depending on context), and to keep vocational options diversified (forms of teaching and ministry can extensively and practically intersect). Fortunately, that versatility may express not just a pragmatic ploy but the dimensionality of theology at its best. And in the honesty and humility of its calling.

So, then, I also want to say that theology has often faced its own fragility. It did for me, and I seem to have thrived in certain margins, to have grown from the unknown. The kind of theology I needed to do wanted radical transformation, not stable tradition. And vastly much transformation did happen, swiftly, rising on the tides of movements against sexism, racism, heterosexism, classism, ecological suicide—movements witnessing to an originative spirit of the prophets, of the Gospels. To the Spirit of creation itself. And this destabilizing creativity has in many cases strengthened the attractive power not just of theology but of the schools and churches enlivened by such ethical metamorphosis. Are these forerunners or mere exceptions? The statistics of institutional religious weakness, not unlike those of climate change, just keep worsening. They cannot predict definite outcomes, but they do portend defining dangers.

The language for the deep stakes of this threat to theology itself is hardly new. It finds clearest voice in the tradition of "the death of God." For, of course, what else does the dimming of the institutions and discourses of *theos logos* mean? It is the *theos* of these institutions, the God whose churches are failing—in mainline fade-out or conservative overkill—who fails with them. The prophet of the death of God, Friedrich Nietzsche, was not recommending but recognizing this death. Declaring that it is "we who have killed him," he was anticipating the dire consequences of such metaphysical violence. Nietzsche's contemporary and friend for a time, Richard Wagner, narrated this death in the final opera of the *Ring of the Niebelungen: The Twilight of the Gods*. He cloaked the demise of gods and their human creations in the ancient Norse myth of Ragnarok. The hearer celebrates with Brunhilde the death of the divine and human patriarchs who betrayed her. The twilight of *those* gods, *those* guys, becomes the climax of history.

And it is tempting to read the death of God in the light, the twilight, of those nineteenth-century visions. A death of *His* institutionalized apparatus, *His* sputtering omnipotence, *His* absorption of the power projections of two millennia of Western Civilization. But I do not read them as the death of all possible faces of divinity, facets of God, and so of any plausible *logos* of *theos*. That "death of God" may have been, may still be, sine qua non of some improbable resurrection.

Still. Truth be told, you young theologian, for all its modernist iconoclasm, the death of God always felt *old* to me. Its theological prophet, Thomas Altizer, was a member of a church I attended at age thirteen. I saw the *Time* magazine cover *Is God Dead?* at my local drugstore in 1966. When, decades later, I found myself teaching at Drew's Theological School, I learned of Altizer's participation in 1960s conferences there, openly discussing that death among many hermeneutical options for greater theological honesty. Again, this all felt interesting but old—like a brave, brilliant, but faded white male drama.

I did and do not celebrate the death of "His" institutions, only of their deadened and deadening patrimony. I have never done theology outside of the liveliness of an alternative. Beyond the secularizing dregs of the Enlightenment lurks still the possibility of an Age of Enlivenment . . .

It will not be predicated upon the atheism signaled by God's death, even if undersigned by radical theology. Nor will it come down to a reprise of some older theism. There are many verbal clues to the possibility, none of them quite satisfactory, all capturing some hint of ancient and coming theophany. It comes in all the colors and sexes and species of a liberating theology, even of a God-saturated cosmology of all that is. That All whispers the mystery of an unspeakability of "God"—an ancient apophasis, a knowing that you do not know. Its darkness shines upon so many ways—intersecting and diverging, sometimes brusquely, from each other—to open theology experimentally into its future. For me, the way of a process theology was crucial, sometimes called a panentheism—all-in-God. That One in whom "we live and breathe and have our being" (Acts 17:28; my translation). In its theological breathing, that process tunes to its Nazarene materialization of revolutionary love. And to a Word embodied in all creatures, peoples, ways . . .

And so there come clues from every other spiritual path—Abrahamic, Asian, or Indigenous—not blurring together but differentiating that All. Clues may come from ancient orthodoxies, for which "God became human so that the human can become God." Or from an old heretical pantheism, or a fresher pantheology, or from anatheism, a postmodern "God after God." These are all lacking the dogmatism of straight theism or atheism. And by the way, they all lend ways of honoring, not repressing, your sometimes deep-down doubt. Your uncertainty about the existence of God & Co. These clues at the same time keep you mindful of the intuitions, breaths, and glimpses you get of the meaning of it All—meaning here, now, on the ground.

Meaning, however, does not reduce to knowing. The meaning-fullness of asking the Big Questions does not put an end to your quest. The fullness will not harden into final Answers. It wants testing, realizing, actualizing—and altering. And so you permit theological constructions to ripen in you. For if theology is to live, it will be as a constructive art. "Constructive theology" (a twentieth-century evolution of the eighteenth-century term "systematic theology") does not make God up. It does not fabricate a deity ex nihilo—or out of fear of nihilism. But it takes responsibility for the human, contextual, effect- and affect-rich work of theological language. It knows itself as the work of imagination and practice, of aesthetics and ethics, of tradition and of novelty. It may even imagine that something very like what we still call God takes some unknowable part in the construction . . .

But in the meantime, the fragile institutions that host such conversations keep growing—more fragile. Without them, who will facilitate these new waves of iconoclasm and of multiple icons? Who will teach the skills of theological history and debate that enable effectual reformation of our religious bodies and transformation of our world bodies? These bodies, collectives theological and planetary, are ailing. They are in crisis.

Strangely, they are ailing together. Worlds of religion and the bigger worlds they inhabit: social, political, and ultimately, ecological worlds. Yet any honest theology knows itself interconnected with those bigger worlds and responsible to them. These are not just parallel but entangled fragilities. So, then, is there perhaps some advantage, some dark grace, in this togetherness? Can the fragility of our God-talk help us address—with the courage of an honesty born of grief, of losses already suffered and losses to come—the fragility of our larger worlds? Of our shared Earth?

We do not know the future of theology or of the Earth. Yet we may be confident that some form of theology, even if it would seem unrecognizable to us now, will come to be. Perhaps it is becoming already, there in the margins of our uncertainty, our struggle, our hope. We cannot guarantee a future of a particular form of ecclesia, of religious gathering or of teaching.

We *can* work to make sure that no matter what, in whatever materialization, the best of theology—the most just, the most loving, the most All-embracing—will persist in forms that we cannot predict, that we might not even recognize. And this counts because it lets our present breathe the open future. To live fully in the present, to wrestle with its challenges, means to affect possible futures.

So it is with the earth, now, when we do not know what futures are possible for our species. The ghost of human extinction sits on the horizon. Or—not much better—the specter looms of some small percent of humans, likely of the same class and race whose economy brought on climate change, surviving in some bubble at the expense of the rest. I won't indulge here in apocalyptic prognostications—except to remind us that *apokalypsis* does *not* mean "The End of the World." It means the "unveiling"—therefore, "revealing"—of our civilization's pattern of destruction, ultimately suicidal, and of the possibility of transformation. Disclosure, not closure.

Christian misreadings of apocalypse have set up a predetermined movement from a beginning point, through a Christ climax, on to The End. That linearity takes overt fundamentalist forms; it takes subliminal secular forms. So as a theologian, I have found little more important than deconstructing that destructive timeline—and reconstructing the time of creation as an open creative process.[1] The *theos* of such a *logos*, such a

Word, calls us to make the best possible choices. Us singly and together. To choose the better possibility in, say, the case of climate change will not mean returning to some prior norm or normalcy. Yet we humans may still choose to alter the relentless course of ecosocial destruction. To get on course for a world of revitalized and reconfigured local communities vibrant with solidarity, across and within the life of the earth. And as theologians, we must keep repeating the following: humans cannot make that choice if we hold out for an omnipotent solution—either by supernatural intervention or supersecular technofix.

Your life and work, dear young theologian, will matter, not in spite of the crisis of theology and of its material world, but because of it. Our critical vulnerabilities may sometimes feel weak, impotent. Yet in that very vulnerability, that opening, might a small seed of potentiality—sown so freely—be germinating?

Catherine Keller

Note

1 See my *Facing Apocalypse: Climate, Democracy and Other Last Chances* (New York: Orbis, 2021).

32

John de Gruchy

I have been asked to write a letter to "young theologians," but I have found it difficult to do so without thinking about some of the young, and now not so young, theologians whom I have had the pleasure of teaching over the years. So I have chosen to write to you by name—Malinge, Lyn, Steve, David, Thabo—and have your faces in front of me, even though as I write, you may well be wearing a mask to keep Covid-19 away. I do so because theology is a very personal matter; it is a calling, not a profession. It may be a necessary subject to study to become a minister or a priest, but it is far more than that, and not all my students, among them some of you, have been ordained. Indeed, sadly, some ministers and priests I know do not have much interest in theology, and I think that is because they don't exactly know what it is other than a subject to study to get a diploma or degree. How sad that is! They have missed out on one of the most exciting and challenging pursuits there is. They have never developed the passion for the subject such as you have had ever since you started studying.

As you know, theology is far more than a subject to study in order to get a job; it is about the mystery of the universe, the mystery of life, the mystery of who we are and what we are doing on this planet earth. It is looking at the sun, moon, and stars and wondering what it is all about. Every person who begins to ask and explore such questions is already in the process of becoming a theologian. For theology is all about "being led into mystery," as Karl Rahner once put it. And only those who are passionate about this journey, a lifelong journey, will really become good theologians. If you are not someone who marvels at the stars on a dark night or the beauty of a flower and majesty of a bird or is deeply moved by some haunting melody, then you have not really begun to know what theology is about. Such stargazing or studying theology might not open many doors for you to get employment, though I know it has opened a door or two for some of you about which I am delighted. But it is not the reason why you have been and remain a student of theology. If it were, you would have given up long ago.

So I write to you by name and you will recognise who you are, as will some of the others who were part of my graduate seminar at one time, loosely known as the "Bonhoeffer Circle." But in writing to you by name, I am also writing to them all, and to all would-be theologians who are already theologians simply because they really want to be. This letter is meant for them as well, as it is for whoever wants to be a theologian today elsewhere whose names I do not know.

What a privilege it is to write to you all, because I have been passionate about theology for the past sixty years and more—indeed, ever since I became a Christian one starry night and started to try to understand what that has meant for others and could mean for me as well. Yes, indeed, theology is being on a journey into the mystery of life and therefore trying to understand that journey better. If it were only a journey into mystery, a journey into the "cloud of unknowing," then it would be better described as mysticism. Of course, every true theologian is something of a mystic because "knowing God" cannot be reduced to a syllogism or two. It is entering through the narrow gate that leads us to know the One "in whom we live, move and have our being." Yes, theology is all about getting to know God! And Christian theology, and that is what we are all engaged in, is knowing the God who we believe is revealed in Jesus Christ. Once you say that, then you immediately begin to discover why theology is a journey of "faith seeking understanding," as Anselm has taught us.

Now I am beginning to drop names (Rahner and Anselm, and I have not yet come to Bonhoeffer), but I do so because I am aware that in studying theology, we engage with other persons, theologians from long ago— for theology has been part of the human story from the beginning—and from times closer to our own time. For theology is not only about "knowing God," it is that above all else, but it is about a conversation with others who are on the same passionate journey and who are only too willing to share their insight with us. People who we love to read, people who we enjoy talking to, and people about whom we write essays and dissertations. If it were only us chosen few who were passionate about theology, we might conclude that we are barking up the wrong tree. But as we "get into theology," we soon discover that there are others who are passionate about the subject as well. Indeed, many others have been engaged in the task over the centuries. And part of the joy in studying theology is to discover them and learn from what they have said.

Yes, among the names of the noble army of martyrs and the great company of saints are also the names of great theologians. In studying their theologies, we also get to know them as persons, and we even read biographies and autobiographies to get to do so. We not only want to understand what they wrote or said; we want to know who they are and why they wrote or said what they did. That is also why we attend seminars and conferences, for how exciting it is to come face-to-face with others who share our passion and engage them in conversation. And how wonderful it is when these conversations evolve into theological friendships. That, of course, is part of the joy of teaching theology, for in the process, students become friends and colleagues, and we learn from each other because we are all on the same journey, and we need each other to find the way forward. I certainly have learnt much from students like you, and I continue to do so.

Being on the "journey into mystery" in company with others who share the same passion is like being on a pilgrimage, such as that described by Chaucer or the modern-day Santiago or its equivalents—for there is one here in the Western Cape that goes through Volmoed. As pilgrims on this shared journey, we not only help each other find the way, but we also begin to discover who we are. For our knowledge of God and our knowledge of ourselves is inseparable, as Calvin tells us at the beginning of his *Institutes*.[1] Oh, dear, there I go again dropping names, and so far they have all been white males. That tells me something about myself. But it also is a reminder that doing theology is, and must be, inclusive because those we meet on the pilgrimage are not all the same as we are. And thank God that is so. For if we only listen to and engage with people like ourselves, doing theology would become very boring. That is certainly my experience. In fact, it is often the case that when I enter into conversation with "the other" theologian—whether the other is defined by gender and sexuality, by race and ethnicity, by faith tradition and denomination—I suddenly see things differently and break out of the theological box that I have constructed. If that does not happen, theology will remain a comfortable "talking shop," not a shared journey, indeed, a shared struggle into mystery.

Which brings me to my final paragraphs, for this letter is already far too long. Studying theology is one thing; it can be passionate and personal, and it can be exciting and sobering, but doing theology takes us a step beyond studying, a critical step. We really start doing theology when we move beyond talking about going on a pilgrimage and start walking along the road. And we do that when we live life theologically; that is why Barth tells us to read the Bible and the newspaper at the same time. Theology is and must always be a reflective praxis, a way of engaging reality, and a way of seeing reality differently—a guide to changing reality. Some of the best (maybe all of the best) theology has originated when theologians have engaged in the struggle for a more just and peaceful world; or engaged with people who are suffering, whether from cancer or poverty; or simply engaged with students setting out on life who are beginning to get personal and passionate about studying theology. And they do so because they suddenly discover that this is all about the journey into that ultimate mystery that gives meaning to life.

I end with one final thought: don't forget that doing theology is always both a journey backwards and forwards. We cannot do serious theology if we do not always go back to the sources of our faith. "Back to the Bible" should be, for us, more than a slogan we use to prove a point. It is recognising that the faith we are seeking to understand has its roots in a journey that began a very time ago when someone called Abraham set out from his comfort zone in search of a place where he could be at home. It is, indeed, the journey home of the prodigal who is dissatisfied with life as it is and is wanting to discover what it means to live life differently. It is a journey that paradoxically entered through a narrow gate but then opens up broad perspectives that help us embrace life in all its fullness. As Bonhoeffer (at last I have got to him) said, we need to hold fast to the *cantus firmus* that Jesus Christ provides in order to discover the polyphony of life.

Your friend, colleague, and sometime mentor,
John de Gruchy
Hermanus

Note

1 John Calvin, *Institutes of the Christian Religion*, trans. Henry Beveridge (Peabody, MA: Hendrickson, 2008).

33

Michael Mawson

In mid-1933, following Adolf Hitler's appointment as chancellor and the beginnings of the takeover of the Protestant churches, Dietrich Bonhoeffer composed a short essay for his students, "What Should a Student of Theology Do Today?" Much of this essay straightforwardly reflects upon the nature of theological study as well as the temptations besetting young students eager to prove themselves through their studies. At various points, however, he makes reference to the wider crisis engulfing church and academy: "One must learn to recognise where and when the church of Christ reaches the hour of its decision, when it is time for confession—the *status confessionis*."[1] In light of the challenges of this new situation, the student must learn to discern when and how to take a stand.

One way of reading Bonhoeffer's essay is as a reflection on how theological study supports and sustains Christian witness during difficult times. How can study help Christians find a way forward, to remain faithful to Christ's call in the midst of things? In particular, Bonhoeffer proposes going back to the basics: "One should, in such times of confusion, go back the very beginning, to our wellsprings, to the true Bible, to the true Luther."[2] In times of crisis and confusion, the student should return to Scripture and to those voices from the tradition that remain close to Scripture: "the company of honest theologians from Paul to Augustine, from Thomas to Luther."[3]

As is well known, Bonhoeffer himself sought to follow Christ faithfully during the next decade under National Socialism. His theological education and commitments were central to how he made sense of this evolving context and what it required: assisting with the formation of the Confessing Church, pursuing peace through ecumenical activities, and running an illegal seminary in Finkenwalde as well as his conspiratorial involvement in the plot to assassinate Hitler. Bonhoeffer's theological commitments were central to his ability to adapt, to reassess and relinquish previously held assumptions and positions, and to be open to following Christ in new and unexpected ways.

Almost a century later, we too are in a situation of crisis. In 2020, the extent of the challenges that are confronting us became especially apparent. In Australia, for example, the year began with a series of bushfires that destroyed homes and livelihoods, devastating many rural communities. In New South Wales, fires consumed 5.22 million hectares of bushland. Estimates indicate that more than a billion animals, birds, and reptiles perished, including many from endangered species.[4] These bushfires, of course, were just a symptom of wider processes of anthropogenic climate change. Unless these processes are arrested and reversed, the continued existence of human beings is uncertain.[5]

This same year, a global pandemic swept the world. As well as its direct impact through illness and loss of life, the wider effects of Covid-19 have been catastrophic. Attempts to respond through closing national borders, implementing social distancing and lockdowns, and shutting down schools and businesses have interrupted every aspect of life.[6] Statistics suggest that rates of depression and mental illness have skyrocketed during the pandemic.[7] Many countries have documented escalating levels of violence and domestic abuse.[8] And incidents of suicide have similarly increased.[9] During and after the pandemic, large numbers of people are facing unemployment and financial insecurity. The virus has also exposed the deep inequities already present in our societies, disproportionately affecting people of colour, women,[10] those without access to health care, and those without the freedom to work remotely and in safety.

On May 25, 2020, the killing of George Floyd in Minneapolis, Minnesota, gave renewed focus to problems of systemic racism in the United States and beyond. Floyd became the latest in a long list of African Americans killed while in police custody. When the graphic footage circulated of an officer kneeling on Floyd's neck—for seven minutes and forty-seven seconds while he cried out repeatedly, "I can't breathe"—protesters began gathering to call for recognition and justice. These largely peaceful protests have remained ongoing, with Black Lives Matter and other groups drawing attention to the plight of Black and Indigenous lives.[11]

We will be grappling with these crises and the realities they represent well into the foreseeable future.[12] The fallout from Covid-19 alone will likely take years to assess. And political leaders and regimes have also begun taking advantage of these crises to consolidate power and advance their agendas.[13] The world as we know it has changed. And Christians must again be prepared to discern when and how to declare a *status confessionis*.[14]

What should a student of theology do today?[15]

Before even addressing this question, we should consider whether anyone should be devoting time and resources to theological study. This should remain an open question. Those who are beginning theological study do so today without any real prospect of stable employment or advancement. And this is especially the case for those committing to the slow and painful work of advanced research. For many of us, there may be better ways of following Christ and responding to the current situation.

Those of us who do continue should, like Bonhoeffer's students, be wary of several temptations. First of all, theological study can easily become a means of simply avoiding the crises and challenges that surround us. Theology can become a means of retreating into speculation or abstraction, of exchanging the concerns of the present for an idealised vision of the past.[16] As Bonhoeffer sympathetically notes in a lecture contemporaneous with his essay, "When life begins to be difficult and oppressive, one leaps boldly into the air and soars, relieved and worry free, in the so-called eternal realm."[17] If one continues with studies and research, this must be in a way that eventually presses back into the world and the present challenges.

To be clear, this is not to suggest that study and research should at every moment be directly orientated to and by a given issue. The work of faithfully understanding and responding to the present situation may at times require long excurses into unfamiliar territory. Unravelling the anthropological assumptions underlying and contributing to climate change, for example, may involve closely reading and grappling with figures such as Karl Barth or Maximus the Confessor.[18] Alternatively, as Willie Jennings has shown, understanding the logics of race and racism as well as how such logics keep Christians separated from one another may require attending to fifteenth- and sixteenth-century figures such as Gomes Eanes de Azurara or José de Acosta.[19]

Similarly, if theological study is to assist with faithfully following God and responding to the world, this may require convoluted and indirect ways of speaking and writing. Judith Butler has drawn attention to how familiar, commonsense language too often serves the status quo: "Why are some of the most trenchant social criticisms often expressed through difficult and demanding language?"[20] If theological study is to aid in responding to these challenges in all their complexity and to help us begin to see and act otherwise and differently, this will require pressing beyond the utilitarian language that is prevalent in our churches and societies. Following God into the unknown will require complex and nuanced patterns of thinking and speaking. We should resist the temptation to think that theology can always be done in ways that are straightforward and accessible.[21]

In addition, those who proceed with studying theology should be alert to certain institutional pressures. At this time of economic rationalisation, with universities cutting funding and shedding staff, there is a temptation to pursue only projects that make a clear and positive contribution to our churches and societies. Increasingly, theology is being promoted and defended for its ability to build resilience, promote flourishing, or contribute to the common good.[22] If such justifications are at times expedient and even necessary, they can begin to direct our efforts away from more risky and critical ventures.[23]

Finally, pressure in the form of global rankings and research frameworks can tempt institutions to value "internationally recognised" research at the expense of local and situated forms of engagement. This is a particular challenge for those of us studying and working in the antipodes.[24] As Mark Brett has recently suggested, "We need a deliberate strategy to link international research to local interests and to local understandings of shalom/salaam. As part of that strategy, it will be necessary to deconstruct the hierarchy that currently separates elite, internationally recognised scholarship from lower-status efforts that reflect community engagement in a local context."[25]

What should a student of theology do today?

How can theological study proceed in a way that remains alert to these temptations? In his short essay, Bonhoeffer provides us with some guidance. In particular, he suggests that genuine theological study proceeds only from the cross: "The real study of *theologia sacra* begins when, in the midst of questioning and seeking, human beings encounter the cross; when they recognize the endpoint of all their own passions in the suffering of God at the hands of humankind, and realize that their entire vitality stands under judgment."[26] That all Christian theology ultimately proceeds from the cross and attends to Scripture and other voices in their witness to the cross has implications for how we understand and pursue the work of theology.

First, the cross has significance for the *disposition* of those studying theology. The cross makes clear that theological study is not simply and primarily about our own efforts and abilities but about allowing our thinking to be interrupted and shaped from without. As students of the cross, we are called to engage Scripture and other voices in ways that keep the encounter with Christ at the centre. Among other things, this means that we should proceed without a view to mastery, without needing to know at the outset where we are being led. Similarly, the cross frees us to hold lightly our cherished commitments and conclusions, recognising that these stand under God's judgment.[27] And for those of us accustomed to a level of privilege and control, the cross disposes us to begin surrendering power and making room for others.[28]

Second, the cross has implications for *how we approach and engage Scripture.*[29] Specifically, it frees us from needing to understand Scripture simply as a deposit of divine wisdom or truth, something we from our side must take possession of, interpret, and make our own. In other words, studying theology does not primarily involve deriving dogmatic truths or moral principles *from* Scripture.[30] Rather, as students of the cross, we are free for more fluid and open-ended styles of engagement and immersion, ones that remain closer to the irreducibility of the diverse biblical texts and forms, thereby allowing ourselves to be formed by these texts in their witness to Christ.[31]

Third, the cross has implications for what we should be *reading beyond Scripture.* (On this point, Bonhoeffer's "company of honest theologians" is in need of a little expansion.[32]) If the pluriformity of Scripture testifies to the diverse ways God is present and at work in the world, the particularity and scandal of the cross lend priority to disruptive and confronting voices. While as students and theologians we should read widely, in and beyond theology, we should pay particular attention to voices challenging and destabilising assumptions and norms.[33] In light of our current situation and crises—to update Karl Barth just a little[34]—we should "read with the Bible in one hand" and with the prophetic speeches of Greta Thunberg or Kimberly Jones in the other.[35]

On this question of reading, I have found Stephen Lim's idea of "reading from elsewhere" to be salutary. Engaging the Malay (Muslim) poet and writer Alfian Sa'at, Lim has shown how reading Scripture in dialogue with marginal voices can disrupt and displace "objectivist desires of reading from *nowhere*" and "nativist inclinations of reading from *here*."[36] Such an approach, he reflects, "has at the very least edged me out of my comfort zone to re-read the text [of Daniel 1] as an ambivalent one rather than the superficial triumphalistic message that it most probably is trying to project."[37] Attending to particular voices from elsewhere can open up Scripture and press us into the world in richer and deeper ways.

Fourth, the cross also has implications for *theological writing*. As mentioned previously, following God into the unknown will at times involve complex and indirect forms of writings. As students and theologians, we are of course required at times to adopt set forms and conventions. Nonetheless, we should still be prepared to write in ways that are riskier, that run closer to the ground. On the one hand, this may involve writing in ways that stay close to the poetical, performative language and forms displayed by various biblical texts. On the other hand, it may involve kinds of writing that expose the hybridity and fluidity at the heart of all language, that attend to how the very ruptures, limits, and spaces of language can be places of God's presence.[38]

Finally, all of this means that as students and theologians, we need not fear or withdraw from the challenges confronting us. As Amy Laura Hall has reflected,[39] "Jesus' suffering invites his followers powerfully to refuse a cautious, calculated distance from suffering." And "those who follow Jesus," she continues, do not "run in the other direction or distract ourselves from the misery of domination of people around us."[40] If all Christian theology is ultimately oriented to and by Jesus's suffering, then in our studies and lives, we are free to acknowledge suffering and confront the domination that surrounds us.

And this is because the cross gives us grounds for hope. As students and theologians, we hold in faith that suffering and crisis do not have the final word. James Cone has profoundly articulated the nature of this hope when reflecting on Black experience in the United States: "Christ crucified manifested God's loving and liberating presence *in* the contradictions of black life—that transcendent presence in the lives of black Christians that empowered them to believe that *ultimately*, in God's eschatological future, they would not be defeated by the 'trouble of this world.'"[41] For

Christians, God's presence and work on the cross remind us that God comes to and encounters us in the midst of contradiction. They remind us that ultimately, those who suffer now will one day be redeemed. Accordingly, in light of our current situation and pressing challenges, and to quote Bonhoeffer's final words in his essay, "one should keep on, ever more undaunted and joyfully, becoming a theologian ἀληθεύοντες δὲ ἐν ἀγάπῃ [speaking the truth in love, Eph 4:15]."[42]

Michael Mawson

Notes

1 Dietrich Bonhoeffer, "What Should a Student of Theology Do Today?," in *Berlin: 1932–1933; Dietrich Bonhoeffer Works*, English ed., ed. Larry Rasmussen, trans. Isabelle Best and David Higgins (Minneapolis: Fortress, 2009), 434.

2 Bonhoeffer, 435.

3 Bonhoeffer, 433.

4 "Have More Than a Billion Animals Perished Nationwide This Bushfire Season? Here Are the Facts," RMIT ABC Fact Check, January 30, 2020, https://www.abc.net.au/news/2020-01-31/fact-check-have-bushfires -killed-more-than-a-billion-animals/11912538.

5 See Clive Hamilton, *Defiant Earth: The Fate of Humans in the Anthropocene* (Crows Nest, Australia: Allen & Unwin, 2017).

6 See, for example, Ed Yong, "How the Virus Defeated America," *Atlantic*, August 4, 2020.

7 For example, see Rachel Schraer, "Depression Doubles during Coronavirus Pandemic," BBC News, August 18, 2020, https://www.bbc.com/ news/health-53820425.

8 For example, see Australian Associated Press, "'Alarming but Not Unexpected': Increase in Domestic Violence in NSW during Covid-19 Crisis," *Guardian*, June 4, 2020, https://www.theguardian.com/society/ 2020/jun/04/alarming-but-not-unexpected-increase-in-domestic -violence-in-nsw-during-covid-19-crisis.

9 Leo Sher, "The Impact of the COVID-19 Pandemic on Suicide Rates," *QJM: An International Journal of Medicine* 113, no. 10 (October 2020): 707–12, https://doi.org/10.1093/qjmed/hcaa202.

10 On the impact of the virus on women in particular, see Gabrielle Jackson, "How Covid-19 Could Set Back Women by a Generation," August 27, 2020, in *Full Story*, produced by Ellen Leabeater and Laura Murphy-Oates, podcast, https://www.theguardian.com/australia-news/audio/2020/aug/28/how-covid-19-could-set-back-women-by-a-generation.

11 In Sydney, several protests centred around the case of the twenty-six-year-old Aboriginal man David Dungay, who died in Long Bay Jail in 2015. Dungay is reported to have called out "I can't breathe" twelve times while being restrained by guards, none of whom faced any disciplinary action.

12 While I've chosen to highlight these three examples from 2020, there are obviously other crises with which we need to continue to wrestle, including realities highlighted by the MeToo movement.

13 Timothy McLaughlin, "Where the Virus Is Cover for Authoritarianism," *Atlantic*, August 25, 2020. McLaughlin's examples include Hong Kong, Thailand, Algeria, Hungary, and Israel.

14 While Bonhoeffer uses *status confessionis* to refer to how confessing Christians need to break with the established church, I am using it a little more expansively.

15 I have in mind here students in the formal sense, but also all of us who pursue theological study as a central part of our activity.

16 This accusation has often been levelled at the Radical Orthodoxy movement. For example, see Douglas Hedley's review of John Milbank, Catherine Pitstock, and Graham Ward, eds., *Radical Orthodoxy: A New Theology* (Routledge 1999) in *Journal of Theological Studies* 51, no. 1 (2000): 405–8.

17 Dietrich Bonhoeffer, "Thy Kingdom Come: The Prayer of the Church-Community God's Kingdom on Earth," in *Berlin: 1932–1933; Dietrich Bonhoeffer Works*, English ed., ed. Larry Rasmussen, trans. Isabelle Best and David Higgins (Minneapolis: Fortress, 2009), 286.

18 I have in mind here Willis Jenkins's *Ecologies of Grace: Environmental Ethics and Christian Theology* (Oxford: Oxford University Press, 2013), esp. 154–206.

19 Willie Jennings, *The Christian Imagination: Theology and the Origins of Race* (New Haven, CT: Yale University Press, 2010).

20 See Judith Butler, "A Bad Writer Bites Back," *New York Times*, March 20, 1999. Butler is here responding to her being awarded first prize in the Bad Writing Competition, sponsored by the relatively obscure conservative journal *Philosophy and Literature*.

21 While I'm committed to an understanding of theology as in service to the church, this is a service that must also at times cause discomfort. This is perhaps difficult to accomplish in contexts like Australia, where theological education remains so closely tied to denominational structures and identities.

22 This is perhaps a particular temptation and problem for those of us working in the subdisciplines of Christian ethics and public theology. These framings can too quickly come to substitute and displace language that runs closer to both Scripture and the complexity and messiness of lived existence.

23 My concern relates to how these framings can begin to locate theological study within horizons that have already been set. Can we really know at the outset what resilience, flourishing, or the common good even are? Do these framings limit an openness to how theology should more radically disrupt and reconfigure general notions of what resilience or flourishing entail?

24 Especially in New Zealand and Australia, far too much time and attention is given to trying to replicate the kind of work being done in elite northern hemisphere institutions.

25 Mark G. Brett, "Past and Future of Biblical Studies in Australia," *Australian Biblical Review* 67 (2019): 96.

26 Bonhoeffer, "What Should a Student," 433.

27 And for many of us, theological study should take the form of acknowledgement of guilt and repentance. For a recent example of this, see Ross Halbach, *Bonhoeffer and the Racialized Church* (Waco, TX: Baylor University Press, 2000). See also Jenny McBride, *The Church for the World: A Theology of Public Witness* (New York: Oxford University Press, 2014).

28 There have, of course, been important critiques of this kind of *kenotic* divestment by feminist theologians and others, as well as more recent attempts to recover and reframe *kenosis*. For example, see Sarah Coakley, "*Kenosis* and Subversion: On the Repression of 'Vulnerability' in Christian Feminist Writing," in *Powers and Submissions: Spirituality* (Oxford: Wiley-Blackwell, 2002), 3–39.

29 I've explored some of these ways of thinking about Scripture in more detail elsewhere. See Mawson, "Scripture," in *The Oxford Handbook of Dietrich Bonhoeffer*, ed. Michael Mawson and Philip Ziegler (Oxford: Oxford University Press, 2019), 123–36.

30 Or at least, this should not be our primary posture with respect to the text.

31 We can see examples of this kind of fluid, immersive engagement in Bonhoeffer's *Creation and Fall* (Minneapolis: Fortress, 1997) and in Martin Luther's expositional theology. For a reading of Luther along these lines, see Brian Brock, *Singing the Ethos of God: On the Place of Christian Ethics in Scripture* (Grand Rapids, MI: Eerdmans, 2007), esp. chaps. 5 and 7. For a different kind of example of this immersive approach, see Jione Havea's recent *Jonah: An Earth Bible Commentary* (London: T&T Clark, 2020).

32 As quoted previously. Bonhoeffer, "What Should a Student," 433.

33 To be clear, it is not that disruptive or destabilising voices have priority in and of themselves. Rather, as Christians, those who see the world through the cross, we are able to attend to such voices as a place that God is encountering and challenges us.

34 While Barth is often attributed with saying that "one should read the Bible in one hand and the newspaper in the other," this has not, in fact, been substantiated.

35 I have in mind here Greta Thunberg's 2019 speech to the United Nations, "Watch: Greta Thunberg's Full Speech to World Leaders at UN Climate Action Summit," PBS NewsHour, September 23, 2019, https://www.youtube.com/watch?v=KAJsdgTPJpU. See also Kimberly Jones's speech in Atlanta in June 2020, "How Can We Win Kimberly Jones Video Full Length David Jones Media Clean Edit #BLM 2020 What Can I Do," CARJAM TV, June 9, 2020, https://www.youtube.com/watch?v=llci8MVh8J4.

36 Stephen Chin Ming Lim, "The Impe(/a)rative of Dialogue in Asian Hermeneutics within the Modern/Colonial World System: Renegotiating Biblical Pasts for Planetary Futures," *Biblical Interpretation* 25 (2017): 663.

37 Lim, 676. See also Stephen Chin Ming Lim, *Contextual Biblical Hermeneutics as Multicentric Dialogue: Towards a Singaporean Reading of Daniel* (Leiden: Brill, 2020).

38 Rowan Williams, *The Edge of Words: God and the Habits of Language* (London: Bloomsbury, 2014).

39 Amy Laura Hall's short book, *Laughing at the Devil: Seeing the World with Julian of Norwich* (Durham, NC: Duke University Press, 2018), exemplifies the kind of theological engagement and writing that I have in

mind. In this book, Hall allows Julian of Norwich's complex, vernacular theology to shed light on her own personal experience and contemporary political realities, even while these realities press her into the detail and substance of Julian's text and language.

40 Hall, 87.

41 James Cone, *The Cross and the Lynching Tree* (Maryknoll, NY: Orbis, 2011), 3.

42 Bonhoeffer, "What Should a Student," 435.

34

Douglas F. Ottati

My letter casts us in roles that can make for difficulties. As an advisor, I risk succumbing to inordinate self-assurance and pride. As an advisee, you risk overconfidence in others (most notably, me) as well as too little regard for your own judgments and experiences. But there are also pitfalls of *not* giving and receiving advice. If I refuse to offer, I risk underestimating the importance of speaking to you from my own place and time. I also fail to be your companion in a longer living tradition, neglect my responsibility to participate with you in the activity of "handing-on." If you refuse to seek advice, you risk overconfidence in yourself and your place and time, and you neglect your responsibility to be my companion in a longer living tradition. We therefore find ourselves bound together in a risky enterprise.

But the enterprise has also been a hallmark of the historic Christian community as well as an important part of what it means to be a Christian theologian, and fortunately, there are ways to mitigate the dangers. I may advise with a sense of my limitations and corruptions, realizing that I have gained much from listening to others and hoping that I may yet have opportunities to learn from you. You may listen with a sense for your own limitations and corruptions but also with a reluctance to accept my remarks uncritically. That is, we may try to speak and to listen knowing that we share similar vulnerabilities and that, by the grace of God, each of us stands in a particular place and time with our own judgments and experiences. My Protestantism shows when I say that this is as it should be. To stand in a living tradition means to speak with a keen sense of one's own fallibility and, with a similar awareness, to listen to others attentively and critically. Then our theologizing resembles a continuing conversation.

OK, you are a young Christian theologian, and you intend to participate in a dynamic tradition of conversation and reflection through the ages.

Good. The light shines in the darkness, but both church and world still need a few theologians. So my advice to you is simply this: be a theologian.

Theology, or *logos* of *theos*, means "discourse and reflection about God or the gods"; *Christian* theology is discourse and reflection about the God disclosed in the gospel. Now, in Jesus Christ, *ho theos* is "the God of grace." A Christian theologian should talk about and reflect on this God and therefore also know that the gracious God disclosed in Jesus Christ always already goes out to create and redeem. This is God's gracious tendency or dynamic, and so it makes little sense to talk about and reflect on the God of grace in isolation. Your charge as a Christian theologian, then, is to talk about and reflect on God and all things in relation to God, to talk about and reflect on families, corporations, cultures, governments, seas, mountains, animals, plants, humans, and the wider cosmos in relation to the God of grace. Your task is to indicate how this dynamic relationship with and reference to the divine yields *a distinctive theological view* of all things.

Why? One reason is practical. For people to live faithfully, for them to interact appropriately with the God of grace as they move in the midst of all the many things in the world, they need a vision or a picture of how they and all of the things with which they interact are related to God and God's purposes. Christian theology is the reflective enterprise that constructs this picture, and in this sense, it is reflection in the service of the faithful formation of the people of God, or of the church's pastoral aim. Here we begin to see how Christian theology and ministry interconnect. There is no Christian ministry without a theological vision and no Christian theological vision that doesn't suggest a direction in ministry.

I hope that for you, doing theology is or becomes a way of faithfully acknowledging and praising God and so has a kind of compelling, even intrinsic interest. But the world and the church do not always value genuine theological discourse and reflection, and sometimes they will suggest that you do something else more to their liking. Both also may offer you incentives to do so or, what historically has been more likely, incentives to press your theological talk and reflection into the service of other causes, ends, or goals.

It may happen like this: As a theologian, you will reflect on the histories, promises, and perils of movements and institutions as well as on the theological and moral arguments and ideas they engender. You will not limit your inquiries to practices, movements, and ideas generated by Christian communities precisely because you intend to reflect on the universal God who always already stands in relation to all. And you will engage in and also enjoy these wide-ranging reflections in order to formulate a normative vision or picture of life in relation to this God of grace, a picture that may help you faithfully engage your own place and time. But a number of culturally respected institutions—say, of scholarship or of higher learning—may encourage you to relinquish your constructive reflections in the service of faithful living and instead merely chronicle and compare Christian and/or "religious" movements and ideas. Again, prominent cultural, economic, and political institutions may encourage you to equate faithful devotion to the God of grace with the pursuit of commercial success, with bolstering the glory of the nation, or with making a case for the superiority of one ethnic group over others. The church, when it has been infiltrated by alien devotions such as these, may do the same. Or again, adopting a specifically ecclesiastical mode of corruption, perhaps the church will conclude that its primary cause is not the kingdom of a gracious God, not the increase of love of God and neighbor, but simply the increase and promotion of itself. Then it may require its theologians simply to advance its own truncated orthodoxies and ideas.

If and when these things happen, listen and observe. Monitor the many causes and devotions as well as the directions in life that they engender. Try to understand why they hold the attention and elicit the commitment of persons and communities. Analyze the many causes and devotions in light of the gospel. Engage the preferred utilitarian pieties of your day and learn from them. But don't capitulate. Continue being a Christian theologian. Stick with talking about and reflecting on all things, including education, commerce, politics, and religion, in relation to the God of grace.

I think your "sticking to" will be helped by remembering that the gracious God disclosed in Jesus Christ and in the longer epic of the Scriptures is the God who creates and redeems. God creates and thus graciously bestows existence and life. The world, therefore, is a good gift, and all things have a value or worth in relation to God that does not reduce merely to their utility for us and our communities. Humans are good creatures, endowed with significant and distinctive but also limited capacities. God redeems, and redeeming grace makes use of chronic human misdirection in order to re-turn and renew. Just how is bound up with mysteries of crucifixion and new life, of reconciliation, renewal, and hope beyond tragedy. But the God who redeems refuses to give up on wayward creatures. One thing this means is that people have inalienable worth in relation to the God who creates and redeems, a relationship that neither falters nor fails. This is why the societies and nations are called, not to bestow worth on persons, but simply to recognize the worth that persons already have.

In any case, the great affirmations of a gracious Creator and Redeemer clearly presuppose persistent corruption and sin. They presuppose that there is something we need redeeming from, and this supposition turns out to be an elemental feature of Christian vision that often goes missing in progressive, comparatively naive, and overly optimistic views of history and human possibility. But note too that for Christian theology, as also for ancient Christian creeds and astute liturgies, sin and grace go together. We are sinners and God is Judge, but divine judgment aims to re-turn and renew rather than simply destroy. The judgment of the gracious God is not vindictive; it aims at redemption.

Additional points follow. For one thing, while we affirm the goodness of creation as well as grace abounding, we remain realists who are aware of human limitations and who also lament chronic human corruption and self-righteousness. We know that persons and communities wield significant capabilities and that with these capabilities come distinctive responsibilities. (This, in fact, is a lesson reinforced by our age of environmental degradation and crisis.) We are suspicious of chronic corruption in all, including ourselves. Repentance therefore remains the primary Christian principle of self-criticism. Forgiveness, or the willingness to bear evil in the other without vindictiveness because evil in the self is known, remains a basic (and also potentially reconciling) principle of Christian social ethics. Nevertheless, just because we affirm the goodness of creation and the persistence of grace abounding, we also remain hopeful. We also give thanks for the goodness of persons made for eccentric lives of attentiveness to God and to others in the midst of creation's interdependent interrelations, and we hope to see that goodness in action. We also watch for possibilities beyond tragedy that renew the good and abundant life for which we have been created.

So, in my vocabulary anyway, a good Christian theology, one that tries to envision all things in relation to the God of grace disclosed in Jesus Christ, yields a stance in life called hopeful realism. Hopeful realism acknowledges our distinctive, considerable, but also limited and dependent powers and capabilities. It therefore recognizes not only our significant responsibilities but also the likelihood that occasionally, we shall be overwhelmed—say, in the midst of a pandemic. It expects diminishment, conflict, fragmentation, and death, but it does not fail to look for enlargement, reconciliation, and life. A Christian hopeful realist recognizes the persistently destructive bents as well as the promising possibilities and traces of grace that all persons and communities encounter in God's world. She therefore subjects all persons and communities to criticism even as she affirms them all. She summons all to repentance as well as to a reconciling and eccentric life of attentiveness to God and others.

Are many or even some of these things approximately correct? If not, what different affirmations and patterns of faithful living and reflection commend themselves? If so, what important revisions nevertheless need to be entered into the scheme I have outlined? Questions such as these, as well as many more that no doubt will emerge from your encounters with additional companions, are for you to answer in your own place and time as you exercise your own gifts of sensibility, faith, and reflection. Exercise them vigorously, and may we both praise the glorious God of grace as long as we live.

Best,
Doug

On Public Life, Science,
Interreligious Dialogue

35

Heinrich Bedford-Strohm

First I want to congratulate you for choosing theology as your subject for your studies. Maybe you are not sure whether this will be the professional path that you will take—for example, as a minister or as an educator. However, no matter how certain you are about your future professional vocation, I dare to give a prognosis: you will not regret it. Maybe this prognosis is primarily based on my own biographical experience. But maybe it also has to do with the content of your studies. For me, they have shown to be ends in themselves. I am rather sure that if I had ended up not as a presiding bishop but as a taxi driver, I would not have regretted to have studied theology. The worlds that theology opens up are simply too fascinating.

When I began to study at the university, my choice was the study of law. After one semester, I realized that the most interesting questions were not in the centre of the law studies I had engaged in but had their place more in voluntary studies in our free time. Why are we doing what we are doing? What is the ethical basis? What if my conscience is in conflict with my duties as a lawyer or judge?

I intensified my reading of the Bible. I went more regularly to worship services. And slowly, I developed the wish to study theology. After the second law semester, I changed to theology. And I have never regretted it one day. Not because law wouldn't have been an interesting subject—later in my studies, the philosophy of justice became a central topic for me—but because I could finally engage in studies that reached the bottom of my heart. Maybe more accurately, the bottom of my soul.

In my studies, and then later in parish ministry, in my academic work as a university professor, and now as a bishop, I was always engaged in something that was not primarily a way to make my living but something I passionately stood for. Something I burned for.

What is the calling God gives me in my existence as a human being in this world? This very personal question is at the same time the question that is at the very basis of my professional life.

I have found my personal answer: I feel called to work for a church that does not only speak of the love of God, visible in Jesus Christ, but actually radiates this love with its very existence. Since this love is a love not only for Christians but for every human being created in the image of God, it means for me also the struggle for justice, peace, and the integrity of creation, the struggle for a world in which hunger is overcome and in which every human being can live in dignity. I cannot imagine a spiritual life without being touched by the suffering of fellow human beings and human creation.

This is the very spiritual basis for what has become my most important devotion in academic theology but also my daily task now as the presiding bishop of the German Protestant churches: public theology.

I do not know what special interest you will develop or even have already developed in your studies. But let me tell you more about mine and explain its theological significance. And since I write in the time of the Covid-19 pandemic, let me also elaborate briefly on the implications of public theology for dealing with this pandemic.

What Is Public Theology?

Public theology is a paradigm in theology that has gained importance more and more in the last decades. This is the case in academic theology, where we founded the Global Network for Public Theology in 2007 at a conference in Princeton, including institutes for public theology in all continents of the globe. But it is also the case in church life all over the world. How the church can gain a public voice in modern pluralistic societies and responsibly deal with its public influence are questions church leaders but also local representatives of the church are confronted with daily. The sudden challenge of a new coronavirus spreading quickly around the globe is the most recent and maybe the most challenging example for this in recent history.

Why we need a public theology has been described by Dietrich Bonhoeffer with words so telling, I repeatedly quote them. In his *Ethics*, he writes, "In flight of public controversy this person or that reaches the sanctuary of a *private virtuousness*. Such people neither steal, nor murder, nor commit adultery, but do good according to their abilities. But in voluntary renouncing public life, these people know exactly how to observe the permitted boundaries that shield them from conflict. They must close their eyes and ears to the injustice around them. Only at the cost of self-deception can they keep their private blamelessness clean from the stains of responsible action in the world."[1]

Bonhoeffer's words are rooted in the experience of Nazi Germany, where grave injustice could happen without vivid protest of those who would have seen themselves, in their majority, as good Christians. Contextual public theology in Germany has been deeply motivated by drawing the consequences for the future of this massive spiritual and moral failure. I myself was raised by my family with the clear value basis of never again looking away when grave injustices around us are happening.

In 2006, I was invited to give the David de Villiers Memorial Lectures in Pretoria and in Stellenbosch. The two lectures I gave there were the starting point for my later, more developed approach to public theology. I came up with five guidelines for public theology, which I later expanded into six guidelines.

For letting you understand what is central in public theology for me, I want to briefly describe each guideline and then give an idea of its relevance for dealing with the pandemic.

Six Guidelines for Public Theology in Times of Pandemic
Public Theology Must Be Grounded in Tradition

Public theology needs to give public witness to the sources from which it speaks. Defending oneself for religious claims or emphasising the ethical profile at the cost of the spiritual profile is therefore not the appropriate basis for public theology. The authenticity of the public voice of the church includes an explicit account of the tradition it comes from. Simply adapting to general society by hiding one's own heritage would make it irrelevant. The special value of contributions of the church to public discourse lies in the vitality of its heritage and the particular insights it potentially carries for the whole of society. Therefore, the beauty and poetic and prophetic power of biblical narratives is a strong resource for orientation not only for the church but also for society in general.

Let me illustrate that with a Bible verse and its significance for coping with the Covid-19 crisis. For me, a verse from 2 Timotheus 1:7 has gained special importance since the pandemic began to develop. I have repeatedly quoted it in public: "For God has given us not a spirit of fear but of power, love and prudence" (my translation). Even though it is a verse from the Bible, which is a spiritual source only for one part of our pluralistic society, it finds resonance in the souls of more people than just Christians. Inner *power* is what people yearn for in times of insecurity. *Love* is certainly one of the primary resources in a society looking for coping strategies in experiences of threatened health and danger of death but also of drastic economic decline, loss of jobs, and destruction of many people's life plans. *Prudence* is heavily needed in dilemma situations that cannot be resolved but always imply unsatisfactory consequences no matter what decisions you make. Substantial values accompanied by good information and sober judgment are the necessary ingredients for prudence.

The most controversial example in Germany was the contact restriction in nursing homes. Should the hospitals and nursing homes be shut down for visitors in order to keep the virus out? A large number of deaths from the virus in some nursing homes led to such a policy. But then, can it be responsible to leave old or sick people without physical company by their relatives? What if the protection from physical death leads to social death? There is no clear solution. All the more, there is a place for prudence.

Thus we see: a biblical verse can be a resource that transcends the horizon of religious communities. "For God has given us not a spirit of fear but of power, love and prudence"—this sentence can radiate energy against the crisis, even when people cannot affirm the *God*-word in its full sense.

Nevertheless, biblical language is not sufficient in the public voice of the church. Then the question arises: What can be the complementary language in which the church's public witness can be given?

Public Theology Must Be Bilingual

Public theology needs to be bilingual: it needs to be eloquent in its own biblical and theological language and, thus, needs to give an account of its origin. But it also needs to speak a language that can be understood by the public as a whole, using reason and experience to show that biblical perspectives make good sense and give helpful orientation beyond the boundaries of a specific religious tradition. As much as the public must be open for the semantic potential of religious language, religious communities in general, and the churches in particular, must translate their contributions to public discourse into a generally accessible language.

A good example of how this becomes relevant in times of pandemic is the debate around the question of solidarity. Many people lose their material existence. This is the case in the affluent Western societies where shop or restaurant owners are facing bankruptcy even though they have done whatever they could to make their small businesses work, sometimes over decades of hard work. Even more, poor people without any savings are struggling hard to make it. In countries where the level of absolute poverty is very high and where national resources in general are very limited, this challenge is even more drastic.

The biblical option for the poor is a clear guideline for how to deal with this situation of injustice. Solidarity is a clear mandate of faith. In order to make this basic orientation plausible for all people of goodwill and be a voice to be heard in the public discourse, the language of reason is needed. In the Sermon on the Mount, Jesus himself gives a good basis for this. He explains the commandment of love with the so-called Golden Rule: "Do unto others what you want them to do unto you. This is the law and the prophets" (Matt 7:12; my translation). If you put yourself in the position of the other, what would you wish for?

The American philosopher John Rawls has used the philosophical method of the "veil of ignorance" to form an original position in which people try to find good rules for the society in which they want to live. They know everything about how societies work. But they do not know who they will be when the veil of ignorance will be lifted. This idea is very helpful in finding reasonable strategies for dealing with the pandemic. Will they be a restaurant owner losing their material existence? Or will they be owners of a company that sells software for video conferences and thereby makes a fortune in times of pandemic?

The most reasonable rule for the distribution of wealth will be the "difference principle," which promotes the maximization of the worst position rather than using luck as the decisive distribution principle. Once the veil of ignorance is lifted, it will be much easier to live with a higher taxation of the immense additional earnings based on the video conference boom than with being left alone with the financial catastrophe caused by the pandemic.

In the end, it becomes clear that the biblical option for the poor is the most reasonable and intelligent strategy to deal with the material consequences of the pandemic.

Public Theology Must Be Interdisciplinary

If public theology intends to speak to the wider public, and if it claims to speak of realities, it needs to engage in a vivid dialogue with the other scholarly disciplines. If public theologians want to understand societal trends, they need to study empirical sociological research and understand theoretical interpretations of such research in theoretical sociology or social philosophy. If they aspire to engage in public debate on economic issues, they need to have a basic understanding of economic processes, even if it leads to unmasking seemingly objective facts as ideological constructs to be challenged. Since public theology is more than a confessional self-expression of believers and seeks to be heard in the publics of a democratic society and its political decision bodies, it needs to take account of political science.

The most obvious and relevant dimension of interdisciplinary exchange in times of pandemic is medical research. For an ethically sound reaction to the pandemic, the most recent and substantial results of virological research are extremely important. Knowing how effectively certain political strategies such as lockdowns or contact rules and mandatory hygiene habits can fight the virus is decisive for finding the right measures. For a responsible public voice of the church, it is necessary to take into account what virologists see as increasing the danger for people's health and what they see as saving their lives. Conspiracy theories of all kinds are on the rise that poison public discourse. Only a clear and solid account of scientific research can be the basis for guidelines in public life, which protect the lives of all people, especially the weakest members of society.

Public Theology Must Be Prophetic

One of the most impressive stories of the Old Testament is the so-called Nathan parable that the prophet Nathan tells to King David after the king's affair with Bathsheba. The parable tells about a rich man who does grave injustice to a poor man by taking the only sheep of this poor man to prepare a meal for his own guest. King David becomes very angry about the injustice the rich man has done. The story ends with Nathan's courageous and challenging words: "You are the man!" (2 Sam 12:7). Public theology follows the track Nathan set. It does not legitimise injustice but speaks up to power in favour of justice.

Like prophets, public theologians are "connected critics"[2]—that is, people who are at home in a certain society, know its values and deficiencies, and speak up in public against what goes wrong.

Whether prophetic critique is needed or basic affirmation of government policies in dealing with the pandemic must be judged in each case. In Germany, there were some voices that criticised the churches for not having spoken out prophetically against the massive contact restrictions in nursing homes—thus the accusation of leaving people alone even when they were dying. But many ministers tried their best to keep in contact with people in nursing homes without risking their health. And should the churches have protested the restrictions, knowing about the thirty to forty people who had died from the virus in some nursing homes because the protection was not effective? Such grave situations are reasons for grief and empathy but not for headlines criticising a government trying to do its best to prevent a collapse of the health system. In this specific case, churches in Germany chose a different path that is based on a fifth criterion.

Public Theology Must Make Politics Possible

A social ethic that only works if you never have to apply it is a bad social ethic. It is important to note that public theology is not fundamentally opposed to power. As opposed to liberation theology in times of dictatorship, public theology as a contextual theology for democratic societies makes use of the possibility of going public and voicing concerns of justice and peace and the integrity of creation in the public debate. Thus it might be appropriate to say that public theology is liberation theology for a democratic society.

Refraining from a fundamental opposition strategy necessary in dictatorship situations, public theology can mean even backing the government in certain situations. During the beginning of the pandemic, when the way to go was completely unknown, the churches in Germany decided to back the government in trying to encourage the population to voluntarily support efforts to prevent the spread of the virus and to stick with legal restrictions serving the same goal. Not celebrating worship services in the churches but rather developing all kinds of new worshipping formats—mostly digital based—was a conscious theological decision honouring the commandment to love one's neighbour. When the signs of love we were used to, like handshakes or hugs, became the enemy of love, it was time to restrict physical contact.

While these physical-contact restrictions apply to personal relationships, they are based on the same logic that applies to the global horizon.

There is probably no institution in which personal connectedness in community is more local and at the same time universal than the church. It is the connectedness of the concrete experience of abundant life in relationships with a sense of universal brother- and sisterhood that makes me believe that the church plays a crucial role in the healing of the world. Being rooted in local parishes all over the world and being at the same time universal in the fullest sense make the church an ideal agent of a global civil society.

Besides giving the comfort of God's ongoing love and care for everyone in times of pandemic, it might be the most important task of the church to open local people's eyes to the suffering of those far away. When hunger increases and the number of people dying not only because of the virus but also because of the consequences of the economic breakdown, it is the church's task to direct attention to this situation and speak up for global solidarity. In times in which many people struggle themselves at home, this is not easy. But if the biblical theological assumption is true that each human being is created in the image of God, this is not a side issue. It reaches to the very core of the Christian tradition and the call that comes from it.

Daring to Act

I do not know where you will be when you have finished your studies of theology. Maybe you will publicly carry responsibility for the church as an institution—for example, by serving as a minister. Or you simply are a witness to the gospel in a professional life somewhere else. Wherever you are, you are called to take a stand in spiritual and moral questions. So public theology will be relevant for you.

Doing public theology is always risky. It is all the more risky when academic reflections meet the daily issues of public church life. That is what I am confronted with every day. As a church leader, I have to take a stand and give answers to journalists whose task it is to critically confront those who hold public offices—whether in politics or in the church or in another societal institution—and need to be held accountable for their actions. Sometimes I can draw from clear judgements based on firm convictions and passionately stand for what I say. At other times, I need to give answers on a much more fragile basis, because either biblical theological reflection leads me to no firm result or the assessment of the facts includes many unknown factors or both.

As the example of dealing with contact restrictions in nursing homes shows, the answers I give—if people listen to me—can have grave consequences for people's lives and even for how they die. Practicing public theology—this conclusion, then, becomes all the more evident—always means being ready to make mistakes, or even to become guilty. If doing public theology is a venture, then, the hope for forgiveness is a prerequisite for it. I could not practise public theology without it. As Dietrich Bonhoeffer has described so thoroughly, nonaction due to uncertainty of judgment can be the less moral action. Responsibility means acting even under conditions of moral uncertainty. Freedom means knowing about both: the risk of becoming guilty and the courage to act based on trust in the possibility of forgiveness.

Dear young colleague,

I have given you some insights into my biographical and especially my theological journey, which is an ongoing one. Many of the insights, which turn out to be at its basis, come from my theology studies at the university. Equally important, however, were my experiences in social and political contexts. May I encourage you to use your time at the university by fully engaging in both? There is a time for quiet reflection in libraries or at the desk at home. And there is a time for engaging in community commitments, which make us understand what is going on in society. Both are needed, each at its time.

You will find your own way. I wish you—from the bottom of my heart— God's blessings for your journey.

All the best!
Heinrich

Notes

1 Dietrich Bonhoeffer, *Ethics*, ed. Clifford Green (Minneapolis: Augsburg Fortress, 2004), 80.

2 M. Walzer, *Interpretation and Social Criticism* (Cambridge, MA: Harvard University Press, 1987).

36

Graham Ward

First of all, thank you for this invitation to write. As someone for whom retirement is now on the horizon, the question of nurturing the next generation of theologians is very much at the forefront of my thinking. I have been in a fortunate position in being able to teach many graduates and see them placed in early career positions in universities across the world. The hope is that they will foster the generation below them and attract their own graduate students. But the kind of theology being done now has an increasingly complex question to tackle, and future theologians will find themselves in contexts shaped by the answer to this question. The question is, *Where* is the study of Christian theology to take place institutionally? I began my own training by being sponsored by the Anglican Church to take a second degree in theology through the affiliation between my seminary at Cambridge and the university faculty. But what I see happening at present is (a) a desire by universities to put clear water between faculties that teach theology at the undergraduate level and seminary education and (b) an increasing lack of interest in the churches in theological education at the research level. I don't think initiating some blame game is going to be productive. This is just the situation Christian theologians find themselves in: the global marketing of university education, on the one hand, and the church resources focussing more on the practical and pragmatic management of the institution, on the other. It will no doubt be possible in the future to gain doctorates from universities in theology, but they may well be understood within the church as more about professional development than genuinely feeding theological expertise into church life. Other than regularly preaching and occasionally being asked to speak at clergy conferences, I am not called upon by the church that paid for my training. And that break between the research-led study of theology and church life is concerning. Faith must seek understanding in each new generation and the matrices of new cultural, social, economic, and political contexts. The great figures of twentieth-century theology (Barth, Tillich, Rahner, and von Balthasar, to name only a few) can inspire the theologies being done today, but they cannot answer the theological questions being posed in the world now—questions to do with being white, male, western, and inheritors of privilege fostered by colonialism, for example. These figures are part of a tradition that moves forwards the theologies they taught on the basis of what was bequeathed to them. It is a tradition in which the church too is embedded, so the greater the gap between the academic and the ecclesial, the more theologians are divorced from exactly the place where faith is faced with questions it needs to grapple with and understand.

Where this most evidently impacts the theologian is that there can be no assumed readership for their work beyond other theologians and students of theology. A readership has to be cultivated, and that has implications for the way theology is written. I work with my graduate students on finding their voice, which means attention to style and avoiding any reliance on a local ingot. That is humbling because I am myself not always "easy" reading. Theology has no language of its own to think through matters concerning God or what we name "God." We are borrowing a language all the time, a language shared with other sciences. We share methodologies of investigation with these sciences—literary, philological, hermeneutical, for example. We have always been and have needed to be interdisciplinary, even when it comes to examining our sacred texts and our sacred practices. The developments in critical theory and philosophy have added to the repertoire of strategies for exegesis and analysis and opened conversations across disciplines, not just with respect to the humanities. We share a concern with therapy with medicine. We share the physical science's concern with "nature" (human and nonhuman) when reflecting upon creation, our place and role within it. Materiality matters, flesh matters, so how the material comes to be, is composed, and operates impacts theology. We need to cultivate these cross-disciplinary conversations to expand and contextualise our specifically Christian or Judeo-Christian or monotheistic investigations. Liturgy studies needs to be aware of the work done by anthropologists in ritual studies, theological studies needs to engage with religious studies, just as studies of the Hebrew or Christian Scriptures need to engage with literary studies, history, philology, and the relationship between any textual production and the complex fields and forces in the production of culture more generally. At the same time, Christian theology has to be true to itself: it has a gospel. The interdisciplinary work that theology has to and has always engaged in is not simply a matter of use and co-option. These other disciplines raise theological questions, and those questions need engagement. Let me give an example: The relationship between theology and literature or theology and film is not simply a matter of showing theological tropes and themes in certain novels or films or genres or an individual author's or film director's work. There is a question about what makes literature or film theological—what is theological about these media, these modes of cultural expression? What is the relationship, ultimately, between a Creator God and creativity itself? And that creativity can be extended beyond the human to nonhuman cultivators: the organisation of ant colonies or beehives, the lines of communication and interdependence in any ecosystem within the fabric of time and space itself as it composes and organises forms, patterned regularities, fractals and emergent entities. What are we learning in all this dynamic creativity about creation and God as Creator?

Finding that voice as a theologian concerns understanding one's vocation as a theologian. That is a matter of being nurtured deeply by the Christian tradition and listening in and through that nurturing to what is being said in the world. At its most profound, theology is inseparable from discernment and spiritual formation. It is responding to the work of God in, through, and above all things created. This *is* faith as it seeks understanding. It is a participation in what Saint Paul called the stewardship of the mysteries of God, the hidden and nonvisible operations of the divine that subtend all things. Here comes a complex but vital sentence: if God is love (and we have to examine what we understand by love and its relation to desiring, wanting, needing, and willing), and caring is written into creation (the threefold Godhead working in and through that which has been brought into being that requires thinking through the nature of predation, sin, and evil), then the theologian's vocation is the way in which they enact that caring. Theology becomes an act of caring, an act of responding to the call within and upon all creation. There is a formation inextricably linked to fulfilling this vocation, living out this careful attentiveness that is listening for the inaudible in the audible, attending to the invisible within the visible. This caring, like this level of attentiveness, involves the whole of the body (and raises a question about embodiment both individual and corporate). The tradition has known this: the theologian is someone who prays. If I would slightly modify this is, then I would say everyone and everything prays. The theologian is one of the human creatures who focusses the prayerfulness that is the beating, doxological heart of all things living (and I count rocks and water, wind and electromagnetic fields as living things). All human acts of creative caring and attentiveness are prisms through which divine light passes. The theologian tries to bring into as great a clarity as possible the ineffability of that light, relating it explicitly to what we name as God. Other people, enacting their own vocation and responses, do it differently and less explicitly. We are all groping to understand.

To my mind, this responsiveness and level of listening have profound pneumatological consequences. In and through sentience, all things live in and towards the habitat systems that compose the world. A spiritually emerges in and through the material that informs, transforms, and reforms. And it can be deformed (by paying little or no attention to it). That means experience counts. Over the last few decades, there has been something of a turn towards the respectability of investigating experience theologically, in part led by phenomenology and in part by attention to affect and the neuroscience that lies behind much work in embodied cognition. This attention has challenged subjectivism versus objectivism, which wormed its way into theological anthropologies and, inevitably, into doctrines of God (the *duplex ordo* of nature and grace, for example). Moods and emotions are contagious and impact communities that have established practices in which certain affects are encouraged (love, mercy, compassion, etc.) and certain affects are discouraged (lust, envy, anger, etc.). Affective communities, with porous boundaries and constant modulation of form, generate, whether consciously or not, spiritual exercises. Theology, as a cultural product of the affective communities and spiritual exercises of the various shared Christian commitments, is inseparably bound to these communities and their practices. Some theologians would argue for theology as a second-order reflection upon these communities of piety and their liturgical practices. I would wish to challenge the reductive cause-and-effect logic that lies behind this understanding of theology, but if we are looking to examine the movement of the Spirit in and through the materiality of practices, affects, and embodiment (that would include "objects" from icons to chalices), then the relationship between the work of a theologian and spiritual formation becomes highly significant.

The relationship between "academic" theology and spirituality has, until recently, been underappreciated, if not attacked. Throughout modernity, the two practices were separated entirely, which led to a compartmentalism of theological expertises in the new university—fundamental and dogmatic theology, liturgical studies and homiletics, scriptural exegesis, ethics and practical or public theology, for example. Happily, with attention to well-being, mental health, and formative praxes in other human sciences (colonial mentalities, for example, in subaltern and postcolonial theory), theologians today are in a different place. And that place offers a space for reflection upon the formative work of the Spirit *within* theological production. Spirituality is best seller material, as many of the more famous religious naturalists demonstrate. But there are rich and more ancient Christian traditions that we have forgotten and need to recover, from the mystagogic theologies of late antiquity that were still being practiced in the work of John Scotus Eriugena (ninth century CE), to the monastic understanding of manuduction evident in Latin works from Augustine to Aquinas. Pedagogy beyond catechesis was recognised as fundamental. Christ as Teacher gave rise to a Christian *paideia* that turned philosophical knowledge towards wisdom traditions. Here, the relationship between theological reflection and spiritual direction was strong (if also, no doubt, abused). But if being a theologian is recognised as a particular calling, then there is a responsibility by a theologian not only for their spiritual formation but for the pedagogical formation of others cultivated by their work. There is good scriptural testimony that we are taught by the Spirit and that that teaching is for the benefit of the church: formation is in Christ through the Spirit, an *imitatio Christi*.

I must admit, I find this responsibility utterly daunting, and while I recognise, theologically, the relationship between training the would-be theologian (through a doctoral study, for example) and spiritual direction, I try to keep the two tasks entirely separate. I would argue for that practice on the basis of professionalism and a sort of checks and balances with respect to the potential overuse of authority. There have always been hierarchical structures within the church that attempted to mitigate the risks of spiritual abuse through an overzealous director: everyone was to be accountable to someone and, ultimately, to Christ. Traditions of mentoring and spiritual friendship were cultivated, which are now making something of a comeback through traditions of Christian faith and piety like the Jesuits, who have always maintained their importance. But if a theologian is one who prays and her theology emerges out of meditation and contemplation, then understanding and engaging in some form of spiritual exercise (which is an extension of the liturgical *lex orandi*) are crucial. Pseudo-Dionysius coined a word I find helpful: *theo-mimesis*. Theology needs to participate in and practice this *theo-mimesis*, as all else created from birds to angels also participate and practise it. Thereby, the relationship among Creator, creation, and creativity is sustained. And we can learn to appreciate more about these spiritual exercises from historians like Werner Jaeger and Pierre Hadot as much as social theorists like Michel Foucault and, in their own ways, Frantz Fanon and Paulo Freire. The more we are aware of our habitus (a term recently recovered by the French sociologist Pierre Bourdieu) and the way it operates and continually undergoes modification, then the more our theologies are responding to what God is saying and doing now. If we ignore the habitus, then we can get ourselves stuck in theological and conceptual logic-chopping, asking and answering questions that are fanciful at best and self-serving at worst.

Which brings me to my final point, which is not at odds with what I have just written, though certainly in some tension that one hopes is productive. That is, for theologians to take risks in the creative connections they make and participate in, they need to be imaginative. We treat beliefs, emotions, hopes, and aspirations, all of which are, in themselves, invisible even if they are less so in their material effects. God too is not visible to us—neither as Father nor as Spirit and not now as Son. Living is stippled with invisibilities, whether theological in nature or not. Even the most reductive empiricist is forced to work and trade in invisibilities: thinking is invisible. The theologian works with myths, metaphors, and narratives in weaving a cultural production on the invisibility of the divine. They need to cultivate the imagination—and I say *cultivate* because the imagination has to be fed, weeded, hoed, watered, and tended like any animate entity. We return to practices again, for the practice of faith as it seeks (grubs and gropes for) understanding demands certain disciplines that take time to be embedded. You cannot rush an intuition; it emerges, sometimes slowly and painfully. Discipleship, and that is what being a theologian requires commitment to, costs. But it is hoped (and here is the risk) that in trying to be faithful, something is born of the theological imagination that gives life to others, something beautiful and good like an act of love. Then the theology is mimetic, and as we know now from understanding the contagious nature of mimesis fostered by those much-remarked-upon mirror neurons, it sends out ripples of resonance to others that broaden the communication. And none of us can calculate a fraction of the consequences of any of our acts with respect to others, human and nonhuman. Especially when that is an act of love.

I think I have said enough, and I have welcomed this opportunity, as I draw nearer to retirement, to reflect upon what the theologian is attempting to cultivate. We go on, and we try to go on faithfully, and theology will always fail as it will always recover from failure and find itself wanting to speak again. In living in and towards the world, questions will inevitably arise that challenge faith, forcing it out of platitudes and the turgid rehearsal of formulas. The theologian's work, like the gardener's labour, is never done: they are planting seeds and seeing trees that, at the moment, are just staked to the ground and (maybe, hopefully) rooting. All Edens are eschatological. That is the metaphor I leave behind for the theologians to come: "make a garden."

Graham Ward
Christ Church, Oxford

37

Gijsbert van den Brink

A retired professor of practical theology once told me that he would not recommend his teenage grandchildren to embark on a theology program in order to subsequently become a minister or church leader. He would rather see them enrolling in some other program and pursue a more worldly vocation. He himself had been a minister for a couple of years, and afterward, as a professor, he had studied and published widely on pastoral theology, catechesis, and so on. He had even written an engaging book on the profession of being a minister (*dominee*). Had he eventually lost confidence in his lifelong mission? I myself had just started as a young professor at a Faculty of Theology at the time, and I remember that I was shocked. How could he say this? Wasn't theology the most engaging, most encompassing, and most enriching study one could think of? My older and wiser colleague must be going through some kind of depression, I figured.

Later on, however, it dawned upon me that his view was not so strange after all. For one, the number of students enrolling in theology programs had gradually been decreasing over the years. The glorious times of dozens of Reformed theology students packed in a classroom, which my retired colleague had been part of in his youth, had gone—most probably forever. Second, and related to this, theology is no longer seen as a relevant academic discipline by many people. Even pastors seem to read more self-help and leadership books than theological work. Third, after having finished one's theological studies, one may easily end up in a greying community with more funerals and fewer churchgoers every year, working hard for an ever-smaller group of people and being regarded with some compassion by outsiders. Apparently, my retired colleague wanted to save his grandchildren the fate of dying away in a "soft" and intellectually nondemanding job in some rural village. Fourth, it is not just ongoing secularization (like Daniel Dennett's famous "universal acid") that corrodes the relevance of theology as training for the ministry. For even where Christian communities still flourish, the need to maintain a well-educated ministry—steeped in biblical languages, the history of the church, dogmatics, and so on—is ever more questioned. Many committed believers would rather have an outgoing pastor with empathy (irrespective of their level of education) than someone who (on top of that) is able to truthfully preach the gospel from its original sources.

Theology as a Fascinating Blend of Humanities

So was my retired colleague right? Should we indeed discourage young people to study theology and become involved in the ministry of the church? I do not think so. In accounting for my view in the remainder of this letter, I will limit myself mainly to the study of theology, since the challenges to be faced by a contemporary minister are of a different nature. So why should a young modern person consider enrolling in a theology program?

First of all, the study of theology as an academic discipline continues to be one of a kind in that it consists of a fascinating mix of the various humanities. For those who love languages, history, *and* philosophy and who want to be trained in each of them, it seems there is only one way to move forward: the study of religion and theology. Unless one enrolls in one of the recently revived liberal arts programs (or "university colleges"), the Faculty or Department of Theology and Religious Studies is the place to be. This is even the case for those who do not consider themselves religious. Secular students may deeply enjoy and profit from programs in religious studies and even in theology because such programs will help them understand and relate to the views, behaviors, and most deeply felt convictions of others.

Along such lines, in her wonderful piece "Study Theology, Even If You Don't Believe in God," Tara Isabella Burton describes theology as "an ideal synthesis of all other liberal arts" that is attractive for all lovers of the humanities. One is taught how to look at the world with the eye of a historian, becomes familiar with philosophical questions and systems, and is trained as a skillful interpreter of both texts and people. In that sense, theology can still be seen as "queen of the humanities." In particular, Burton argues that whereas religious studies provides us with an outsider's view of world events, theology "offers us a chance to study these same events from within: an opportunity to get inside the heads of those whose beliefs and choices shaped so much of our history, and who—in the world outside the ivory tower—still shape plenty of the world today."[1]

If this makes sense, studying theology does not so much require faith as it requires—and fosters—*empathy*. It helps you understand the most profound thoughts and feelings, worries and desires of people living in entirely different circumstances from your own. And it may even help you find out what values and core convictions are at the bottom of your own heart.

Thus studying theology may be a deeply rewarding endeavor to those who are interested in people. The scope of its object need not even be restricted to *religious* texts, traditions, beliefs, and practices, since other worldviews may be included as well. Ideally, in a theological program, nonreligious views of life such as atheism, agnosticism, scientism, and humanism are also being studied—the core idea being here that somehow, everyone has a view of life as determined by whatever, at the end of the day, matters most to us or is our "primary determinant of meaning" (Vincent Brümmer). Therefore, in order to highlight theology's relevance, we do not need the stereotyped reference to "the important role religion still plays today," as testified by various (usually negative) contemporary phenomena and developments (e.g., religiously motivated terrorism). True as this may be, even if it were not the case, theology's questions and concerns remain relevant, since what should matter most (i.e., who or what is or should be our *god*) is, of course, a very important and rational question to ask.

In this way, theologian John Webster has argued that theology is the queen of the humanities, since questions such as what the humanities are good for and why we should pursue academic studies in the first place can only be answered in theological terms (i.e., in terms of what is or should be valuable to us). Or to give an example from ordinary life, think of what you would say at someone's funeral, where all language that refers to money making and economic targets to be met all of a sudden sounds trivial. In retrospect, comments like "he worked hard all the time" necessarily come with a ring of superficiality unless a higher purpose or overarching value that was really worth striving for was involved. For all of us, it seems, there are choices to be made concerning the sort of life we want to live—or in theological terms, regarding the god or gods we want to worship. If we just want to worship the god of our own ego, we almost certainly end up in loneliness. In any case, theological description and analysis provide us with the tools and language to make such choices explicit, to analyze and discuss them.

Theology's Constructive Task

Yet in its best expressions, theology goes beyond the descriptive and analytic level in that it also has evaluative and constructive dimensions. It is one thing to investigate the views of others; it is another, more daunting task to investigate one's own view in interaction with these. When we shape our own views on what really matters, we always do so in interaction with relevant others surrounding and preceding us. In other words, as a student of theology, you typically participate in the search for theological truth by joining a *tradition*. I use this word here in the sense coined by Alasdair MacIntyre—that is, an ongoing practice of inquiry and investigation characterized by certain sources and methods, rules and goals—a kind of craft or discipline. Note that *tradition* stands here not for any form of fossilized conservatism but for an ongoing story of debates, arguments, and techniques about how to perform these in the best possible way. In the case of theology, there are ongoing debates and arguments as to where the good life, or salvation, is to be found; how it can be attained; how we can live up to it; and how we can relate in appropriate ways to its source (in monotheistic traditions: God).

God, of course, is the proper subject of theology (*theology* meaning a *logos*, or "reasoned account," about *theos*, or "God"). Rather than trying to circumvent or conceal the G-word, I believe theologians should, in the end, be open about their ultimate subject matter. That is nothing to be ashamed of if it is true that God is the all-determining reality, or our ultimate concern (as famous theologians like Pannenberg and Tillich put it). In fact, we might even join Evelyn Underhill in claiming that the only interesting thing about religion is God. Yet—and here is an important caveat, since this point is often overlooked—theology can never be narrowed down to "studying God" in isolation. In part, it is this persistent misunderstanding of theologians as all the time studying some mysterious invisible object called "God" that may explain theology's current decline in reputation. As Thomas Aquinas already put it, theology is about God *and everything in relation to God*. Thus it is the attempt to make sense of our lives, the world, and all its dimensions—biological, sexual, economic, political, historical, or whatever—in the light of God. And obviously, it belongs to the most crucial debates within theology where this God is actually to be found. But anyhow, theologians develop proposals that try to make sense of things from this transcendent perspective.

In elaborating, refining, and defending their sense-making proposals, theologians necessarily operate in a self-involving way. Far from being a detached pursuit of "objective knowledge," theology consists of a deeply passionate search for growth in understanding. Theology shares this search with the other humanities. Investigating what is going on in the process of *interpretation*—for example, interpreting art or history—philosopher Hans-Georg Gadamer argues that acquiring knowledge and understanding in the humanities typically takes the form of a "fusion of horizons" in which we expand our intellectual horizon by engaging with the horizon of the texts or artefacts that we study. Precisely because these texts or traditions are initially strange to us, there is a lot to be learnt. The very reason why we start studying some tradition may even be that somehow, we feel implicated or intrigued by it (note that one can only be intrigued by what is alien, not by what is familiar). Such personal factors should not be bracketed as nonessential but be taken into full account, since, as Gadamer puts it, we are always already affected by history. It is this type of "engaged scholarship" (as we call it at my own Faculty of Religion and Theology at Vrije Universiteit Amsterdam) that is typical for theology. Here as well, we always find ourselves immersed in some tradition—a religious tradition and/or a tradition of doing research—prior to our professional engagement with its debates and concerns. And standing at its front edge, we are the ones who continue this tradition in novel directions that can nevertheless be recognized as truthful to its deepest tenets. In this way, becoming a theologian amounts to taking up responsibility for a certain tradition, for a way of believing, perceiving, and doing things that one wants to make relevant for one's own context.

We may even consider that theology—or the study of "divinity," as it used to be called—goes beyond the humanities in that its object indeed eludes us because of its very transcendence. We may acknowledge a transcendent aspect to art, literature, and even history (e.g., it is impossible to come up with a final, once-and-for-all interpretation of a historical event or period). But when it comes to theology, doesn't it belong to the very nature of God to escape and thwart all our attempts to come to grips with Him? Even using the common personal pronoun *Him* in this connection seems deeply inadequate . . . We cannot do without common language, frameworks, and thought forms in theology, whereas at the same time, we know that all of these fall short. As Alfred Lord Tennyson famously puts it,

> *Our little systems have their day*
> *They have their day and cease to be*
> *They are but broken lights of Thee*
> *And Thou o Lord art more than they.*[2]

In that sense, doing theology is even less "objective" and more self-involving than engaging in any of the other humanities. (But note that this is a difference in degree and not in kind!) Given the elusiveness of its transcendent object, the only legitimation for theology as a scholarly discipline seems to be that it starts from God's self-disclosure to humans.

Thus after we have gone all the way from theology as a mixture of humanistic studies to its proper object and goal, we cannot escape this appeal to the concept of divine revelation as its only possible starting point. And even so, it remains a daunting challenge to speak about *God* instead of projecting our own ideas on a heavenly screen. As the young Karl Barth once wrote, as theologians, "we ought to speak of God. We are human, however, and so we cannot speak of God. We ought, therefore, to recognize both our obligation and our inability and by that very recognition give glory to God."[3] In that sense, there is probably no discipline that is both more demanding and engaging than theology.

The Tragic Split between Descriptive and Normative Approaches

Now if all this holds water, why has theology's fate been waning over the past decades and even centuries? As far as I can see, there are at least two reasons for this.

First, since the end of the nineteenth century, the study of theology has gone through a tragic split between one-sidedly normative approaches on the one hand and one-sidedly descriptive methods on the other. In their compelling analysis of the current state of theology, *For the Life of the World* (2019), Miroslav Volf and Matthew Croasmun see the retreat to descriptivism especially in the transformation of theology into religious studies. The ineffectiveness of this "coping strategy" is clear from the fact that religious studies departments have even more difficulties than theology programs in the struggle to attract sufficient numbers of students. In the eyes of many, religious studies scholars assemble very detailed pieces of knowledge that hardly interest anyone beyond their own circle.

The one-sidedly normative approach to theology is located by Volf and Croasmun both at the conservative and at the liberal side of the spectrum. Theologians from conservative circles often reduce the task of theology to nostalgic attempts at shoring up *that old-time religion*—usually conceived of as "the beliefs, practices, and cultural mores of their pious great-grandparents."[4] These past articulations of the faith have to be defended at all costs against the eroding influence of new cultural and scientific developments. Even though the rearticulation of ancient creeds and Scriptures *does* belong to the theological task, reducing this task to it is to undermine theology's reputation as a serious academic discipline. For in doing so, the quest for truth is actually given up: the truth is known already well in advance, and all forces are marshalled in order to bolster it. It is little wonder that the outsider (and the general public) usually does not feel attracted to this way of doing theology. Normatively engaged theologians in the liberal camp, on the other hand, do not do much better. They tend to water down religious views to politically correct normative values that are identical to those articulated with more rhetorical skill by influential secular thinkers.[5] Their approach to the Bible, the church, and even God is often characterized by an ongoing critique in which they unmask and problematize whatever topic they examine. Even though this posture may have its background in the fierce criticisms of sinful human behavior by the biblical prophets, the progressive critique differs from the prophetic one in that it does not come up with a positive alternative (for such a positive theological vision would be another target of critique).

Over against these disintegrating tendencies, Volf and Croasmun develop a case for reorienting theology toward its original positive goal: exploring and elaborating visions of the good life—that is, the "life worth living." Here we are back again with our analysis of theology as focused on what matters most or is most valuable, salutary, and fulfilling. Space prevents us from exploring their view in more detail, but it seems to me that it requires a conception that connects (normative) theology and (descriptive) religious studies rather than playing them off against each other. To paraphrase Einstein's famous dictum on science and religion: religious studies without theology may easily become lame (in that it does not help us move forward in our own understanding of life's big questions); theology without religious studies is blind (in that it may build beautiful systems whilst ignoring what is actually going on in people's heads and minds). Thus it is important to move beyond the traditional split between theology and religious studies and restore their unity.

In my own university, an attempt is being made to achieve that. Separate undergraduate programs of theology on the one hand and religious studies on the other have recently merged into a joint program of "theology and religious studies" in which students are being taught by both religious studies specialists and theologians of various stripes. Of course, to some extent, students make their own choices according to their preferences, but quite a couple of courses are mandatory for all of them. Also the graduate programs are based on the interaction between descriptive and normative approaches. Faculty staff members may or may not have a religious outlook themselves, but views of life should matter to them, as they should be prepared to engage in dialogue with their students. Therefore, they should be open about their own view of life instead of suggesting "scientific" neutrality or scientific objectivity. As a result, students do not just acquire knowledge (as in a religious studies department) but also increase in understanding and experience personal growth, along both lines becoming more knowledgeable and accountable academics.

Progress in Theology?

The second reason why in Western contexts theology has become a waning, disreputable discipline is that—in stark contrast to the sciences—it does not seem to make any progress. Issues that have bothered theologians throughout the centuries still bother them today, as can easily be read off from the table of contents of standard dogmatic surveys: they often show the same titles, even in more or less the same order, as similar works from past centuries. This apparent standstill seems to show that "the achievements of theologians don't do anything, don't affect anything, don't mean anything," as Richard Dawkins once put it. But doesn't theology make any progress indeed, and if so, is that a problem indeed? To start with the latter question: one might also argue that not making much epistemic progress makes a discipline's results more reliable. As philosopher of science Larry Laudan has famously argued, the fact that science makes progress and thus changes all the time implies that we can hardly trust its current outcomes, because most probably, these will be corrected by later developments. Theology's results seem much more time-tested. Whereas scientists can only smile at, for example, Aristotle's physics, theologians can still seriously engage with Paul's doctrine of justification or Augustine's view of God. So theology's lack of "progress" may be seen as a sign of stability, strengthening rather than undermining its trustworthiness.

Yet second, in the wake of the sciences, theology evidently does make some epistemic progress. For example, the sciences have shown that the universe is much older than six thousand to ten thousand years, and this fact has helped theology invalidate certain interpretations of Genesis (obviously, epistemic progress is achieved not just by acquiring knowledge but also by overcoming false beliefs). Similarly, many other scientific discoveries have led to adjustments (and, for all we know, improvements) of theological views that were previously associated with assumptions that have become obsolete as a result of scientific developments. In most cases, the scientific developments touched theology at best tangentially so that not much work needed to be done. In some cases, such as that of evolutionary theory, the situation was different. As I tried to show in my recent book *Reformed Theology and Evolutionary Theory* (2020), taking Darwinian evolution seriously implies that theologians must be prepared to adapt at least some of their traditional understandings.[6] So here theology seems to make some progress, albeit in the wake of the sciences.

Third, theology may also make progress by prompting the sciences to explore and test certain "theology-friendly" hypotheses or theories, which may subsequently find empirical corroboration and even become generally accepted. In this way, the Jesuit priest George Lemaître famously suggested that the universe might have started with a "big bang"—a notion that (despite his own denial) was arguably inspired by his theological belief that the universe, as being created by God, had a beginning. More recently, theologians have stimulated quantum physicists to explore various interpretations of quantum mechanics in order to find out which ones are hospitable to the concept of noninterventionist divine action. These are fascinating ways in which theology and science can cooperate instead of excluding each other. For in this way, theological background beliefs may usher in epistemic progress even in the sciences.

Fourth, on closer inspection, theology may also make progress independently of the sciences. For example, whereas in the past, Christian theologians were convinced of the doctrine of divine impassibility, most theologians have now come to see that God is actually "passible"—that is, able to suffer. Epistemic progress is not necessarily limited to cases of emerging *communis opinio*, however, nor is the emergence of near consensus a proof of progress. Thus some theologians, working in another paradigm (or research program), still hold on to divine impassibility, and they tend to see its contemporary rejection as a sign of regress. Conversely, Protestant theologians typically argue that the sixteenth-century Protestant Reformations led to epistemic progress, even though Catholics may disagree. Call such forms of progress "intraparadigmatic"—and compare that according to post-Kuhnian philosophy of science. Progress in the sciences is also mainly intraparadigmatic. Thus it seems that theology is not so different from the sciences after all, even though—due to the complexity of its task and the elusiveness of its main object—it comprises many more paradigms existing next to each other than is customary in the sciences. That, however, is a matter of degree again rather than a structural difference.

One may even consider, fifth, whether it is possible for theology to make progress in a way that goes beyond the intraparadigmatic level. Hopefully this does not happen too often, for in such a case, the reliability of even the most deeply embedded theological assumptions is at stake. Yet it is an intriguing historical observation that many religions that once flourished have now become extinct while others have taken their place. A plausible reason for this is that due to changing cultural conditions, theologians of the previous religion no longer succeeded in making sense of the world in light of its core assumptions. For example, almost nobody seriously worships Wodan or Zeus any longer because their cults were tied to a limited (mostly fertility-related) cultural horizon. In this way, it might be argued that theology makes epistemic progress when it succeeds in convincingly interpreting *new* developments, phenomena, and experiences in light of its core beliefs. Theologians should never just repeat the past but always seek to engage in innovative ways with values and patterns of thinking that have emerged in their own time. In such cases, theology functions as what is called a "progressive research program" in the natural sciences. Arguably, today such progress can mostly be expected if theology is being done in an interreligious context. For that reason as well, doing theology in the setting of a multireligious faculty or department of theology and religion seems most appropriate and promising.

Rewarding

I hope this letter will convince the reader that the resignation of my retired colleague was, after all, misplaced. Theology continues to be one of the most exciting and rewarding academic disciplines, and I have never regretted my choice to enroll in a theology program as an eighteen-year-old student.

Best wishes,
Gijsbert

Notes

1 Tara Isabella Burton, "Study Theology, Even If You Don't Believe in God," *Atlantic*, October 30, 2013, https://www.theatlantic.com/education/archive/2013/10/study-theology-even-if-you-dont-believe-in-god/280999/.

2 Alfred Tennyson, *In Memoriam* (New York: Fords, Howard & Hulbert, 1897).

3 Karl Barth, *The Word of God and Theology* (New York: T&T Clark, 2011), 177.

4 Miroslav Volf and Matthew Croasmun, *For the Life of the World: Theology That Makes a Difference* (Grand Rapids, MI: Brazos, 2019), 52.

5 Volf and Croasmun, 53.

6 Gijsbert van den Brink, *Reformed Theology and Evolutionary Theory* (Grand Rapids, MI: Eerdmans, 2020).

38

Alister E. McGrath

I've been thinking about some things that I might want to say to a young theologian who is beginning to think about the place of theology and the theologian within the churches in particular and the world at large. Forgive me for writing such a short letter, which touches on only a few matters. Rather than overwhelm you with detail, I just want to offer you some pointers to help you find your way and develop your own vision of what theology is all about. Perhaps the most helpful thing I can do is tell you how I became a theologian and reflect on my own understanding of what I was called to do.

I had not the slightest interest in theology during my formative years as a teenager. My academic focus was on mathematics and the natural sciences; my personal belief system was atheism, which I perhaps unwisely—and certainly prematurely—considered to be a proven fact. I became caught up in the unrest of the late 1960s and was drawn to Marxism on account of its expansive intellectual vision and the added rigour it provided for my increasingly dogmatic atheism. I secured a scholarship to Oxford University to study chemistry and confidently expected that my future lay as a research scientist either in one of Britain's leading universities or in one of its specialist medical research units.

But it didn't work out like that. On arriving at Oxford University in October 1971, I encountered a highly articulate and intellectually engaged form of Christianity that captured my imagination and offered both food for my soul and a rich stimulus to my life of the mind. I discovered that, like Marxism, Christianity could generate a "Big Picture" of reality, and I found an able exponent of this view in C. S. Lewis, who remains a major influence on me to this day.

I had no intention of abandoning my love of science and wanted to find ways in which my love of science and new commitment to the Christian faith could be brought together in a richer whole. Would I have to compartmentalise them, allocating them to different regions of my mind so that they did not interact with each other? Or was there a way of coordinating them, bringing them into a creative and constructive dialogue that could lead to intellectual and imaginative enrichment? Happily, conversations with leading Oxford scientists—such as Charles A. Coulson, Oxford's professor of theoretical chemistry—helped me see that I could fit my love for science within a Christian framework. But more work clearly needed to be done.

As I began to explore my new Christian faith in greater intellectual depth, I experienced a deep intellectual longing to explore its conceptual foundations. I continued studying science at Oxford, following my undergraduate degree in chemistry with a doctorate in molecular biophysics. Yet I knew it was now inevitable that I would turn to the study of theology in order to satisfy my deep intellectual curiosity. So in the final two years of my Oxford doctoral research, I began to study theology, gaining a doctorate and an undergraduate degree in theology in 1978. I then went to St John's College, Cambridge, to do some theological research while also preparing for ministry in the Church of England. I began to realise that preaching allowed me to act as a theological interpreter of the "place" in which I and my congregation existed, enabling me to make connections between faith and life.

After serving for three years in an Anglican parish in Nottingham, I returned to Oxford to teach theology, both to Oxford University students and to students training for ministry in the Church of England. Initially, I focussed on developing a deep knowledge of historical theology, especially on the Renaissance and Reformation periods. Yet I never lost my interest in the relation of the natural sciences and theology, and today I hold Oxford University's endowed professorship in this field.

So how do I understand theology? And how do I see my own calling as a theologian? Both of these have emerged and crystallised over a period of nearly fifty years. Let me tell you something about these.

I began to study Christian theology at Oxford in 1976. I found it very difficult to make the transition from the natural sciences to theology for a number of reasons. For a start, they seemed to use quite different methods of inquiry. Yet more significantly, I had a huge amount of information to absorb and accumulate as I studied theology. In my earlier field of chemistry, advanced learning was made easy on account of several excellent textbooks that introduced major fields of study—such as March's *Advanced Organic Chemistry* and Cotton and Wilkinson's *Advanced Inorganic Chemistry*. There was no theological equivalent. I had to learn everything from ground zero.

Happily, Oxford University uses a tutorial system for teaching at the undergraduate level, and I was fortunate to have some of Oxford's leading theologians to introduce me to the field and help me find my way. I gradually began to grasp how theology worked and catch a glimpse of its enormous potential for spiritual enrichment and cultural engagement.

So how do I understand theology? Basically, I see theology as uncovering and exploring the "Big Picture" of the Christian faith that is disclosed in the Christian Bible and as the long Christian tradition of wrestling with this text. As I read early Christian writers such as Athanasius, Augustine, and Gregory of Nyssa, I am impressed with the fact that they are deeply rooted in the Bible yet are able to articulate its insights in such a way that they open up and allow us to inhabit a wider and deeper vision of reality. Theology is biblical, yet it is *more than biblical* in that it seeks to weave biblical themes together and discern the richer picture that results—one that cannot be fully disclosed by a single biblical passage. If biblical themes are the threads, the theology is the tapestry that results from weaving them together. If individual biblical passages are brushstrokes, then theology is the picture they disclose.

I spoke earlier of my realisation that Christianity could generate a "Big Picture" of reality, paralleling and perhaps even rivalling that offered by Marxism. I found this view set out in the writings of C. S. Lewis, which I first encountered in February 1974. The first of his essays that I read—"Is Theology Poetry?"—ends with these words, which have become almost the leading motif of my understanding of theology: "I believe in Christianity as I believe that the Sun has risen, not only because I see it but because by it I see everything else." Theology is about the articulation of this grand vision, which illuminates reality, allowing us to see things as they really are and live meaningfully and appropriately within this strange world.

So let me tell you about just three of the core themes that have emerged for me over the years, which shape my understanding of the role of theology and my own place as a theologian. The three themes I will mention are (1) the importance of theological education, (2) the need to connect Christianity and Christian communities with wider intellectual projects and cultural concerns, and (3) the place of theology in communicating and commending Christianity through apologetics.

Let me turn to the first of these—namely, the importance of theological education. Back in 1976, I needed help to break into the study of theology and was unable to find a textbook that met my needs—a book that assumed its readers were interested in learning about Christian theology yet knew nothing about it. Having discovered the importance of studying theology to enhance my own intellectual well-being, to enable me to preach more effectively, and to engage major cultural issues, I naturally wanted to help others do the same.

During the 1980s and 1990s, I gave an introductory course of lectures on theology to Oxford students and those preparing for ministry and gradually developed teaching approaches that they found accessible and ways of explaining core theological ideas that they found persuasive. An Oxford publisher heard of the impact these lectures were having and asked me to develop them into a textbook. We gave it the unimaginative title *Christian Theology: An Introduction.*[1] It appeared in 1993, is now in its sixth edition, and has been translated into twenty languages. I had found a role: someone who was able to open up the riches of the Christian theological tradition for others. Rather than adding to those riches myself, I could help others appreciate and make use of them.

Yet I also found myself focusing on relating the Christian faith to other aspects of life—above all, to the world of the natural sciences. While this was of considerable personal relevance to me, it was clearly of wider intellectual and cultural significance. I felt that I, as someone who was deeply steeped in the worlds of both science and theology, might be able to explore ways of understanding their relationship that might be helpful, especially in challenging the hideously simplistic cultural mantra of the "warfare" of science and religion. Although this is now widely regarded as a myth created by nineteenth-century rationalists who didn't like religion, it is clearly important to do more than point out its deeply flawed historical credentials. It is necessary to offer alternative and more reliable frameworks of seeing their relationship.

Over the years, I have developed three main ways of framing this relationship and regularly explore their potential (and their limits) with scientists and theologians who want to bring together their disciplines in an intellectually robust manner. These ways are quite simple to set out, although each of them has an imaginative depth and intellectual reach that cannot adequately be conveyed in this short account. None of them are original; in every case, I draw on existing ideas, even if I at times develop them in new ways.

The first is to see science and theology as offering different perspectives on a complex reality. This idea was first explained to me by Charles Coulson at Oxford in 1973. Science, theology, poetry, and philosophy each offer their perspectives of our complex world; the task is to coordinate and integrate these perspectives in order to give a full and reliable account of a greater whole. One perspective offers only a partial account of this larger reality and thus fills in only part of any attempt to create a "Big Picture" of reality.

The second is to see science and theology as engaging questions about reality at different levels. In developing this approach, I drew on the insights of the movement known as "critical realism," which was inspired by the works of the social philosopher Roy Bhaskar. For Bhaskar, each intellectual discipline engages reality in its own way and at its own level, which is determined by the nature of its object of study. As Bhaskar puts it, ontology determines epistemology. The nature of an object determines how we investigate it and how much we can know about it. There is no universal method that applies to everything, so we have to find a way of unifying or integrating insights developed from different disciplines.

The third approach I developed after a conversation with the philosopher and public intellectual Mary Midgley, who argued that reality was so complicated, we needed to use "multiple toolboxes" to investigate it and "multiple maps" to represent it. No single research tool or map was capable of engaging or depicting reality in its totality; a range of research methods had to be used, and their results somehow coordinated—for example, by superimposing different maps so that a richer account of reality could be achieved.

I now turn to the final theme of this letter: the role of theology in defending, communicating, and commending the Christian faith. Let me make it clear that I do not see theology as a defence of a particular church or denomination. I have always spoken of "Christian theology," drawing on C. S. Lewis's notion of a shared consensual orthodoxy that he termed "mere Christianity." I am an Anglican, but do not speak of a distinct "Anglican theology," nor do I use theology to buttress my denominational identity. Theology is there to serve the Christian church, and I do not use it as a weapon to claim privilege on the part of any specific church or tradition or any specific group of people. At its best, theology holds us all to account.

What I have in mind here is theology's important role in enabling us to identify the core themes of the Christian faith and, hence, challenge the intellectual authority of rival worldviews (an important aspect of the theology of the Swiss theologian Emil Brunner) on the one hand and allow us to identify and articulate some of the key themes of the Christian faith on the other. Let me explain.

I am a great admirer of the scientific vision of Isaac Newton. One of Newton's more interesting achievements was to identify the colours of the rainbow: red, orange, yellow, green, blue, indigo, and violet. Newton showed that a glass prism broke a beam of white light down into its constituent colours so that each of them could be identified and appreciated in its own right.

I see theology as enabling us to grasp the distinct identity and importance of the multiple themes of the gospel while at the same time affirming their coherence and interconnectedness. Apologetically, this means that we are able to appreciate the apologetic significance of each evangelical theme and its potential impact on a wider audience. In this sense, the apologist needs to be theologically informed, since this enables us to have an optimal appreciation of the dynamic range of the Christian faith and its potential impacts on multiple audiences.

Yet theology also plays another apologetic role—namely, in countering what are often well-entrenched negative cultural tropes about Christianity. Perhaps the most famous of these is Tertullian's famous aphorism "Credo quia absurdum" (I believe because it is absurd). Tertullian, of course, never wrote this; its invention dates from the time of the Enlightenment, and it has become a predictable element in the atheist polemic against religious faith, such as Richard Dawkins's *Devil's Chaplain*.[2] A good knowledge of historical theology is useful in many ways, as I discovered when calling into question the reliability of Dawkins's criticisms of religion back in 2006, when the "New Atheism" seemed poised to gain cultural credibility before its more recent implosion.

Now I could tell you more about how I understand theology, but I don't want this letter to become very dull. Instead, let me end with a piece of advice: please realise that theology is not going to give you a clear-cut, unambiguous account of everything. The landscape of faith is not a sunlit upland in which everything is clear and distinct; it remains partly obscured by mist and shadow. There are parallels here with the biblical descriptions of Moses approaching God, who is shrouded in cloud and darkness. We are wrestling with the living God, who overwhelms our capacity to understand and to depict. Theologians use the term *mystery* to speak about God and salvation—not because our faith is irrational but because our limited capacities mean we cannot hope to grasp this in all its fulness.

We see, as Saint Paul puts it, "through a glass, darkly." If we try to clarify what cannot fully be grasped, we end up distorting it. I really like a quote I found in the works of the Franciscan theologian Thomas Weinandy, who I knew when he was based in Oxford: "Because God, who can never be fully comprehended, lies at the heart of all theological enquiry, theology by its nature is not a *problem solving* enterprise, but rather a *mystery discerning* enterprise." There's a lot of wisdom in those words.

But I have said enough. As you will have gathered, I am an accidental theologian in that I never had any ambitions in this direction. For me, theology is intellectually fulfilling, spiritually satisfying, and apologetically useful. It expands our vision of God, challenging our natural instincts to reduce God to what we can cope with. It helps us make sense of ourselves and our world and make connections with a wider culture. And finally, it offers us a vision of God that leads to worship and adoration. I hope you will enjoy this journey of discovery, exploration, and transformation. I know I have. And it's not finished yet.

Best wishes,
Alister McGrath
Oxford

Notes

1 Alister E. McGrath, *Christian Theology: An Introduction*, 6th ed. (Oxford: Wiley-Blackwell, 2016).

2 Richard Dawkins, *A Devil's Chaplain: Reflections on Hope, Lies, Science, and Love*, reprint ed. (Boston: Mariner, 2004).

39

Veli-Matti Kärkkäinen

Introduction: Religious Diversity as a Challenge and Asset to Christian Formation and Vocation

The world in which theological education and ministerial training find themselves in the beginning of the third millennium is vastly and radically different from what it was throughout centuries in the Western world when it was assumed that the prospective ministers only need to know about Christian tradition in order to prepare for the work in the church.

Just think of the statistics: at the time of this writing, about a third of the world's population belongs to the Christian church (2.4 billion), and about a quarter is composed of Muslims (1.6 billion). The 1 billion Hindus make up about 15 percent, followed by Buddhists at half that number. Jews number fewer than 15 million, and among the remainder, over 400 million belong to various kinds of "folk religions." Only about 15 percent (1 billion) label themselves religiously unaffiliated (even though the majority of them entertain some kind of religious-type beliefs and practices). This means that our world is currently more religious than ever, even if forms of secularism are also flourishing—though, number-wise, in a much more modest manner.

I believe theological education and ministerial formation have much to do with preparing men and women to work and live in a world in which not only ethnic, national, political, and economic differences divide and cause conflict but also religious diversity is a potential source of conflicts and wars. And even more: apart from alleviating the danger of battles and fights, astute theological training could also play a profound role in shaping the vocation and identity of Christian leaders preparing to minister in a religiously pluralistic world.

This need for cultivating vocation and designing formation for the sake of the pluralistic world, however, has not been at the forefront of theological training. On the contrary, to be honest, by and large it has been ignored altogether. Even during times in the history of the church of heightened tensions with the religious other, such as those in North Africa with Islam in the seventh century or when new opportunities were looming large as with the neo-Hindu Reform's interest in Christ in nineteenth-century India, the opportunity was missed. And yet making religious diversity an asset rather than an obstacle in the formation of men and women is a deeply *theological* mandate—as much as it is also practical and virtuous in itself. The reason it is a theological issue is simply this: "Our theological understanding of religious plurality begins with our faith in the one God who created all things, the living God present and active in all creation from the beginning. The Bible testifies to God as God of all nations and peoples, whose love and compassion includes all humankind."[1] How could we ever fail to notice this as theological educators?

An Autobiographical Note: How I Was Awakened from My Slumber

The need for a theological formation and vocation fit for the pluralistic world of ours was brought home to me decades ago when I first lived with my family and ministered in the religiously diverse context of Thailand. Teaching theology and doing church ministry in the "home" of Theravada (the original form of) Buddhism, with a significant minority of Muslims and Hindus and a mix of folk religions, awakened me from the slumber of falsely assuming that we only deal with all things Christian but do not have to be concerned about other faith traditions. Indeed, this awakening did not come first from books or even my primary work of training Thai ministers in a Christian college. It rather came to me through ordinary experiences living as a young family in a large town house in Bangkok amidst Thai families. (Against the assumption and expectation set up by the established missionary community, as newcomers to a strange country eagerly learning the new language, we refused to live in the college compound alongside other foreigners. Instead, we always rented an apartment in the city itself among ordinary Thai families.)

Coming home from the college for dinner, I recall having seen my then young daughters happily playing on the streets with Thai kids. True, the two blonde, long-haired, fair-skinned girls stood out in the midst of a group of children. But they also fit in not only because of having gained fluency in the language but also because they themselves felt like they *fit in*! Christian and Buddhist kids bonding together.

Sharing a bowl of rice with moms and dads of the playing kids in the neighborhood—the most intimate mode of fellowship in that culture—made us feel like we were welcomed. Sure, the neighbors knew we were Christians and they were Buddhists. But the difference of religion never came up in the conversations about the children's schoolwork, an upcoming flood, constant traffic jams, and similar everyday topics. Or to be more precise, religion itself could be, and often was, a natural part of everyday conversations. The conversations, however, were not conflicted.

Having been invited for the first time to a dedication of the neighbor's home on the other end of our town house—an hours-long, elaborate religious ritual with a number of monks, led by a chief monk of the neighboring Thai monastery—I first hesitated. I wasn't sure if it was appropriate for a Christian minister to attend. For sure it is, the family conference decided. And I am happy we decided to go! After a most gracious welcome and introduction of this foreign family to the extended family and the religious, I was offered a plate full of incense and fruit and was then invited to say a blessing upon the household. I said the prayer respectfully and boldly in the Christian mood. A number of people came to thank me for this hospitable gesture. Several of them mentioned to me later that the importance of having a *Christian* minister's presence in the feast was very meaningful for them.

With the advancement in Thai language, culture, and religious knowledge, debates and discussions with Thai experts further gave me opportunities to learn not only of this great religion but also of my own. Yes, we debated, but we did it in a civil, hospitable matter. No wonder my classroom experience in the college began to shift in focus: the little knowledge and experience I had gained about this host culture and religion began to "talk back" to me and, at the same time, to inspire and invigorate the teaching of the basics of Christian doctrine.

In this process, my own vocation and calling as a Christian minister and theological educator began to be reshaped. Integrating the challenge and asset of religious diversity as part of my own vocation not only immensely enriched my own scholarly and pedagogical work but also inspired and challenged my own Christian faith. Indeed, it did not make me abandon my deepest convictions but rather helped clarify and modify them.

Returning from Thailand first to Europe and then to the United States gave me an opportunity to further reflect on the implications of this reshaped vocation and how to best help my students and parishioners catch a vision suitable for their particular needs and contexts. My first training in ecumenism—the theological discipline that studies and seeks to find resources for pursuing Christian unity in the midst of endless divisions and prejudices among Christian communities—has served me well in this continuing journey. Against misconceptions, neither ecumenical dialogue (inner-Christian unity) nor interfaith dialogue has as its goal the cancelling out of differences or seeking a compromise at any cost. Indeed, a fruitful result of either ecumenical or interfaith exchange could be a clarification of real differences of whose existence the parties were not aware of before the hospitable encounter. And even when the dialogue results in a consensus or convergence, the distinct identities of all parties are being honored and respected.

Ways and Means of Shaping Interfaith Sensitivity in a Theological Seminary Setting

The challenge of religious diversity and religious pluralism understandably can be treated in more than one way in higher education. I am speaking from my own context, theological seminary, which has only Christian faculty and students while at the same time seeks to widen the curriculum to include interfaith aspects as part of its ministerial training.

A key issue for the seminary setting is the availability of faculty with some interfaith experience. Particularly valuable are those faculty members who have a working knowledge of at least one living world religion (beyond Judaism, which, understandably, is somewhat more familiar to theologians than other faiths, although it is also the case that ancient Israel's religion based on the Torah encountered in biblical studies programs is hardly to be equated with the Judaism[s] of today).

Some of the ways I am incorporating interfaith sensitivity and knowledge as an integral part of my work both as a scholar and pedagogue include the following. Over a number of years, I have worked with producing a new kind of full-scale presentation of Christian doctrine in a way that would be dialogical not only within Christian resources but also in relation to world faiths. The end result is the recently finished multivolume work titled *A Christian Theology for the Pluralistic World* (2013–17): *Christ and Reconciliation* (2013), *Trinity and Revelation* (2014), *Creation and Humanity* (2015), *Spirit and Salvation* (2016), and *Hope and Community* (2017). This series puts all Christian doctrines and basic teachings in a vital and mutual dialogue with Jewish, Muslim, Buddhist, and Hindu views.

I am convinced that as long as the basic texts and materials used in seminary classrooms are focused merely on Christian resources, the student does not have the opportunity to begin to learn one's own faith dialogically. The student is exposed only to Christian materials. In contrast, should the student be exposed to, say, Muslim interpretations of Jesus or theistic Hindu visions of the avatars (divine embodiments) when speaking of Christology and incarnation, the possibility for dialogical learning would offer itself naturally.

Indeed, over the years, I have become convinced that it is not only that theological seminaries should imagine ways to plan and organize new courses in interfaith encounters—as important as those are for all institutions of higher learning. The more important way of cultivating vocation is to make diverse religious perspectives an integral part of everything studied in the curriculum. Since I am not a biblical or historical or pastoral scholar, I do not know in detail how other disciplines should execute this task. I am just wondering if, for example, the study of Scripture could be approached also from the perspective of other faith traditions. And the same with church history; I don't think history courses should necessarily be limited to the Christian tradition. And so forth.

Another way I am seeking to help students shape their vocation and calling with regard to other faiths has to do with theology courses focusing on learning about world religions and the basics of doing the work of comparative theology. Comparative theology entails a careful comparison of beliefs, doctrines, and ideas between two or more faith traditions.[2] In early 2000, soon after having joined Fuller Theological Seminary's faculty, I created a course titled World Religions in Christian Perspective, which subsequently has been taught, and still is being taught, by a number of other instructors as well. That course consists of two uneven parts. The first part, about two-thirds, is devoted to a basic introduction to fundamental teachings and traditions of Islam, Buddhism, and Hinduism. The reason is obvious: most theological seminary students possess either very superficial or no knowledge at all of any other faith tradition. The latter part of the course focuses on comparative theology and gives the students an opportunity to learn the basics of comparison between Christian faith and the three other traditions. Ideally, this kind of course would be co-taught in order to ensure enough expertise in various topics; indeed, that is the way I myself have always taught it (except for the online version).

An essential part of this course involves mandatory visits to temples and sacred places of these faith traditions. The visits include, whenever possible, participation in the weekly service, a presentation by the local religious leader with a Q&A session, and fellowship around a meal. For most Christian seminary students, this might be the very first time they enter a sacred worship place of another religion.

Not seldom a few students raise the question of the propriety of a Christian exposing oneself to the worship experience of another faith tradition. I can recall occasional instances in which the student might have also raised doubts about the potentially negative and harmful spiritual influence that an exposure to a "foreign" religion might entail. Rather than dismissing, let alone ridiculing, such doubts and fears, the instructor can take them as an excellent platform for discussing the underlying issues, exposing hidden fears, and correcting misunderstandings and so help cultivate interfaith sensitivity and maturity. It is likely that after graduation, the student will find him- or herself helping congregants deal with similar kinds of issues. Furthermore, discussions in the classroom after the visits also provide an excellent arena for processing the students' impressions, reactions, and experiences.

This course also requires the student to read some carefully chosen texts in the sacred scriptures of the three traditions. As strange as it may sound, for most seminary students, this is likely the first time ever they have opened the Holy Qur'an, let alone the extant Buddhist or Hindu writings. Even the "bible" of the common folk all over India, the Bhagavad Gita, is virtually unknown to Christian students. Beginning to read the texts of other faith traditions is usually a daunting task, and some help is needed from the instructor for it to make sense. The reasons for the difficulty are many and well known: neither the Qur'an nor the Hindu Vedas has a plot, Hindu and Buddhist scriptures are so exceedingly vast that even to begin locating something is almost impossible for the beginner, terminology and forms of expression are very different, and so forth. Notwithstanding the obstacles and difficulties in trying to understand the scriptures of other faith traditions, this exercise is absolutely necessary for any meaningful attempt to get even to the basics of religions. Indeed, a key goal of this part of theological training is to help the student read rightly religious texts. Fortunately, access to the scriptures is easy in this internet age.[3]

Again, some Christian students may feel trepidation in opening up the Holy Qur'an or other holy scriptures. Similar to the visits to sacred sites, this fear may turn out to become a learning and formation experience.

As said, there are a number of ways that theological seminaries—let alone other institutions of higher learning in religious and theological studies—could incorporate the interfaith aspect as a part of their vocational formation. Here I have shared some specific ways I as a theologian teaching in a typical theological seminary setting have for a long time sought to cultivate the Christian vocation and calling in ways that would open up to other faith traditions. Summatively, the benefits and fruits of such comparative learning and experiences are many:

> First, Christians can and should learn something about non-Christian religious traditions for the sake of the religious other; in fact, both the license and the imperative to do so rest on a biblical foundation. Second, Christians can and should expect to learn something about God in the course of that exploration, and the basis for such a belief can be found in who God has revealed Godself to be and how Christians have traditionally understood that divine self-revelation. Third, Christians can and should expect that their understanding of their own faith tradition will be stretched and challenged, but at the same time deepened and strengthened through such interreligious dialogue.[4]

In Lieu of Conclusions: Dealing with Differences, Holding on to One's Own Identity

It has already been made clear that a robust orientation to the interfaith challenge is not a pretext for leaving behind or compromising Christian identity and faith convictions. We are speaking here of Christian formation taking place in a Christian setting, led by Christian faculty, forming Christian students. That said, there is no denying a deep, built-in dynamic between unwavering commitment to one's own tradition and bold openness to dialogical engagement and learning from others. As Francis X. Clooney says, "In our religiously diverse context, a vital theology has to resist too tight a binding by tradition, but also the idea that religious diversity renders strong claims about truth and value impossible."[5]

Rightly understood, Christian comparative theology—as long as it is both *Christian*, rather than a "pan-religious" mixing of insights from here and there, as well as *theological*, rather than a sociological description of church practices or merely an analysis of human interpretations of human religiosity—is both an act of faith and a spiritual practice.[6] At the same time, that does not deny or compromise its status as an academic discipline, which follows the strict procedures and principles of any similar academic field in the humanities. Depending on the seminary's Christian distinctiveness, emphases may vary. But I have a hard time imagining how any seminary's Christian orientation would, in principle, thwart the enterprise.

Previously, I mentioned the utmost difficulty in learning to read and understand the texts of other traditions. The same difficulty of understanding and interpretation also applies to any conversation between persons of two traditions, let alone a more formal interfaith dialogue. It is ultimately about the right interpretation. As the German hermeneutical philosopher H.-G. Gadamer has reminded us, interpretation is an encounter between two "horizons," mine and yours—and true "understanding is ultimately self-understanding."[7] Rather than external, understanding is an "internal" process that also shapes us. Knowledge in religion is a process not between "subject" and "object" but rather between two "subjects" whose horizons of (self-)understanding cohere and mutually influence each other. In relation to interfaith dialogue, this means, on the one hand, that I as a Christian should not—and cannot—imagine putting aside my convictions and, on the other hand, that those very convictions are in the process of being reshaped, sometimes even radically altered. As Gadamer says, "In understanding we are drawn into an event of truth and arrive, as it were, too late, if we want to know what we are supposed to believe."[8]

In order for the comparative approach to be *comparative*, and hence useful and interesting, one has to resist the modernist fallacy of the "common core" and "rough parity" of religions. Modernist ideology does not honor the Otherness of the Other and thus fails to prepare the student for our diverse and pluralistic world. A truly dialogical mode, rather than denying differences, is an essential asset in the pursuit of truth and conviction. This is an important lesson to our students and a value to be minded in our training that seeks to resource students to engage an interfaith dialogue in their own settings. The German theologian Jürgen Moltmann puts it well: "Dialogue has to be about the question of truth, even if no agreement about the truth can be reached. For consensus is not the goal of the dialogue. . . . If two people say the same thing, one of them is superfluous. In the interfaith dialogue which has to do with what is of vital and absolute concern to men and women—with the things in which they place the whole trust of their hearts—the way is already part of the goal."[9]

Moltmann rightly contends that the only people capable of dialogue— "merit dialogue," as he puts it—are those who "have arrived at a firm standpoint in their own religion, and who enter into dialogue with the resulting self-confidence."[10] Thus "it is only if we are at home in our own religion that we shall be able to encounter the religion of someone else. The person who falls victim to the relativism of the multicultural society may be capable of dialogue, but that person does not merit dialogue."[11]

What the willingness to engage the religious Other entails is that one is able to step out of one's own comfort zone. The human intuition and desire is to stick with those who are like-minded. Everything foreign and strange scares us. An astute theological training in a safe seminary setting may resource and empower the student for such a lifelong adventure to step out. Cultivating interfaith sensitivity is thus much more than merely conveying information about other religions or even teaching the skills of an interfaith dialogue, as important as they may be. It is a matter of attitudinal formation—to which belong the exposing of one's fears and strengthening the will and desire to venture into new experiences. The leading American comparative theologian the Jesuit Francis X. Clooney puts it succinctly:

> If we are attentive to the diversity around us, near us, we must deny ourselves the easy confidences that keep the other at a distance. But, as believers, we must also be able to defend the relevance of the faith of our community, deepening our commitments even alongside other faiths that are flourishing nearby. We need to learn from other religious possibilities, without slipping into relativist generalizations. The tension between open-mindedness and faith, diversity and traditional commitment, is a defining feature of our era, and neither secular society nor religious authorities can make simple choices before us.[12]

Veli-Matti

Notes

In this letter, I glean from my "Teaching Global Theology in a Comparative Mode," in *Teaching Global Theologies: Power and Praxis,* ed. Kwok Puilan, Cecilia González-Andrieu, and Dwight N. Hopkins (Waco, TX: Baylor University Press, 2015), 45–53; and "Dialogue, Witness, and Tolerance: The Many Faces of Interfaith Encounters," *Theology, News & Notes* 57, no. 2 (Fall 2010): 29–33, https://fullerstudio.fuller.edu/dialogue-witness-tolerance-many -dimensions-interfaith-encounters/. Hence references in the current text have been kept to minimum.

1 "Religious Plurality and Christian Self-Understanding," World Council of Churches Ninth Assembly, Porto Alegre, Brazil, February 14– 23, 2006, https://www.oikoumene.org/resources/documents/religious -plurality-and-christian-self-understanding.

2 There are three interrelated yet distinct disciplines that facilitate an interfaith engagement: religious studies / comparative religion, Christian theology of religions, and comparative theology. First, *comparative religion* is a subset of the larger domain of religious studies. Religious studies employs various subdisciplines and approaches in investigating the phenomenon, spread, spiritual life, practices, teachings, and other facets of living religions. Comparative religion's focus is—as the name indicates—on a scientific comparison of religions' doctrines, teachings, and also practices. It seeks to do the work from a neutral, non-committed point of view. Second, *Christian theology of religions* is a confessional Christian discipline. It seeks to reflect critically and sympathetically on the theological meaning and value of religions. To this task also belongs reflection on what it means for Christians to live with people of other faiths and the relationship of this faith to other traditions. Third, since theology of religions operates usually at a fairly general level, another discipline is needed, *comparative theology.* Gleaning resources not only from Christian theology and theology of religions but also from comparative religion, it complements the more generic approach with an effort to consider in detail specific topics in religious traditions. Whereas comparative religion, as mentioned, seeks to be "neutral" on faith commitments and look "objectively" at the features of religious traditions, comparative theology (similarly to the theology of religions) is a confessional discipline. It is rooted in and works from

the foundation of a particular faith tradition, in this case Christianity, while also learning from others. The confessional nature of comparative theology, however, does not mean that comparative theology doesn't qualify as an academic discipline because, similarly to other humanistic disciplines—say, history and philosophy—it follows established scholarly procedures.

3 All important Hindu scriptures can be found on the Sacred Texts website: http://www.sacred-texts.com/hin/index.htm. Some (mainly Mahayana) Buddhist texts can likewise be found in the same database (http://www.sacred-texts.com/bud/index.htm), and a major part of the necessary portions of the Tipitaka (Theravāda) is available on the website Access to Insight: Readings in Theravāda Buddhism: https://accesstoinsight.org. The Qur'an (with several modern versions) can be easily found, for example, at http://altafsir.com, and much of Hadith is available in the Hadith Collection at http://www.hadithcollection.com.

4 Kristin Johnston Largen, *Baby Krishna, Infant Christ: A Comparative Theology of Salvation* (Maryknoll, NY: Orbis, 2011), 9.

5 Francis X. Clooney, *Comparative Theology* (Oxford: Wiley-Blackwell, 2010), 8.

6 For fine insights, see Clooney, 10–11.

7 Hans-Georg Gadamer, *Truth and Method*, 2nd rev. ed., trans. Joel Weinsheimer and Donald G. Marshall (New York: Continuum, 2006), 251 (emphasis removed). For reminding me of Gadamer's importance to interfaith conversation, I wish to acknowledge Kristin Johnston Sutton, "Salvation after Nagarjuna: A Reevaluation of Wolfhart Pannenberg's Soteriology in Light of a Buddhist Cosmology" (PhD diss., Graduate Theological Union, 2002), 2–16.

8 Gadamer, *Truth and Method*, 484.

9 Jürgen Moltmann, *Experiences in Theology: Ways and Forms of Christian Theology*, trans. Margaret Kohl (Minneapolis: Fortress, 2000), 19–20.

10 Moltmann, 18.

11 Moltmann, 18–19.

12 Clooney, *Comparative Theology*, 7.

On Fun, Joy, Imagination

40

Johan Cilliers

If I had any advice to give to you as a young theologian, it could be summarised in three words: *focus*, *freedom*, and *fun*. With *focus*, I mean that all theologians should, at least at a certain stage in their academic journey, find and explore that which ignites their passion the most. It could be many things, but it should not be all things. You can do a lot of things from time to time, but you should be doing only one thing most of the time.

With *one thing* or *focus*, I do not have a reductionist approach to theology or creativity in mind, on the contrary. This focused space-that-ignites-passion could and should be wide and open, like God's grace, and linked to life, real life; but it should not become a labyrinth in which you are perpetually lost. There needs to be some streamlining and therefore progression in your academic journey. The Egyptians started to build their pyramids not from the top but at the bottom, laying the triangular foundation. But they also did not stop at the foundation. They worked their way up towards the apex. Without the foundation, they could not have an apex. And as we all know, even after centuries, they had a foundation solid enough to reach a rather sharp and streamlined apex! As a theologian, you need a foundation, but you also need an apex, or at least a trajectory towards an apex.

There is a certain tension here, in particular if you are starting out on your journey as a theologian. The layout of the foundations of theology is larger than life. Theology, if it is good, offers so much that it can become bewildering. There are so many possibilities that it might lead to academic confusion. Bewilderment and confusion are not necessarily bad—chaos always precedes creation—but you should not remain in a state of bewilderment and confusion forever.

Chaos is not bad; it is actually beautiful, given the fact that it harbours (the possibilities of) creation. But chaos is not and should not become an eternal site of building blocks lying strewn around or haphazardly being carted to and thro. Nietzsche spoke about the beautiful chaos of being but not about the beautiful chaos of chaos. There is a being there, a becoming, a formation—in view of an apex. Within and on the basis of this chaos, you receive what could be called your calling—to build on and above the first foundational layout, towards the apex.

Let me take a cautionary step back: it might happen that you may have to return to the chaos from time to time in order for you to discern your building plan with new eyes. In a sense, theology should always come with a sign attached to it: "Caution—building under construction." In a sense, one could even say that the process of doing theology is as important, if not more so, than the product. But the process hopefully implies progress; and progress should have the satisfaction of at least reaching a summit from time to time, with panoramic views.

The tension deepens: On the one hand, you should seek out your passion amongst the plethora of possibilities; you should start by selecting the building blocks of your theological pyramid. On the other hand, you cannot force it, and you cannot "find" it—it finds you. This is part and parcel of the (paradoxical, wonderful) space that we call "theology." It calls, before all else, for a stance of openness, a hermeneutics of expectation, a willingness to be surprised by what was unthought-of and unsought-for, a flexibility to alter your apex trajectory.

Let me put this in another way: to acquire focus means not only going "up" but also going "deeper," which is not the same as becoming unintelligible. Many "theologies" are exactly that—no human being can understand a word of it. They are so deep that they are covered in mysterious darkness. It simply does not make sense to people anymore and has no real meaning for their lives. To focus means going deeper, but that means becoming simpler. Simplicity and profundity are not contradictory; on the contrary, they are flip sides of the same coin. Theologians need to relearn the art of simplicity, which comes through focus and leads to profundity—that is, wisdom and "depth." One of your greatest challenges as a theologian will be to think and speak and write about God in such a way that the inexpressible becomes expressible and the profound palatable. Or else, only the angels will be your audience.

You should have a focus, a simplicity of depth, an intelligibility of profundity. Which means that you should also seek, and guard over, your own (academic) *freedom*. It is good and important to listen to many people, in particular to the voices of the wise ones, but never to the extent that you lose your own voice. Nobody can do what you can do, and anything that curtails your freedom in this regard, be it academic or cultural or ecclesial, should be resisted.

As a theologian in particular, you should guard against the tendency to fixate theological structures or God-images or ecclesial creeds—as if they can encapsulate who and what God is. At exactly this point, it is opportune to deconstruct my own metaphor: as theologians, we are not called upon to create eternal God-like pyramids. God cannot be monumentalised, or cast in stone. No apex can aspire to surpass God. Our best theo-panoramic views are but glimpses, moments—fleeting but simultaneously fulfilling. This is theology (*theos logos*)—speaking words about a God who is more than our words, deeper than our foundations, higher than our apexes, and of a different order than all of our theological constructions.

In exactly *this* sense, you should guard over the freedom of your thoughts, and tongue, and pen—forever open to the possibility to be surprised by yet another glimpse of God's grace and yet another discovery that shatters your set structures and monumentalised images of who God is or should be. Be free to be—a theologian. That is, someone who speaks (stammers) about God in the full knowledge that this stammering is just that: the articulations of a pleasantly surprised child and never that of a theological know-it-all. If we lose our capability to be amazed by amazing grace, we should be seeking out another occupation.

This freedom from fixation should remind us that we do not know everything about God, and we do not know everything about people. We do not even know everything about ourselves. We should be slow to speak and even slower to judge. We should not stereotype, or stigmatise, or exorcise on the grounds of our so-called knowledge—neither of God nor of humanity. On the contrary, we—theologians—should not forget how small we are, how little we know . . .

Be aware: freedom from fixation might make you controversial at times. You might find yourself swimming against the tide often. The status quo thrives on fixations and resists fluidity. The establishment establishes what it believes to be the "truth." But never allow your freedom to be torpedoed by those who think they know the "truth." We, theologians, do not "have" the truth—it is given to us, continuously. When we think that we "have" the truth, we have already lost it. When we "grasp" the truth, as if with a firm and eternal grip, we already have lost sight of grace. The truth sets you free, not vice versa. This lifelong journey of being liberated by truth is called grace, the grace of freedom, and the freedom of grace.

Do focus and freedom contradict each other? After all, *focus* means "narrowing down," and *freedom* means "opening up." No, they do not contradict each other if the link between them remains one of *fun*. Yes, I am serious—about fun. With this linkage through fun, I have not superficial frivolity in mind but a playfulness about life, about yourself, and in particular, about our ever-so-serious thinking about God. Fun links focus and freedom because we have been created to play (as *homo ludens*) and because God is the playful God (*Deus ludens*). Our theological constructions are probably so irrelevant and alien to life, or simply just so boring, because we are so serious. We are often so seriously "correct" that we are so seriously wrong. We think we have to keep God upright, have to construct the theological scaffolding to keep God's statue—or pyramid—from coming tumbling down. God does not need us; but God does want to play with us. Perhaps we could even "define" theology as such: because God plays with us, we become part of the divine joy, and we may participate in the divine play.

If you only had focus, you would end up being a theological know-it-all, or worse, a theological killjoy. Then you operate under the misunderstanding that you are called to be a security guard, patrolling along the borders of theological constructions and ecclesial creeds and synodical declarations in order to safeguard God's interests. Then you are ready to strike down any sign of dissent (from your view), ready to condemn any suggestion of an alternative, poised to obliterate that which does not coincide with your standard and standpoint. If we operate in this way, our "theology" could even become dangerous—in some cases, extremely so. People who wage war on the grounds of their "theology" are known to be deadly serious and notoriously joyless. Focus without freedom and fun falls prey to fanaticism. Then we indeed represent a God set in pyramid blocks, a God in granite. That, young theologian, is *not* the way to go.

But—on the other hand—if we only had freedom and no focus, we could end up being theologians without gravitas, or worse, theologians filled with fluff. We will end up being all over the place and, in effect, nowhere. We do need gravitas, but not granite; freedom, but not fluff. Fun—divine joy—links focus and freedom, connects gravitas and grace. Fun—entering the playgrounds of the playful God—prevents gravitas from becoming granite and freedom from going up in fluff. Fun—divine play—prevents theological fanaticism. Fun exemplifies the fluidity of grace. *That*, young theologian, is the way to go.

Have fun.

Postscript: having fun, as a theologian, is not to be equated to superficial frivolity. On the contrary, divine joy and tears of human suffering are, more often than not, two sides of the same coin. Laughter and lament are not and should not be strangers to one another. In the Christian tradition, this seemingly paradoxical state of affairs has often been linked to the figure of the clown, being a metaphor for the foolishness of the gospel (cf. 1 Cor 1:17–25). The clown turns things upside down in order for us to see better. It often is a painful, exposing experience—for both the clown and those observing. Holy wit is not without weeping, and the comical not contra crying. On the contrary, clowns are known for crying, their oversized red noses strangely emphasised by tears in their eyes, and vice versa. Clowns remind us of our vulnerability and, as such, point towards an alternative—the Vulnerable One, crying out and crucified for us:

The clown, in fact, bodily interrupts the splendor of the trapeze artists, the magicians, the lion tamers. That is, the clown bodily interrupts the symbols of breathtaking human achievements. Foolish clowns represent another world, another side of humanity. With their red noses and oversized shoes, their stumbling about and fooling around, they highlight the oddness, frailty, vulnerability, and resilience of embodied human life. Their very presence relativizes the mighty and clever, unmasking them as mere mortals, in need of comfort and help. Their colorful adornment and brightly painted faces bring together joy and tears, laughter and lament. After falling down, the clown always gets up and has the last laugh. Clowns transform the circus arena into a more human, livable space.[1]

Johan Cilliers
Stellenbosch

Note

1 Charles L. Campbell and Johan H. Cilliers, *Preaching Fools: The Gospel as a Rhetoric of Folly* (Waco, TX: Baylor University Press, 2012), 158–59.

41

Cynthia L. Rigby

First, allow me to tell you how honored I am that you are taking the time to read my thoughts and reflections. As so many of us do, I suffer from a bit of imposter syndrome. It still startles me, even after twenty-six years of teaching theology, when people ask me what I do, and I hear myself telling them that I am a theologian. It makes me feel like I'm overstepping somehow. And of course I am, as all of us who call ourselves theologians are. I mean—who are any of us to say words about the infinite God?

If you were anxiously to ask me this question, I would, of course, have a ready answer. (Have you already noticed, as I have, that being able to help others with their questions doesn't necessarily mean they are resolved for yourself?) I would likely say something along the lines of "I believe you are called to speak words about God. But remember that none of us generates these words on the basis of our own wherewithal. God comes to us and shows us God's very self; our job is to pay attention and to bear witness." And then I would probably remind you not to forget that what we know about God never exhausts who God is—there's always more to learn, always the possibility we are wrong or incomplete in our understanding. Our task, young theologian (I hope it's all right if I address you as "YT"), is to keep seeking understanding of the things that continue growing larger and more incomprehensible to us even as we learn more about them. The search for understanding, when it comes to God, doesn't end with understanding but continues with further seeking (Anselm, twelfth century).

The way I see it, YT, this way of thinking has been quite alien to the mindset of American culture through most of the twenty-first century. This mindset seems almost to promise that if a person invests ten thousand hours practicing something, they will gain mastery over it. How can we compete with this enticement of influence and prestige when our students and parishioners ask what kind of takeaways they will receive from the study of theology? "If it is impossible to come to a complete understanding of God even if one invests a great deal of time and energy, why bother trying to understand God at all?" they might ask you, as they do me. And their solution to this conundrum is simple and straightforward, I'd say: They don't renounce their faith (at least, most of them don't). Instead, they throw up their hands with cries of "Mystery!" and renounce their search for understanding. This is not acceptable if for no other reason than because here, mystery functions as an exhaustive answer for who God is and thus betrays itself.

What those who cry mystery don't seem to realize is that theology facilitates not only an imperfect description *of* mystery but also participation *in* it. It is through trying to understand the "So what?" of the Trinity, for example, that we come to understand how much greater the reality is than our own capacity to embrace it. And it is this realization, I believe, that gives way to our participation, through Christ, in the life of the triune God and the transformation of ourselves and the world.

Even more troubling to me than the fact that these transactional ideals are so prevalent in culture is that so many Christian leaders buy into them. Worried that our numbers will decline if we can't deliver measurable outcomes, we borrow from the corporate world suggestions for how better to brand our churches and seminaries and convey our core message. Don't get me wrong, YT—I don't have a problem with learning from the corporate world or being held accountable for the quality of my work. But when we start handling the gospel as though it is a manageable commodity rather than the "quick and powerful Word of God" that reorients us by "judg[ing] the thoughts and intentions of the heart" (Heb 4:12; my translation), we're getting off track. We've forgotten, again, that God is the infinite Creator and that we are finite creatures (see paragraph 1). To be perfectly blunt, if you teach a seminary class, don't allow the aims, goals, and rubrics you are required to create get in the way of the work of the Spirit, which will often come through your teaching. One of the problems with these transactional, self-protected systems is that we teachers are called upon to name outcomes before we are through listening so we have a way of being assessed on the basis of what we set out to do. This method *might be* effectual for teaching facts, information, and strategies, but it is more damaging than helpful for teaching people to be theologically reflective because it sets mastery as the goal rather than focusing on the search for understanding itself.

I worry, YT, that what lies at the core of problems like this is a widespread disbelief (or, possibly, distrust) in the power of the gospel to "undo and remake" us, as Serene Jones has put it. There are, in my view, too many Christians in the world who have given up on trying to understand God because they fear living with open questions will lead to a loss of faith. It is part of my job and yours to help them see that faith *provokes* questions. I'm saying not only that it *allows for* occasional doubts; it also precipitates lament, skepticism, and uncertainty whenever it witnesses injustice or suffering, whenever it sees reason to remind God of God's promises.

I'm also suggesting that all theologians have the responsibility to help Christian disciples realize that faith is not meant to serve merely as a personal coping mechanism or to help us "do our best" and let God "take care of the rest." I agree with Christian Wiman, who said that believing in Jesus can be like having "a shard of glass in your gut"—you can no longer see a hungry person and turn the other way without feeling pain. Jesus insisted that even the smallest amount of faith has the potential to move mountains, to transform us, to power our participation in God's transformation of this world.

"Wait a minute!" you might be thinking. "Did you say, a couple paragraphs back, that 'it's part of my job' to challenge people to deepen in faith?" Perhaps you are an academic who doesn't feel especially gifted as a spiritual caregiver and are happy, therefore, to rely on more-qualified pastors. Or maybe you are a theologian who pastors a church full of folks who are, as Kenda Creasy Dean has put it, "almost Christian"—meaning they think having faith is "nice" as long as it doesn't require too much of an investment. Either way, to be a theologian is not just to disseminate information, teaching theological terminology, the history of doctrinal development, and theological systems of everyone from Gregory of Nazianzus to Catherine Keller. It is to be with and be for those to whom we speak words about God, to love them even before we feed and tend them (John 21). YT, will you love those whom you will teach and to whom you preach?

Thankfully (and I hope you agree), there seem to be many counterexamples to this graceless, transactional way of existing that is symptomatic of global capitalism and surreptitiously funding our culture and churches. In recent days, for example, the mindfulness movement continues to gain in strength, offering grace a little space to push into the room—and sometimes even find a chair. I'm thinking this might be because people are recognizing they are being made tired and unwell by having to prove and re-prove their value day after day. "I Am Enough" read many mindfulness T-shirts. "Just Be" read others. I think these sayings are arguably less about the wearer being either grandiose or lazy and more about them wanting to be known by who they are. (By the way, I have the *Calm* app on my phone and the *Breathe* app on my Apple Watch and actually use them!)

If I am right that a new space for doing theology is emerging, I think it will be important for you and your generation of theological teachers and ministers to keep an eye out for new examples of the Holy Spirit working in and through culture in ways that are not explicitly Christian. This is an important aspect of the theologian's work as noted by Gustavo Gutiérrez, who (I hope you remember) reminds us that the church is wherever the Holy Spirit is at work—whether in the *ekklesia* (the church that identifies itself as embodying Christ) or the *koinonia* (the church outside the institutional church). You, YT, are entering the stage as a theologian at a time when the great sins of the church are being named and raged against. The most consistent criticism of us is that we are a bunch of hypocrites. We say we want to do justice, love kindness, and walk humbly with God (Mic 6:8), but we actually come across as self-righteous, unkind, unmerciful people who talk a good game when it comes to justice but actually don't do much to help. That must be why David Barron, in his wonderful TED talk titled "You Owe It to Yourself to See a Total Solar Eclipse," finds it necessary at both the front end and back end of what I would say is a very spiritual presentation to assure us he is "not religious." He doesn't even want to be associated with you and me, YT. That hurts, because I really like the guy. He talks about conversion, transformation, and Sabbath. Similarly to Eric Weiner, he says he "wishes" he believed in God. Do me a favor and listen to the talk (just google "TED talk" and the title). Then maybe we could write to him? Ask him for another chance? Maybe if we met him at the next global eclipse . . .

I know it seems a little weird to bring up such a specific example as Barron and his talk. But you, I'm sure, have had teachers who have pointed out that this is often how God works. A particular burning bush, talking donkey, pregnant woman. In the case of the Jewish carpenter, God makes Godself known in ways that are scandalously particular and don't fit into any rubric or theological system. So don't think you can just keep your eyes on the big stuff, YT. That's just what got the Pharisees in trouble. They were looking for someone grander than Jesus and, in doing so, missed their Messiah. YT, my recommendation is that you commit yourself every morning, anew, to be present to the particular things of this world—beautiful or base—as you choose what words to speak about God. Sometimes this will seem a little awkward. Like when a pastor has prepared a glorious poem of a pastoral prayer and has no choice but to include intercessions about Ms. Jones's bunions, the problem of the air-conditioning insulation blowing into the balcony, and conflicts over a sexual harassment charge made by a member of the staff. I know I'm being very, very Protestant when I say the real church is not perfect. It has blemishes all over it. But Protestants are very, very right about this, IMHO. All of our efforts are provisional; we still await the second coming of Christ, when all will be made whole (see paragraph 1).

What amazes me and gives me hope for the future of our discipline, YT, is that the testimony of Scripture is that the Christ, without whom all of our efforts are provisional, will come and take we who are finite to himself as *essential players* in the work of God. I don't know exactly what this looks like, but I believe it will *not* look like a powerful man relegating to his side his weaker bride and reassuringly saying, "Nice try. Now step back and let me show you how it's done." We as theologians—we as *Christians*—are already agents in shaping the new normal that continues to be born of God's creative desire. A new normal that is not normal insofar as it turns inside out even our very best practices for managing the Spirit's transforming work. A new normal we are free to imagine, and then playfully to enact, and finally to bring to earth as it is in heaven.

Let me, here at the end of this letter, risk telling you something I've hardly told anyone, YT. It is my joyful testimony that I've experienced a feeling of utter freedom pretty consistently when lecturing on the "So what?" of various theological doctrines. I know this is kind of odd for a Presbyterian theologian to share, but I figured in some way, it might be an encouragement to you. If you have not yet experienced the freedom that comes with going deep into trying to explain the "So what?" of Calvin's *extra calvinisticum*, or Rosemary Radford Ruether's *kenosis* of the Father, or James Cone's concept of redemptive suffering, I surely wish this for you. Do you want to know what it feels like? I'll try to describe it: It can happen when I'm lecturing, writing, or preaching, but more often when I'm with people and watching their expressions change from boredom to joy. They usually stop taking notes without even being aware of it. For my part, I'm off the detailed outline I've handed out but even more on point than the outline is. I lose all self-consciousness and most self-awareness even as I feel filled with the Word in which I am participating—and I am inviting those present, with me, into the bigger reality that is connected by the Spirit to but never exhausted by my actual frail but powerful words. I lose track of all time when this happens. I participate, somehow, in eternity.

I probably should do some work seeking understanding of this, YT. But for now, what I can say is this:

1. I have witnesses in my students, who confirm that something is happening that's pretty mystical for a systematic theologian who is a "T" (a Thinker, as opposed to a Feeler, on the Myers-Briggs Type Indicator, the Enneagram of my generation).

2. This experience is probably related to my reason for getting ordained as Minister of Word of Sacrament. Because I started working toward ordination after I became a professor who had never planned on being a pastor and already had a teaching position, I wondered to myself, *Why?* The best reasons I could give myself were (a) it felt wrong for me to preach and not be able to go from there to the table and break the bread and (b) it felt wrong not to be able to lay hands on my students after preaching at their ordination services.

YT, I do not know whether you are called to be ordained or not, but I know the God who likes to work in very particular ways is calling you not simply to be a theologian in general but to particular tasks, to particular commitments. To particular joys and to particular struggles. So I charge you not only to keep an eye out for the Word you are called to proclaim to others but to keep an eye out to the Word directed by the Spirit smack-dab to you. Barth was fond of saying theologians should begin each day not by formulating questions for others but by asking themselves the key question: How is it with your heart? Marilynne Robinson (Pulitzer Prize–winning author of *Gilead*) points out that theology, as we understand it through the practice of worship, never divorces the metaphysical from the mystical—Word from sacrament, mind from heart, or intellect from experience. Each of these pairs is integrated in people of faith and perhaps especially in theologians. We've got to start doing a better job of showing this to people, though, I think, because we too often come across as cold fish due to the fact we're more introverted than our students. Nontheologians tend to think that theologians are more dispassionate than they are. But they know we're smart, so they start thinking theologians disassociate intellect and passion. YT, will you commit to modeling the integration of passion and substance? Will you show the world that one can speak with conviction without being simplistic and can speak complexly without being obtuse? If you could do just this one thing in these polarized days, it would be a real help. But I know you and I can accomplish much more if we remember not to try to show off but to rely on Christ to strengthen us.

I look forward to being friends, to supporting one another in ministry, and to having lots of good theological conversations.

In hope and with joy,
Cynthia L. Rigby